A

I Am Hip-Hop

Conversations on the Music and Culture

Andrew J. Rausch

THE SCARECROW PRESS, INC.
Lanham • Toronto • Plymouth, UK
2011

Published by Scarecrow Press, Inc.
A wholly owned subsidiary of The Rowman & Littlefield Publishing Group, Inc.
4501 Forbes Boulevard, Suite 200, Lanham, Maryland 20706
http://www.scarecrowpress.com

Estover Road, Plymouth PL6 7PY, United Kingdom

British Library Cataloguing in Publication Information Available

Library of Congress Cataloging-in-Publication Data

Rausch, Andrew J.
   I am hip-hop : conversations on the music and culture / Andrew J. Rausch.
      p. cm.
   Includes index.
   ISBN 978-0-8108-7791-7 (cloth : alk. paper) — ISBN 978-0-8108-7792-4
(ebook)
   1. Rap musicians—United States—Interviews. 2. Rap (Music)—History and
criticism. I. Title.
   ML394.R387 2011
   782.421649092'273—dc22   2010053563

∞™ The paper used in this publication meets the minimum requirements of
American National Standard for Information Sciences—Permanence of Paper for
Printed Library Materials, ANSI/NISO Z39.48-1992.

Printed in the United States of America

For Michael Dequina,
Henry Nash, and Aron Taylor,
three of my oldest
and best friends.

Every age has its own poetry;
in every age the circumstances of history choose
a nation, a race, a class to take up the torch
by creating situations that can be
expressed or transcended only through poetry.

—Jean-Paul Sartre

CONTENTS

CONTENTS

FOREWORD

E lton John starts his song "Crocodile Rock" with the verse, "I remember when rock was young." I've heard that song thousands
of times, but never really thought about the implication and true
meaning behind that statement. I never really thought much about what
it would be like to remember when rock was young—when this new form
of musical expression rose up and captured the imagination of America's
youth, forever separating from the generation that came before them. At
least I never really thought about it until very recently.

Not that long ago I was having a conversation with someone more than
twenty years my junior, and the topic turned to hip-hop. And at some point
I actually found myself saying, "I remember when hip-hop was young," as
thoughts of Elton John's "Crocodile Rock" passed through my mind.

At the risk of dating myself, I remember when hip-hop was young. I
was young, too. A child really, when I first heard Sugarhill Gang's "Rapper's Delight." Everyone knows that song now, as it is pretty much the
ultimate classic of hip-hop, having come along at a time when the sounds
emitting from the streets of New York hadn't even been labeled hip-hop
yet. To be ten or eleven years old, having been raised on a steady musical
diet of Earth, Wind & Fire and Billy Joel, and hearing for the first time,
"I said a hip hop the hippie the hippie to the hip hip hop, a you don't stop
the rock"—well, that was just something else altogether.

It's difficult to truly convey what I felt about this music, other than to say it sounded "right" to me. It was new and young, and it didn't sound like it was meant for people my parents' age. And so I started flirting with this new music, which came with its own unique style of dance, as well as art that was a bold expression of wild colors that defied the conventions of what art could be, where it could be, and if it could even be legal.

By the time Grandmaster Flash and the Furious Five dropped "The Message," I was done flirting with hip-hop—I had fallen in love. These were the days of trading tapes with my friends, writing my own rhymes, practicing backspins on old pieces of cardboard, and planning my graffiti masterpiece. And to be perfectly honest, the only thing I did well was trading tapes. My aspirations of being a great emcee or a great breaker or a great graffiti artist faded in time, and I resigned myself to being nothing more than a lover of hip-hop.

When I think of what hip-hop means to me, I think of a culture of artistic expression that rose up in places where no one expected there to be art. Hip-hop, in all of its permutations, is the creation of something from nothing. It is the transformation of ugliness into beauty. It is a defiant stance against a society that seeks to marginalize the poor and disenfranchised, only to find that the poor and disenfranchised have created their own kingdom.

Hip-hop to me is so many things. It is possibilities. It is about finding your way when you're lost. It is knowing that deep down inside of you there is a message that must be delivered to the world, on your terms, in a language that you speak. It is hearing a song like "Street Justice" by the Rake for the first time, and being transported to another place through the sheer might of lyrical force.

For those of you too young to remember when the Fat Boys were still the Disco 3, or when Kangol Kid and Dr. Ice were backup dancers for Whodini, I feel sorry for you. Sure, you can love hip-hop and immerse yourself in every aspect of the culture, but you will never be able to say you remember when hip-hop was young. You will never be able to say that the first time you experienced hip-hop was the first time the world experienced it, as well.

For those of you old enough to remember when Kurtis Blow first dropped "The Breaks," or when Run-DMC first appeared on *Soul Train* and blew the spot up, try not to get too caught up in lamenting the days gone by. It is difficult at times to not look at the current commercialized state of hip-hop without becoming cynical. We old guys now talk about how things were "back in the day" and we wax nostalgic about the old school, but we need to keep in mind that everything must change and grow—even if it changes and grows in ways we don't always understand or appreciate.

One last thought before I wrap this up—just as I remember when hip-hop was young, I remember when people said it was a fad that wouldn't last. There were naysayers who discounted all of it—the music, the dance, the art—dismissing it as nothing more than junk. But what they were really dismissing was a culture that had found its voice—a voice that those within the establishment could never fully comprehend. And they were wrong. Hip-hop has lasted. It has thrived and flourished and spread all over the globe, and when all is said and done, hip-hop to me is about being alive and finding a way to express yourself to the world.

—David Walker, author of *Reflections on Blaxploitation*

ACKNOWLEDGMENTS

I would like to acknowledge the following people: Stephen Ryan, Marilyn Allen, Louis L. Gregory, David Walker, Michael Dequina, Henry Nash, Aron Taylor, Ronald Riley, Charles Pratt, Kerri Rausch, and all of the artists whose interviews are included in this book, as well as all of the agents, managers, and publicists who helped to make it happen.

INTRODUCTION

The unifying question found in each of the following interviews is "What does hip-hop mean to you?" Some of the interview subjects dug down deep and came up with thorough, well thought-out responses about the nature and historical meanings of hip-hop. But the answers I like best are the ones in which the interview subjects simply say something to the effect of "It's my life." Those are the responses I can best relate to. You see, hip-hop has long been my life, as well. Many of you may be questioning that statement, unable to believe that a white guy from Kansas would even have the audacity to write a book on the subject of hip-hop, let alone claim it to be a defining factor in his life. But it's true. That I could have been so personally affected by this urban music and culture is perhaps a testament to the widespread popularity and worldwide embracing of hip-hop, as well as its raw power.

As you will discover within the pages of this book, hip-hop means something different to everyone. It is likely that inner-city b-boys will find difficulty in recognizing or appreciating that people of other races who live in places like Nebraska or even Japan have grown up with this music and identify with it in much the same ways that they do. But again, it's true. And while hip-hop must be recognized as a black art form and culture first and foremost, it cannot be denied that a great many people of varying races from a wide variety of countries define themselves through hip-hop. What was once an underground movement in the streets of New York City is now a phenomenon which reaches around the globe. It has been said that hip-hop music is the soundtrack to modern America, and that certainly appears to be true. Hip-hop music is now used in advertisements for everything from automobiles to dish soap, and it is quoted and referenced freely in virtually every corner of American society. When right-wing conservative Bill O'Reilly says "Fiddy" Cent or country singer Trace Adkins uses the Keith Murray–originated phrase "badonka-donk" in a hit song, it is a testament to the power and universal nature of hip-hop music.

To answer my own question, hip-hop is very time specific to me. I will forever see hip-hop in the way it existed in what is now known as the "golden age" of hip-hop, which lasted from approximately 1986 to 2003. Baggy Girbaud jeans were in fashion, as were oversized hoodies and Timberland boots. Classic albums like Wu-Tang Clan's *Enter the 36 Chambers* and Black Moon's *Enter Da Stage* blasted in our car stereos and Walkman cassette players. Groups like Public Enemy and Tribe Called Quest made us see hip-hop as the legitimate art form that it is; rather than making asinine dance songs like so many artists today do, these artists (and they truly were *artists*) continually pushed the creative boundaries of this new music.

Like many of the kids who grew up on a steady diet of hip-hop music, I fancied myself an emcee. I recorded a number of demos between 1993 and 1998. And although I came close to a record deal, did a show with Tech-N9ne, was featured in *Rap Sheet* magazine, and even managed to get one of my songs played on Chuck D's radio show, the dream never materialized for me. In the end, it turned out that I was a much more talented writer than I was an emcee. But that love of all things hip-hop has never died.

And that's what this book is about—passion. It's a heartfelt tribute to this music and culture; a reminder of what it once was, and a discussion on what it now is and soon will be. The older folks in the seventies and eighties called hip-hop a fad, but they were dead wrong. Today the older generation—myself included if I'm being honest—often complains about what hip-hop has become, but again I think we fail to see the larger picture. Just as the older folks who had grown up with the rock music of the 1950s (Elvis Presley, Buddy Holly, etc.) were unable to recognize the rock music of the 1970s (Led Zeppelin, the Who), time has shown us that both styles of music possess merit. And while no one will ever say that artists of today like Soulja Boy or Nicki Minaj rhyme about anything of substance the way guys like Q-Tip and Chuck D did 20 years ago, it is perhaps important for us to remember that they don't really have to. In retrospect "Blue Suede

Shoes" or "Teddy Bear" seem lyrically shallow when compared to something like "Stairway to Heaven," but they are no less classic.

The song says that there is a time for everything, and perhaps that's true. Just as America turned to the lighter fare of comedies and dance films during the Great Depression in the 1930s, maybe it needed a lighter incarnation of hip-hop to get through the financially hard times we have faced as of late. And if the adage that things come in cycles is correct, then perhaps another era of more profound lyricism is just around the corner.

Nas' statement that hip-hop is dead has been heavily debated (within these pages, as well), but the truth is that hip-hop isn't dead. In fact, it's far from dead. It's everywhere we look today. The truth is that it's constantly evolving, and that evolution isn't even close to being finished. Maybe instead of criticizing today's hip-hop music we should take more time to analyze it and appreciate it for what it is rather than admonishing it for what it isn't.

9TH WONDER
Producer

L ittle Brother, a Durham, North Carolina hip-hop group consisting of Phonte, Rapper Big Pooh, and producer 9th Wonder, released their debut album *The Listening* in 2003. The album received critical acclaim, and 9th Wonder's production, which consisted of chopped and manipulated soul samples, drew comparisons to legendary beat-makers Pete Rock and DJ Premier. The producer then remixed Nas' album *God's Son* on a lark, releasing the project as *God's Stepson*. This street album was well received and started the trend of remixing popular hip-hop albums. After 9th Wonder had already received praise from the likes of Pete Rock and DJ Jazzy Jeff, Jay-Z tapped him to produce the song "Threat" for his 2003 effort *The Black Album*. Following the release of this album, 9th Wonder remixed it just as he had done previously with Nas' *God's Son*, titling the project *Black Is Back*. This project, which many believe to be even better than the original Jay-Z album, brought the producer further acclaim.

9th Wonder's stature in the industry continued to grow when he produced three songs ("Girl," "Is She the Reason," and "Game Over") for the 2004 Destiny's Child album *Destiny Fulfilled*. The producer then worked with such noted soul singers as Erykah Badu and Mary J. Blige, winning a Grammy for his work with the latter. He then produced Little Brother's second album, *The Minstrel Show*, which once again garnered acclaim for the both the group and the producer. In 2007, 9th Wonder parted ways with Little Brother. He has since produced the music for the popular animated series *The Boondocks*, and has gone on to work with such noted hip-hop artists as Ludacris, Lil Wayne, Murs, Wale, Drake, Black Moon, and David Banner.

In addition to his work as a producer, 9th Wonder also hosts a radio show in Fayettville, North Carolina, called *True School Radio*. He is the president, founder, and CEO of It's a Wonderful Music Group, which caters to the 28- to 40-year-old demographic of music listeners. He also runs two independent labels, Jamla Records and the Academy Music Group. In 2007, 9th Wonder was appointed Artist-In-Residence at North Carolina Central University, where he began instructing a hip-hop history course. He then went on to teach similar courses at Duke University and Barber Scotia College. 9th Wonder has also been appointed the National Ambassador for Hip-Hop Relations and Culture for the NAACP, where he leads a board of Ph.Ds, hip-hop artists, and Juris Doctorates.

What does hip-hop mean to you?
For me hip-hop is a way of life. It has shaped so much of my life. Its inception was in 1973, and I was born in 1975. It's been so much a part of my life—the true essence of hip-hop; this is what I eat and breathe on a day-to-day basis. I'm talking about the study of the music, the cultural aspect of it—not how much money it's made over the years, but the cultural aspect of it and its worldwide impact, and the impact that it had on the black community, and the messages that it created in the late eighties and early nineties that helped form me in my adolescence. It's shaped a great deal of my life and has formed my way of thinking—artists like Chuck D and KRS-One and Brand Nubian and Tribe Called Quest. And plus it turned me on to a legion of artists that I never knew about through its usage of samples in the music.

Tell me about some of your earliest productions. Most of us used the pause button on our cassette players to make little loops in the beginning. Did you do that?
[Laughs.] Yeah, I did that. I did that in the mid-nineties . . . We all did that because we wanted a way to make beats when we didn't have the proper equipment. That was some of my earliest production, and then I started actually making beats around 1998 or 1999. That led to my messing around with it for a few years until the inception of Little Brother. I've been at it, just from a hip-hop standpoint—actually practicing the dynamics of the hip-hop culture—for about 12 years. As far as knowing about the music

and it manifesting over time within me, whether it was through a clarinet or a keyboard, oh, man . . . we're talking about 24 years! And you were probably the kid like me who had the CD book with about 500 CDs in it. I think it manifested in all of us that way.

What producers would you say have most influenced you, and in what ways specifically?
DJ Premier because I think he's the best in hip-hop at capturing the wintertime sound; just that gritty sound. I can't think of any producer in history that's produced music that was grittier than what DJ Premier has done. If you want the 40 below, Timberland, puff jacket—that type of boom-bap production—then it's DJ Premier. I can't think of anybody else who comes close to that. Then there's Pete Rock, who's the best sample flipper. He uses samples better than anyone else I've ever heard in my life. If you take those two cats together—with a little Beatminerz and Organized Noise and some different cats thrown in there . . . Those are my primary influences.

It must be kind of surreal to be in a position now where people are comparing you to both of those guys.
It's kind of crazy. You take someone like Big Sean, who just signed with Kanye West; he told me, "You're a legend to me. I've been listening to you since I was 15." And he's 22, so that kind of makes sense. I started listening to Tribe Called Quest when I was 14. And that makes sense for cats to say that I am the equivalent of those guys—not in terms of music, but because they grew up listening to my music. To them, I *am* Pete Rock. I mean, I went crazy over Pete Rock and DJ Premier, and *their* favorite producer was Marley Marl. It just goes down the line like that. I think I'm similar to them in that someone who doesn't really know hip-hop may not know my name, and that was what Pete Rock and DJ Premier were to us. I think to this generation I am the one that embodies samples and the boom-bap sound, while all the other producers may do something different. I'm the one that still sticks to that, and so I think that's why they would say that.

What was it like landing your first record deal with Little Brother?
We really didn't know what to make of it. We already had *The Listening* finished. That album was already a year old when we finally signed with ABB Records out of San Francisco. For us to be from North Carolina and sign a record deal with a label in San Francisco was just totally crazy. We never

went into this trying to get a deal. It was just basically, "Let's see what happens." We had so much love for the music that we were just like, "Let's see where this goes." We just tried to make each song better than the last one. We didn't really know what we were doing. So when we got our first deal, and our advance was just $2,000—split four ways because we had to give our manager a piece—it was just like, "Okay." I mean, it didn't really hit me until we actually started traveling and going places and finding that people knew our songs. That kind of hit me more than the fact that we had a deal. We would go to New York or L.A., and people would know our songs word for word. That was when it hit me that we were onto something.

What are some things that you learned as an artist from being a part of a group?
Just that it's hard. [Laughs.] There are just different dynamics with different people. Nobody's right, nobody's wrong. It's a very difficult process. But if you stick with it, it can be a real learning process. You not only learn about people, but you also learn a lot about yourself.

How would you say that your methods of production have changed since you crafted the first Little Brother album?
The formula is still the same, but I've updated it a little bit. I've got a friend who told me, "You still make underground records, but now you make mainstream underground records." And the way that you make it mainstream is by making sure that the listener can learn the record. It's about "if I listen to this song on the radio, can I learn the record?" If it's something that's difficult to learn, then that's when it goes out of the mainstream. So I try to make records that are still me, but ones that people can learn. So that's how I've changed over the years. And I also try to make my sound a little bit bigger. I just believe in my fans, and my fans believe in me. I am the representation of what hip-hop used to be. I try to stick with that and not stray too far away from that, because I believe that trying to appeal to a bigger mass audience would shorten my career. But sticking with my 300,000 loyal followers for 20 years is what will give me longevity, and that's what I want to do.

As a fan of the boom-bap sound of the "golden era" of hip-hop who also owns his own record label, are you going to use that power to try and resurrect that sound in a bigger way?
I think it's going to take more than me. I think everything repeats itself in 20 years, and I think that's where hip-hop is going. Hip-hop goes in

cycles just like history does. We are now at a time where we are 20 years removed from 1990 . . . We were 20 years removed from the seventies and stuff like Curtis Mayfield and the Motown sound when D'Angelo came out and kind of brought that back. I think it takes a generation to have to be removed from that sound, or it takes a generation of children who grew up with their moms' and dads' music. If you ask a 15-year-old right now what the first rap record they heard was, they might say Nas. And you'd ask, "How was that?" And they'd say, "My mom and dad used to play that." So now we're at a point where the 15-year-olds were born in 1995, and their parents are saying, "You're gonna listen to what I listen to in the car." So that means that they're listening to groups like Tribe, De La Soul . . . You follow me? So what's going to happen is that that sound is going to become cool again. You've got kids going to college and wanting to listen to adult music. I mean, when we went to college, we still listened to our Jodeci and Mary J. Blige, but if you *really* wanted to be grown you listened to the Commodores and Bob Marley and John Coltrane and the O'jays. You listened to something kind of vintage that your friends may not have been up on. All the college kids did that. Now it's going to happen again. You might listen to Drake and Trey Songz and J. Cole, but if you really want to be up on it, you need to get up on the *Midnight Marauders* album. We're entering into an era of the new classics now. So that's going to strike a chord and some kid's going to say, "You know what? Let's take off all these chains and start wearing good wood and African medallions again." That's coming back, so I think that whether I try to do it or not, that's going to be the thing to do anyway.

You mentioned the new classics, which makes a good segue for this next question. How did you wind up producing "Threat" on Jay-Z's *The Black Album*?

[Jay's engineer] Young Guru was a fan of Little Brother, and a fan of my production as well. He reached out to me, and he said, "I need you to come to New York and play some records for Jay." So I went to New York, and that's how "Threat" came to be. I actually played 29 beats for Jay first, and he was like, "Man, I need you to make one for me." I made "Threat" for him. That's how I got on *The Black Album*, and that was seven years ago tomorrow, if you can believe that. It was September 22, 2003.

What was that experience like working with Jay on that?

Surreal. It all happened in a span of three or four days, so it's kind of a blur to me. Every time I get to meet Jay or sit around and talk to him, it's a blur. Whether it's three hours or it's 10 minutes, it's all a blur. But it was surreal. I mean, here no one was sampling records anymore, and I was a kid who was labeled as being a backpacker, or labeled as being underground. And here he's asked to produce a record by one of the best rappers, if not *the* greatest rapper walking, on a heralded album that also comes with a movie. It's unheard of. It was surreal. In fact, it's still surreal to talk about it.

You know, anytime I meet somebody it comes up. You talk to someone and someone else says, "You know who this is? This is 9th Wonder." And they say, "Nah, I don't know who that is." And then they say, "He made a beat for Jay-Z," and that instantly validates me. I've made records with everyone from Destiny's Child to Mary J. Blige, and that's the one project that seems to validate me. "He got a beat with Jay-Z." And they say, "Oh, word?" And that automatically makes me somebody.

You remixed both *The Black Album* and Nas' *God's Son*. What was the response to those projects like?

The Nas *God's Stepson* project came along when a friend of mine brought me the Nas a capella CD and said, "See what you can do with these." And I did the whole thing in a weekend. I really didn't think that much of it. And that made a *lot* of noise. Then MF Doom did one after me called *Nasdradoomus*. Then some other cats did the same thing. Then the next thing you know, *The Black Album* a capellas came out and started a whole revolution again. And everyone was like, "You've *got* to do it." And I did. It just started out as something I did in my household that I didn't think was going to be that big of a deal, and it wound up being a type of revolution of remixing albums. And everybody thought I used that to get in the game. Nah, I was just remixing an album because I got tired of hearing Nas over those beats. I wanted to see what they would sound like over mine.

I think the Jay-Z remix album, *Black Is Back*, is really amazing.

I don't know if Jay has ever heard it. I remixed my song twice. Maybe he heard it, maybe he didn't, but it is what it is. I did it because it was fun. That was why I originally got into this game in the first place. I get to make records and live out my childhood dream. I get to be a part of something—not because of the money, but because of the camaraderie and the brotherhood. You couldn't script it any better than this. So that's why I made those records. For me, it was just a part of the craft.

Do you ever hand over a beat to an artist, or are you pretty much there with the artist the entire time?
Sometimes. I mean, we're in an age now where people just take my whole catalogue . . . They just go online and Google my name and find the instrumentals and then make a whole album with them and put my name on it. [Laughs.] And that's without my being there or ever meeting them. They think that's going to get them to the next level. As for my actual productions, sometimes I do that. I mean, I've done it once or twice. I did it with Skyzoo. But really, I'd rather be there while they're recording it. We are producers. That's what we do, so I'd rather have more of a hands-on situation with the music that I produce.

That's sort of the old school mentality. I'm always amazed to hear about all of these artists and producers that never meet. They just go in and record it and then have someone else mix it down.
I was watching something on Herbie Hancock, and he was making an album. I think if Herbie Hancock and Sting could coordinate their busy schedules and get together to collaborate, then anybody should be able to. And they were in the studio together for five days. And this is *Sting* now! Of the *Police*! And that's why the level and quality of their music is so incredible. You know, people are in this game now for the wrong reasons. They'd rather be at the latest big party than be in the studio collaborating and putting together a good record.

You're extremely prolific. How many beats would you say that you create in a month's time?
I'd say 100. No offense to anyone else, but I don't have a lot of vices. I don't drink, I don't smoke. I don't have those things standing in my way. This is what I want to do. I think a lot of us take for granted being a part of this thing, you know? The business side of it sucks. Everyone hates the business side of it. A&R, chasing checks, dealing with the label . . . That all gets on your nerves. But come on, man, we're making music for a living. What is your gripe? There are lots of people who work nine-to-five jobs who hate their jobs. We make beats for a living and people praise us for it, you know? What is your gripe? So that's how I stick with it. Everyone gets

into the game for a reason. Some people do it for money; I got into this game for something different. I got into this game to carry a torch from the guys who passed it on to me. Whether or not I was ready to carry it, that's my position in this game. I make as many beats as I do because I'm always trying to chase the same high that I got when I made this particular beat, or this beat, or this beat . . . I'm trying to get that high again.

What are your favorite collaborations, and why?
"Threat" because of what it stood for, and to actually watch Jay-Z record his verses with nothing written down on paper. Destiny's Child, because that showed me that I could do something else other than hip-hop. I mean, I always wanted to make soul music. I'm labeled as a hip-hop producer, but I want to make soul music, and working with them showed me that I could do that. The record I made with Mary J. let me know that I could not only make soul music, but that I could be recognized for it. I won a Grammy for that. Working with Erykah Badu was special because, look, you never think the people that you adored when you were younger are listening to you. But she had been listening to me for years, and that was how that collaboration came about. And Ludacris showed me to never judge a book by its cover. That's not to say that I did a lot of judging of Ludacris, but he wasn't necessarily what I expected in terms of industry standards of mainstream or underground. And those are all on the mainstream level of things regarding some of my favorite productions.

But I think my number one favorite collaborations have probably been the records that I've made with Murs. I've done four records with him, and we're totally different people. I've heard people say that if you don't agree with 9th Wonder or do exactly what 9th says then it won't work, but that's not true. Me and Murs argue *all* the time, but we've made four albums. I think we just respect each other's space, and we're men about it. And those four albums are my favorite collaborations.

I've read that you've been working at a couple of different universities these past few years as a hip-hop educator. How did you get involved with that?
I went around and spoke at a lot of high schools. That's one thing about growing up in North Carolina—you have a lot of cats that you went to high school with that grow up and become teachers. So obviously they're gonna ask me to come by and speak to their classes. So I had a friend who asked

me to come and speak to a couple of his classes, and the chancellor at North Carolina Central University caught wind of it, and he asked me to come and teach a class at North Carolina Central. And that just happened to be the largest class on campus. I stayed there for three years. Once the chancellor changed, I moved on to Duke, and they totally embraced what I had going on there. We decided we'd do this every other semester. And while I was at Duke, I also volunteered down at Barber Scotia College, which is a so-called black college in Concord, North Carolina. It was the first college for the daughters of slaves, and I volunteered to teach there. It's just the opportunity to do something totally different.

I feel that anything that has been a part of our society for 37 years— whether you want to admit that or not—needs to be studied. It needs to be totally understood on a college level. I mean, the same thing happened with jazz. Jazz was created in the streets, and now it's studied all across the world. I believe that hip-hop is going to come to that. I just wanted to be one of the forerunners of it rather than there be some 60-year-old guy who knows nothing about the art form but teaches about it because he read a couple of books.

What does your course curriculum cover?
The course at Central was called "Hip-Hop in Context," and we talked about hip-hop from 1968 to 1997. Most history courses today don't even talk about black history after Martin Luther King. So it's like, after Martin Luther King died, what happened? So this course covered everything between the assassination of Martin Luther King all the way up to the assassination of the Notorious B.I.G. There were a lot of things that happened from a socio-political standpoint which corresponded with the music. A lot of people like to think the music has nothing to do with politics, and so we talk about the creation of hip-hop and how it affected things like how the black community was viewed. The course covered a period of time that your average 18-year-old knows nothing about. He may have heard some about hip-hop from his parents, but he knows nothing about the history of Cold Chillin'. And all of that is important. It's a part of black history, period. So that's what we studied at Central. The class at Barber Scotia was basically the same class.

At Duke we had a more in-depth class. It was called "Sampling Soul," which meant that we sampled different topics every week. One week we talked about Michael Jackson. The next we talked about *Illmatic*. The next week we talked about sampling geography, and I talked about Gamble and Huff, Motown, Solar Records, Stax. We did that every week.

DISCOGRAPHY

1. *9th Invented the Remix* (2003)
2. *The Listening* (2003) [as Little Brother]
3. *Shake N Beats* (2003) [w/ Spectac]
4. *Legsclusives* (2003) [w/ L.E.G.A.C.Y.]
5. *Murs 3:16: The 9th Edition* (2004) [w/ Murs]
6. *Dream Merchant Vol. 1* (2005)
7. *The Minstrel Show* (2005) [as Little Brother]
8. *Chemistry* (2005) [w/ Buckshot]
9. *Spirit of '94: Version 9.0* (2005) [w/ Kaze]
10. *Murray's Revenge* (2006) [w/ Murs]
11. *Cloud 9: The Three Day High* (2006) [w/ Skyzoo]
12. *Dream Merchant Vol. 2* (2007)
13. *The Formula* (2008) [w/ Buckshot]
14. *Jeanius* (2008) [w/ Jean Grae]
15. *Sweet Lord* (2008) [w/ Murs]
16. *The Corner of Spec and 9th* (2008) [w/ Spectac]
17. *Wonder Years* (2009)
18. *9th Invented the Remix . . . Again* (2010)
19. *Fornever* (2010) [w/ Murs]
20. *Death of a Pop Star* (2010) [w/ David Banner]
21. *Loose Joints* (2010)
22. *Food for Thought* (2010)
23. *The Solution* (2011) [w/ Buckshot]

AKROBATIK
Emcee

Following in the fine tradition of emcees like Ed O.G. and Guru of Gang Starr, Dorchester native Akrobatik set out to represent Boston in the late 1990s. In 1998, the fierce emcee released his first single, "Ruff Enough," on Boston's own Detonator Records label. Akrobatik then released his next two singles, "Internet MCs" and "Say Yes Say Word" on Rawkus Records, with the latter becoming an anthemic favorite that made many hip-hop fans take notice. In May 2003, he released his first full-length album, *Balance*, which featured production from such respected beat-makers as Diamond D, Da Beatminerz, and DJ Revolution. The album was an underground sensation and garnered positive reviews from many noted music publications.

It was during this period that Akrobatik joined forces with fellow Boston artists Mr. Lif and DJ Fakts One to form the group the Perceptionists. The group released a mixtape, *The Razor*, in 2004. That project spawned the single "Memorial Day," establishing the group's reputation as one of underground hip-hop's most talented crews. The following year saw the release of the group's debut album, *Black Dialogue*, which spawned two more singles, "Blo" and "Black Dialogue."

In 2005, Akrobatik inked a deal with Brooklyn-based Fat Beats Records. He then went to work on his album, *Absolute Value*, which wouldn't be completed and released until 2008. The album, which featured production by Da Beatminerz, J Dilla, and 9th Wonder, as well as guest appearances by

Chuck D., Talib Kweli, and B-Real, received rave reviews and finally put Akrobatik squarely in the national spotlight.

Akrobatik's music has appeared in films like the Steve Carell comedy *Date Night*, the hit television series *The Wire*, and on video games such as *NBA Live '06* and *Need for Speed: Most Wanted*. In addition to his work as a hip-hop artist, Akrobatik maintains a daily job rapping about sports news on "The Sports Wrap-Up" on Boston's JAM'N 94.5 hip-hop radio station.

What does hip-hop mean to you?
When I think of hip-hop, the first thing that comes to mind is the beginning of my relationship with hip-hop. I was really fortunate to be born and growing up around the time that hip-hop made its first initial explosion. There was just a real genuine and authentic feeling that came from it because it didn't exist before that. I think about the beginning of the music and how it represented a whole new way to represent one's self musically. When I first heard "The Message" by the Furious Five, that was just amazing. Those guys just sounded so cool. I was used to hearing people sing, and now here were these dudes just saying the words in a kind of rhythm that I had never heard before. I got to witness the whole thing explode with the Run-DMCs and the LL Cool Js and all of those people who were coming up. So when I think of hip-hop, I think of the Fresh Fest era. I think of how excited everybody was about this new thing that was coming out, and how it infected me and made me yearn to become a part of it. And that was *all* I did. As a kid, my life was basically sports, video games, and hip-hop. Honestly, it kind of still is! [Laughs.] So for me, when I think of hip-hop, I think about that initial surge and how it caught fire so quickly.

When you're that young, a time period of five years seems like an eternity. So that time period of like 1986 to '91, '92, where everybody was still kind of learning . . . people were still sampling whatever they wanted to, and it was just a really fun time. Now, for me, it's kind of more a professional thing and definitely something where I have to take my work into account as opposed to just living it. But I definitely still have that initial excitement for hip-hop running through me today.

You mentioned that period from roughly 1986 to 1992. The thing about that period that amazes me is the growth that the music underwent in such a short period of time. And literally every year the sound changed.

Also, there were so many different types of hip-hop existing simultaneously then, from Tribe Called Quest to NWA to X-Clan . . .

The beauty of that, to me, is that all those groups kind of worked with each other, or toured with each other. They shouted each other out on their records. Groups like NWA and Digital Underground could coexist—because of the fact that hip-hop was so new and people weren't really worried about categorizing the different types of hip-hop. They were like, "Yo, we got on, and you guys got on, too, and this is fun. Let's make some money and do some shows." That was something great, and I think we've steered away from that recently. Now it's more about everybody being so desperate to sell records and get attention. So if you make one type of music, then it's the thing now to kind of shit on everybody who doesn't make that kind of music. A lot of that unity is gone. For me, it's music first. I kind of feel like when Tribe Called Quest came out, that kind of changed the way people started making beats. There are a lot of groups from the early days of hip-hop that really formed the music, and what it became, and what it is. Even though they're mostly on the underground, you still have a lot of producers who take that really artistic approach to making music. They aren't just throwing on loops or electronic beats, so props to them.

What do you see as being the contributing factors to that change in hip-hop?

I think the information age changed everything. Back in those days, 1988 or 1995, the average guy couldn't just turn on a computer and make a beat and get their music out to people. Now the industry is so watered down that you have people who are not truly artists at heart, and they have just as much of a capability as a truly talented artist in getting their music out there. So now, any video that ends up on YouTube or any song that ends up on a blog somewhere can really catch fire just as fast as something by an artist who's been grinding it out and doing shows and all that stuff. I think that's what changed hip-hop mostly, and because it's changed in that way, it's put people in the position now where they can pretty much just copy whatever the next guy is successful at doing; they can piggyback off that and get attention and, in some cases, record deals.

Nowadays you have to be a music-savvy fan to find good authentic hip-hop. But there is plenty of rap music out there that is on the menu that is only a click away. It doesn't really bother me, because I know where to go to find good music. But I feel bad for the younger generation because most of them don't have any realization of what is happening. They've just come into the situation, and they don't have the history to distinguish between the two types of music, and they don't have access to some of these other artists who are putting out the more artistic stuff.

You're obviously a student of hip-hop music. In what ways do you feel that having an understanding and knowledge of the music has helped you as an artist?
It's almost like just knowing your heritage as a human being. If you know your heritage, you know what came before you. It's a good indicator of what lies ahead for you. I've been in the music business now for 12 years, and I think part of my ability to survive for as long as I have has a lot to do with my knowledge of the things that came before me. I have a lot of respect for the heritage, and it gives me a more honest approach towards making the music. I don't make music to be famous—I make it because I love it. I would like the people I grew up listening to who loved their music to be impressed by what I do. I'm not just making music to impress the people who live on my block or the people from my city . . . I'm doing it because I love it, and I want my peers and my influences to recognize that and respect me for the same reasons that I respect them. That's definitely one way that it helps. I feel that if I didn't know anything about Big Daddy Kane or Slick Rick or LL Cool J, I wouldn't have those influences. I mean, those guys are direct influences on my music, and I can't deny that. So if you're coming out and the only influences you have are the guys who have been around for the last couple of years . . . then I think your influences are coming from a watered down source. I feel that my influences are coming from a genuine source—the real deal—and you can't really take that away from me. I can quote just about any lyric off of LL Cool J's *Walking with a Panther* album, or the *Long Live the Kane* album . . . Those flows that those guys kicked, those punch lines that they used, they're all in my head. So not only do those things inspire me in regards to what I should do, but I also know what not to do because it's already been done.

In the liner notes to your album *Balance* you stated that you hope to change the perception of the black man in America with your music. I find that fascinating. Tell me about that.

Well, the first thing I'll say about that is I was a really ambitious dude when I put that album out. I was so excited about the fact that I was putting out my first record that in the back of my mind I probably thought I was going to save the world with it. Looking back on it, perhaps I was a little too ambitious making *that* statement. At the same time, I feel like there were a lot of people who heard that record, and maybe a couple of the songs on there did in fact change the way they thought about things; particularly "Remind My Soul." So I don't really know that I was being too ambitious.

When that album was released that was during the era of 50 Cent and G-Unit and everybody was trying to piggyback off of that, and for me, I would be in a lot of situations, whether it be in Europe or the United States, where it got to the point where I didn't want to tell people that I rapped. I mean, it was because what it meant to be a rapper had changed rather drastically. Whereas back in the day you had NWA, and they were like the flagship gangster rap artists and you'd have been a fool to try to copy them because they were so authentic, everyone during this period just wanted to have that gangster swagger and put out drug dealer gangster music. I didn't do that, because that was not what I was about, and the people that I know would not have respected that. There was no reason for me to do that, so I wanted to put out music that would make people say, "Okay, here's a brother who isn't influenced by all the shit that's going on right now. He sees it, he knows about it, but he has a different perspective on it." I didn't really feel like my perspective on drugs and violence in hip-hop was really being represented in hip-hop outside of maybe a couple of artists. It was important for me to get that out there at that time. I don't feel like it's that necessary to make that distinction today; now I just feel like I can make music and have fun.

Do you feel that emcees have a responsibility to address social and political issues?

No. I think music is music. I feel that you should just do whatever you want to do. We're all complex people and we all have a lot of things going on in our lives, and you can take any one aspect of your persona or your character, and that might be all that you're willing to express to people as an artist. You're not obligated to give people anything other than what you want to give them. We're in this era where if you sign up for a Facebook page you feel like you have to give up everything short of your social security number and having someone grab your nuts and tell you to cough. I feel that we, as a people, have sort of lost sight of the fact that our own privacy is something that can be guarded. We have a right to guard that, and we only have to share what we want to share. And yes, the artists that tend to be loved the most are the ones who are fearless and share the most, but, I mean, if you just want to be a dude who only talks about women and relationships, you can do that . . . If sometimes you just feel like you're an angry black man and that's all you want to put out there, then that's fine. I mean, look at Public Enemy; they made music that was socially conscious that was about what was going on around them. Chuck D never made a love song, but I'll bet you that Chuck D has been in love, and he just decided not to share that side of himself. And I respect that, because if that's not what he wants to do—if he feels that it goes against his brand of the music that he's making—that's fine. I feel like people can and should do whatever they want, but it's ultimately up to the public to decide what they're going to accept from someone and what they're not.

You're sort of a throwback to the artists of the nineties in that your focus seems to be on sound lyricism and positive messages. Do you feel that maintaining your integrity in this aspect hurts you in terms of achieving mainstream success?

Well, yeah, because being positive and saying uplifting things is not really something that the media has ever really wanted to get across to the mainstream in any forum, other than maybe trying to make people who are already famous look good. I mean, look at the NBA; all those guys are millionaires and you always see the "NBA Cares" campaign . . . You see that and all the charity work that they do because they have to. They have to maintain a certain level of responsibility because they make so much money and because everybody has their eyes on them. But if you're not famous, it's not going to make you famous to be some good charitable guy that is into all these different things and trying to raise social awareness. Mainstream success is more about grabbing the attention of as many people as you can with your song, and usually that's going to happen with catchy hooks and singing and certain types of beats—danceable music that's played in the nightclubs. And I understand that, but I don't make music for mainstream success. For me, I know that if I make music that I like and enjoy, that there will be enough like-minded people out there like me who are going to hear it and enjoy it and I'll be able to get booked and make some money. It's that simple for me. It's a career. It's something that I want to be able to do for as long as I can; this isn't a get rich scheme or anything like that. But yeah, major labels aren't going to come knocking on my door with the kind of music that I'm kicking most of the time. But that's okay. I don't really feel like I'm missing out or anything, because mainstream success does not necessarily equal happiness or even fortune.

Do you think we'll ever see lyricists finding crossover success the way that they did 15 years ago?
I don't know about that, because I don't think there's a strong enough movement of artists doing that. When they had the "Stop the Violence" and "Self-Destruction" movements, those guys all rocked together—like 30 artists on one song, for one cause; even the gangster rappers. There's not enough unity amongst artists right now because everyone is guarding their own careers so closely that, even amongst the conscious artists, you have cliques. It's kind of hard to crack certain cliques if you're not affiliated with certain people or from a certain area. It's too bad, and I think that has maybe hurt me a little bit, being from Boston, and not really being able to get too close with some of the other conscious artists from places like Philly or New York or Chicago. Everybody's doing their own thing, and on the surface it doesn't really seem that there's an initial reason to reach out to cats outside of your clique. I understand how that works, but because I'm not really part of a deep clique, I have this really kind of independent mind state and individualism is really important to me. Just to see a lot of people come out with conscious lyricism would be amazing when the vast majority of the hip-hop audience has been dumbed down and bamboozled. I think that right now people have been sedated to the point where they don't even know that they're being made fools of as fans. They don't realize that they're being manipulated by the labels who are saying, "You know what? These people are going to go along with whatever dumb shit we put out there. All we have to do is talk about sex and the shit that hustlers do, and people will go for it." Right now audiences are easily entertained by dumbness because they've been numbed to things that have any value in our society. That's just a harsh reality that we have to face. I don't like it, but it's the truth. I mean, if you go to *any* club, that truth will reveal itself immediately. These are our times, and this is what we're dealing with. I don't

want to be the grouchy old guy who's complaining about it all the time; I just want to be able to do what I do and have my audience enjoy that.

It would be nice if we could go back to a time when the artists were 21, and they were mature and coming out with great concepts and saying things that could uplift communities. But the truth is, today the artists are 35 and they're talking about ignorant shit that kids should be ashamed of. Maybe you should talk to some of those artists and have them explain it, because I don't understand it. I don't understand how you can be 30 or 35 years old, and still talking about selling cocaine and all the girls that you've slept with. It's like, where are all the grown-ups in hip-hop? Twenty years ago all the grown-ups in hip-hop were 21, and now the grown-ups in hip-hop are the most immature people that black people have representing them in media. It's amazing.

DISCOGRAPHY

1. *The E.P.* (2002)
2. *Balance* (2003)
3. *The Lost Adats* (2003)
4. *Black Dialogue* (2005) [as the Perceptionists]
5. *Essential Akrobatik, Vol. 1* (2007)
6. *Absolute Value* (2008)

BIG DADDY KANE
Emcee/Producer

I n 1984, Brooklyn-bred emcee Big Daddy Kane befriended another up-and-coming rapper named Biz Markie. They became partners, with Kane penning many of Markie's lyrics, and the two soon joined the Queens collective known as the Juice Crew. Both emcees signed to Marley Marl's Cold Chillin' Records, and Kane released his first single, "Raw," to much acclaim in 1988. He then released his debut album *Long Live the Kane*, which spawned the classic single "Ain't No Half-Steppin'." That same year, Kane also appeared on the legendary posse cut "The Symphony" with Kool G. Rap, Craig G., and Masta Ace. The following year Kane released his second gold album *It's a Big Daddy Thing*, which outsold its predecessor on the strength of the singles "Smooth Operator" and the Teddy Riley–produced "I Get the Job Done." In 1998, *It's a Big Daddy Thing* would be selected as one of *The Source*'s 100 greatest hip-hop albums. The single "I Get the Job Done" would also be selected at number 57 on VH1's list of the 100 greatest hip-hop singles.

In 1990, Kane released his third album, *Taste of Chocolate*. The album, which featured the singles "Cause I Can Do It Right," "It's Hard Being the Kane," and the Barry White collaboration "All of Me," had a more distinct R&B sound than Kane's fans were used to. This change in musical direction, coupled with appearances in *Playgirl* and Madonna's book *Sex*, led to criticism by some within the hip-hop community. In 1991, Kane lent his vocals to Patti LaBelle's "Feels Like Another One." He then released his fourth album, *Prince of Darkness*, which spawned the singles "Groove with

It" and "The Lover in You." For his 1993 album, *Looks Like a Job For . . . ,* Kane enlisted the help of some of hip-hop's most talented producers in Easy Mo Bee, Large Professor, and the Bomb Squad. The album, which featured the hit singles "Very Special" and "How U Get a Record Deal?," delicately walked the line between the R&B crossover sound of *Taste of Chocolate* and the hardcore hip-hop sound of *Long Live the Kane* and was hailed as a return to form for the artist. The following year Kane returned with *Daddy's Home.* Although the well-received album featured production by the likes of DJ Premier and Easy Mo Bee, Kane himself took over the lion's share of production, producing five of the album's 13 songs. Kane then went on a four-year hiatus before releasing his seventh offering, *Veteranz' Day.* This time Easy Mo Bee returned to produce two songs, and Kane himself got behind the boards once again to produce an impressive nine tracks.

Big Daddy Kane is easily one of the finest and most influential emcees ever to touch a microphone. He is routinely selected to media and hip-hop artists' lists of the top emcees of all time. Kane's verbal dexterity, often complex wordplay, and tenacity on the mic make him one of the true greats. He is also credited with discovering Jay-Z, has had an impressive second career as an actor, and led the way for artists who routinely combine elements of hip-hop and R&B today. Big Daddy Kane's impact on hip-hop is immeasurable.

What does hip-hop mean to you?
When I think of hip-hop, I think of a big cultural change where the youth from the streets had an opportunity to go against one another without violence being involved. It could be battlin' rappin', battlin' deejaying, breakdancing. You could still be competitive and keep that drive and ambition to be great without causing anyone any physical harm. That's one of the main things that hip-hop *meant* to me—I won't say means, because it's changed so much—when I first heard it and first got involved. Also, it represents a whole new genre of music.

Considering the fast pace of some of your songs, like "Nuff Respect," I was surprised to learn that you suffer from asthma. Has that affected the way you've had to approach things in the studio or on stage?
To be honest, it never really bothered me until we were shooting the "I Get the Job Done" video. It wasn't because of my rapping, but rather it

was due to the number of takes they did with me doing that dance routine. That's when it kicked in and made it hard for me to breathe. That was the first time in my career that it had ever affected me. In the studio it was never a problem. I guess my asthma isn't as bad as a lot of other people's. I've seen people who've had to have their inhalers on the regular, and they have to stay away from certain places. It's really not been that bad for me.

You've stated in the past that your friend and mentor Biz Markie taught you a lot about the music industry and about being an emcee. What kinds of advice did he give you?
When I was younger, I was always trying to get a deal. I sent demos to different record labels. I sent one to Nia Records. I sent one to Motown. I even mentioned them in the songs; I said something about being the first rapper on Motown. I never heard back from Motown, and Nia declined. So I pretty much gave up on trying to become an artist. Instead I just wanted to be a battle rapper and go from neighborhood to neighborhood battling cats. Then when I met Biz, he was telling me that we could actually make some money doing shows. He said, "We're gonna get a record deal. Just trust me." And, you know, I started believing him. When we were doing shows, he showed me different things. A lot of times I wanted to spit my battle rhymes, and he knew that I also had funny rhymes about girls, which I had been doing since about 1982 when I heard Grandmaster Caz's "Yvette's Story." Later, when Slick Rick came out around 1985 and made "La Di Da Di," I stopped doing that because that was pretty much his thing. But Biz was telling me that these rhymes would work on stage. At first I didn't listen to him, and I did the battle rhymes, and the crowd wasn't paying attention. From that point on, I listened to Biz and did the funny rhymes about the girls and we used to rock every night. He taught me a lot about working onstage. He also taught me a lot about patience, and basically the art form of making a record.

How much did your life change after Biz Markie's "The Vapors" came out? I mean, he did an entire verse about you and you were in the video.
People started noticing the face from the video and that type of thing. I started getting a lot of new friends [laughs], and that type of thing. But I guess things didn't really change until "Ain't No Half-Steppin'."

I remember reading that you and [producer] Marley Marl weren't really sure you liked "Ain't No Half-Steppin'" at the time you recorded it. Is that right?

What happened was I was at Cool C's house, and he had the 45s that Biz had bought. We were over there just going through them, and I heard that one, and I was like, "Yo, that's kind of hot." So C looped it up and I started rhyming to it, putting something to it. A little while later Biz called, bragging about some other record he'd found. And I was like, "Since you found that one, you probably don't need this one right here, right?" And he wasn't even paying attention. He was like, "I don't need it. I don't care." So I got it and took it home and listened to it, trying to figure out where I wanted to go with it. And then I found the Heatwave joint "Ain't No Half-Steppin'," and I was like, yeah, this is gonna be dope on the chorus. But then I wanted some noise on it, too, and I came up with the UFO part. Then I headed to Marley Marl's house to put it down, but as usual, I stopped by Downstairs Records. My man J.C. who worked in there had put a new 45 to the side, and he played that Monk Higgins joint with the horns. I was like, "Give me that." I didn't even know if those horns would fit, but I went to Marley's house and was like, "Try this, try this . . ." Marley was arguing with me. "You're putting too much shit in the song, and it's gonna sound crowded. There's just too much going on. It should just be that Heatwave sample and the beat." And I was like, "Nah, fuck that." And he put it all in and it sounded great. And then he was like, "Yeah, yeah, that's hot."

I'd like to ask you about another famous collaboration you made with Marley Marl. I think just about everyone would agree that "The Symphony" is one of the greatest hip-hop songs ever recorded. At the time you recorded that, did you have any sense of how special that song was?

Nah, at the time we recorded it me and Kool G. Rap wanted to leave the session! We didn't even want to do the song. When I had done my song "Raw," G and myself had then done a freestyle to that beat. And after "Raw" came out, Marley started playing the freestyle. Everyone was calling the radio station asking to hear the remix of "Raw"—they thought it was a remix, but really it was just a freestyle that we had done. So Marley said, "I want you to do a song on my album together." We agreed, but then the next thing you know Marley came back and said he wanted to put Craig G. on it. Me and G just really wanted to do the song by ourselves; we didn't want anyone else on the song. But then Marley played something Craig had done called "Duck Alert," and we were like, "Yeah, that's kind of hot." So I was like okay, yeah. Plus, I liked Craig because he was one of those underdogs that Warner Bros. hadn't really wanted in the beginning, just like me. So I was like, "Yeah, cool." But then on the day of the studio session Marley came with another dude with some big-assed nerdy-looking glasses, talking about, "This is my new artist and I want to put him on it, too." That was when me and G was like, "Hell no, let's get out of here. Let's just go." But then Masta Ace rhymed, and his rhyme was better than Craig's and we were like, "Wow, dude is hot!"

You know, when Kool G. Rap rhymed, his first rhyme ran off the reel. I hadn't even rhymed yet! Marley was trying to convince G to cut his rhyme short, and G couldn't figure out where to cut it. Finally he just said, "Forget it, I'll just say another rhyme." And you know, I think that rhyme worked better anyway.

I read somewhere that Rakim and yourself actually came close to releasing diss songs about one another. What happened?
What happened was, there were people getting in my ear saying, "He's trying to play you with that 'word to daddy' line." And there were people trying to convince him that I was trying to play him with my saying 'rap soloist, you don't want none of this.' So yeah, it got to that point where I had a song ready to go where I was gonna say something about him. And there was word on the street that he had a song dissing me. It was called "Break the Wrath in Half." Eric B.'s brother was my road manager. Me and Eric have always been cool. And one night I went and picked this girl up and she gave me a picture that said, "Dear Kane, I wanna 'Set It Off' and get 'R-A-W,' 'Ain't No Half-Steppin'" cause I'm gonna 'Break Your Wrath in Half.'" And I gave the picture to Eric's brother, Ant, and he read it and laughed.

To make a long story short, at the end of the night he was like, "Yo, this shit is gonna get out of hand. Y'all niggas need to talk." So he called Rakim and put me on the phone with him, and I asked him about the 'word to daddy' line and asked him if that was directed toward me. He said no, it wasn't, and that it was just something that Long Island niggas say. Then he asked me about the 'rap soloist' line and I said, "Nah, I'm not saying that *you* don't want none of this. I'm saying that I'm a rap soloist, and competition don't want none of this. I'm calling myself a soloist. I'm not talking about you. Anyone who rhymes alone is a soloist." So we squashed that, and, you know, at that point that was that.

But then about a year later, after they did *Rap Mania*, they wanted to do *Hip-Hop Battles*. So they asked me and Ra to battle; Kool Mo Dee and LL Cool J; Furious Five and Cold Crush; Shante and Sparky D. And this was gonna be a televised pay-per-view event. And Rakim didn't want to do it. And they called me and asked me to talk to Eric and Ra. So I called Eric B. and was like, "Yo, they're saying that y'all aren't going to do it." [Laughs.] And Eric and his stupid ass gets on the phone and says, "No, we're gonna bust your ass, Kane. We're gonna bust your ass. That's a done deal." So I called them back and told them that Eric said the battle was still happening. Then they called me back the next day and was like, "I don't think it's Eric. I think it's Rakim. Could you talk to him?" And I was like, "I don't know him. Me and Eric are cool, but I don't know Rakim, and we don't have that type of relationship." Ever since then, dude has been like a recluse whenever I'm around.

You've been in some legendary battles, from Freddie Foxxx to a guy named Jazz Fresh. What are some of your fondest battle memories? What are some things that stick out in your mind?
There was this guy I battled at this school called Erasmus Hall. I don't remember his name, but it was one of those battles where I was tearing his ass up every round, but he was just relentless. He was one of those dudes who wrote like a hundred bar rhymes. He wasn't saying anything fly, but it was just that he rhymed so long and he had so many rhymes! He just wanted to stand out there and go *all day*. That's when I realized that there has to be some sort of time limit. This isn't the way fights or basketball games or any other competitions are won—just going until somebody runs out of rhymes [laughs], no matter who's saying the better shit. That dude had a lot of confidence in himself, and even though I was murdering him, he just didn't want to stop.

I remember another time there was this guy at this club in Philly called After Midnight. I had gone like two rounds and had just eaten his ass up, but he just did not want to stop. Lady B, the host from the radio station, had already told him he'd lost, but dude did not want to stop! And I was in the middle of my stage show. Finally it got to the point where I was like, "You know what? I'll tell you what, dog . . . here's a hundred dollars. Just take that and enjoy your fuckin' night."

Do you still get a lot of people trying to battle you?
Nah. I don't even write like that anymore.

I was thinking of the aging gunslinger who tries to hang up his guns, but people just keep coming for him, trying to knock off the best.
It's funny. In the late nineties it used to be like that. I could have been at the mall, anywhere . . . It was the type of thing where at that point and time they were looking at me like I was old and a has-been. It was like, "Here's the perfect time to get this win under my belt." But at that time I was still really heavy into what I do, with that type of love for it.

When you started transitioning into more R&B-influenced music, you caught a lot of flak for that. Today, however, that style is much more accepted—possibly due in large part to yourself. What are your thoughts on that?
I guess really the best way to sum that up is to say that I probably should have waited about five more years to do that and then just linked up with Puffy. I probably should have just stayed with the "Raws" and the "Ain't No Half-Steppin's" until about 1994 and then just linked up with Puffy and said, "Yo, this is my vision."

How did you end up recording "All of Me" with Barry White, and what was that experience like?
One day we were at Quincy Jones' house for this cookout, and Barry was there. We talked. When we got into the car, I was already listening to Barry in there on cassette. When we got in and it came on, he just laughed. "Ha ha, sho' you right, Kane." And he said, "We should get together and do something." I was like, "Anytime." We hooked up about a week later, and we found out that we had a lot in common. You know, my birthday was on September 10th and his was on September 12th. We liked a lot of the same stuff . . . We sent someone to the liquor store to get some champagne and they didn't have it, so I was like, "Shit, then just give me a beer." And I didn't want to say "O.E." in front of him, and he said "O.E." We just clicked.

Then we were just going through the idea and I said, "What if we call it 'All of Me'?" And he just stopped and looked at me like he'd seen a ghost. And then he told me about a song he'd had in the seventies called "All of Me Wants All of You" that he had never released. And that ended up being the hook for the song. We had to switch it around to make it fit that track, but he took part of that song from the seventies and made it the hook for the song. He switched the cadence of it around a little bit . . . We were at Record One, where they have three booths. You know, they have a booth for the main lead, a booth for the background, and a booth for the band, where everyone can do their thing at one time in one shot. So we were in separate booths just going back and forth at each other; no written stuff, just off the top of our heads. We just said whatever the hell came to mind, and it was a wrap. It was that simple.

I think we did our leads in a matter of about 30 minutes, and then it took another six hours just to do the background! [Chuckles.]

You recorded a song titled "Wherever U.R." (also known as "Untouchables") with the late Tupac Shakur for his never completed *One Nation* album. How did that collaboration come about?
Eric B. had given me a call and told me that Suge Knight was going to be starting an East Coast division of Death Row Records, which he was going to be running. Eric said he told him I was a free agent and Suge said he wanted to sign me. He asked me if I would come in and meet with him, and I was like, "Sure." So I flew out to L.A. to meet with Suge and we ended up going to a Tyson fight in Vegas. We were just hanging out and kicking it, talking about what could be done together, and he said, "You and 'Pac need to do something together." And I was like, "That's my man, ever since the Digital Underground days." And he was like, "Why don't you guys go back and do something *tonight*?" And we actually hopped on a plane that night and flew back to L.A. to Death Row studios. We actually banged out three songs that night: that one, a song called "Too Late Player" for Hammer, and something else for Hammer . . . a song I wrote called "What You Gonna Do for Me?" We banged out three joints that night. Then after me and Suge talked about the business side, I decided that wasn't really what I wanted to do.

You played an important role in the discovery of Jay-Z. How did you meet Jay-Z, and what role did he play in your live shows?
I met him through a mutual friend who lived around my way. He wanted me to do a tape with Jaz, and I came through to do it, and Jaz asked if his man could rhyme. Afterwards my man was like, "Do you think you could help Jaz get a deal?" And I was like, "Actually, I like the little light-skinned dude better." And then me and Jay linked up and he came out with me on the road.

I was going through a Patti LaBelle stage at that time where I wanted to do outfit changes during the show. So I would do half the show and then go in the back to change, and then Jay-Z would freestyle on stage while I was gone.

Keith Murray told me a story about his rhyming for you when he was a kid. Do you remember that?
Yeah. Back then Keith was MC Do Damage. There was an artist I was working with who was friends with Keith Murray's uncle. He brought him to one of my shows and then let him rhyme for me in a restaurant. We were playing around, acting like we were battling.

What were your thoughts on Keith at that time?
He was dope, and he was hungry. He was sitting there really quiet the entire time, and then as soon as they mentioned him rhyming . . . It wasn't like, "Nah," or any of that goofy shit niggas say today like, "Yo, I need a beat." He just jumped up and went at it, and spit hard, like he was serious. So I always felt like one day he was going to do something big.

Today everyone mentions you in their lists of the top five greatest emcees ever to rock the mic. How does it feel to receive that kind of universal recognition?
You know, the era where I'm from, that's why we started doing it in the first place. You don't get into it because you want to be rich and famous; you get into it because you want to be the best at it. So for someone to say something like that, it's a beautiful thing. It makes me feel like I accomplished my mission.

DISCOGRAPHY

1. *Long Live the Kane* (1988)
2. *It's a Big Daddy Thing* (1989)
3. *Taste of Chocolate* (1990)
4. *Prince of Darkness* (1991)
5. *Looks Like a Job For . . .* (1993)
6. *Daddy's Home* (1994)
7. *Veteranz' Day* (1998)
8. *The Very Best of Big Daddy Kane* (2001)
9. *The Last Supper* (2011)

BLACK SHEEP DRES
Emcee

Dres and Mista Lawnge, two teens from New York whose families had relocated to North Carolina, established the hip-hop group Black Sheep in the late 1980s. The duo soon returned to New York where they landed a recording deal with Mercury/Polygram Records. The group then made a thunderous entrance into the rap game with their hit 1991 song "Flavor of the Month." The group, an affiliate of the Native Tongues, a collective of jazz-influenced social-minded artists, then released their gold selling debut album *A Wolf in Sheep's Clothing*. The album, released during the heyday of New York hip-hop, spawned two more high charting hits, "Strobelight Honey" and "The Choice Is Yours." The latter single spent 16 weeks on the *Billboard* Hot R&B Singles chart and would become universally recognized as a bonafide classic, as well as becoming the song most frequently associated with the group. Dres and Mista Lawnge then made a memorable appearance on Vanessa Williams' single "Work to Do," which ranked as high as number eight on the *Billboard* Hot Dance Music chart. During this period the group also established their own vanity imprint (One Love) through Mercury/Polygram.

In 1994, Dres and Mista Lawnge returned with their eagerly anticipated second album *Non-Fiction*. With the release of this album, designed to be a counterpart to their debut, the group showed growth and displayed new dimensions not seen on *A Wolf in Sheep's Clothing*. As the two men told *The Source* magazine, they sought to avoid being seen as "just another one of those New York acts with the same old beats." While the album underperformed due to a lack of promotion, *Non Fiction* was praised by critics for offering something more substantial and artistic than most of the albums out at the time. Following the disappointing sales of *Non-Fiction*, Black Sheep soon disbanded. They have since reunited to record the title track for the film *Once in the Life*, as well as the 2002 EP *Redlight, Greenlight*.

Dres, who has since changed his moniker to Black Sheep Dres, has found some work as an actor and has enjoyed a fruitful solo career. In 1999, he released his solo debut *Sure Shot Redemption*. Seven years later he released the album *8 WM/Novacane*, which had started out as a Black Sheep album but then became a solo album after Mista Lawnge once again left the group during its recording. In 2009, Black Sheep Dres dropped his third solo project, *From the Black Pool of Genius*.

What does hip-hop mean to you?
It's kind of grown over the years. I've kind of come upon a revelation that it's the music of the people. I heard this poet—an African cat—who was speaking on hip-hop. He observed that if you flip hip-hop around backwards it's "pih-poh" . . . *people*. I've really embraced that. He's right. Hip-hop is much bigger than a culture of a sect of people. Hip-hop has the power to affect *all people*, as does any form of music. I would even go so far as to say that it's possibly more powerful than other forms of music on a certain level. It can more directly affect the children than other things that are offered to them. Ultimately, that's how I've grown to see music: as something that affects the people—and not always for the best.

In the past you've stated that you see a wide expanse between hip-hop music and rap music. As you know, a lot of people—including the media—tend to see them as being the same thing. In your view, what's the difference between hip-hop and rap?
I definitely see the two as being different. Again, hip-hop is something that speaks to the people and is for the people. It speaks not only of your struggles, but it can also speak of whimsical things. It can be one of a billion things, but it's a voice of the people. The mechanics of such . . . there's a tradition that's been passed down and is adhered to. It's creative, and original, and doing something just a little bit different while still being grounded in these principles.

Rap music, to me, is pop music. It's the cookie-cutter stuff that's all over the radio. Someone combined the DNA of pop music and hip-hop music, and the result is rap music, which doesn't really adhere to that principle. It's made by artists who don't really look at it as an art form so much as they look at it as a hustle or a business. It's work, and it's just work. That's cool, and I'm not mad at those artists. But for me, it's more than just work. We've gone really far . . . it's just too bad we're going the wrong way. We've come really far. Who ever knew there would be hundreds of millionaires because of hip-hop? And that's such a powerful statement, but what's sad is what we're doing with that money. Coming from the conditions that we all came from, it's shameful for us to turn our backs on that and on each other. Someone like Kool Herc or Melle Mel or Kurtis Blow shouldn't want for anything. There are responsibilities to where we come from that we're not adhering to.

You once made a statement that I found profound in its simplicity. You said that you got your record deal for being original, but that today record deals are given to artists for sounding exactly like someone else.
I think everyone's become kind of lazy in approach. Something that's always been in every community, but especially the black community, is that you need to get money. "Get money, we've got to get money." And then a way was discovered to get that money through the music, and it became a hustle. You know, "I don't necessarily have to go to school if I get money" and "I don't necessarily have to adhere to anything if I get money." And that eventually became a blueprint in music, and everyone just set out to make money. Today there are a lot of cats who rap, but there aren't a lot of artists. But don't get me wrong, there are a lot of cats out there who are looking for, and are very happy with, rap music. I would just like to be able to present them with more options.

Does it disturb you as an artist that hip-hop music is often judged from the outside by the more dumbed down stuff? People who don't know anything about hip-hop music tend to see the cookie-cutter pop music as being the same as the more artistic music. To them, it's all the same.
It does disturb me a little bit, but you kind of have to stick to your convictions regarding who you are. It affects me almost like an entourage. If I go out with a bunch of knuckleheads, and somebody slaps the shit out of somebody, it'll be, "Dres from Black Sheep is wild. He's crazy." I might not have even been there. I might have been in the bathroom, but I'm running with this crew that represents me incorrectly. It's the same with the music . . .

I play golf, and I'm playing with an older gentleman. He asked me what I do, and I'm trying to explain to him that I'm a hip-hop artist. And his only point of reference was what he hears, and he started looking at me. Now his attitude was more that he didn't see that in me. "I don't see you as being that kind of person." This was based on what little about hip-hop that he knew or had seen prior. I then spent the next four hours explaining to him that the music comes in different shapes, sizes, and colors. You know, there's good and bad everything. I said, "It's unfortunate that you haven't been introduced to any of the good, powerful music that's out there, but please don't think by any means that even reflects half of what's out there." He walked away with a better understanding, but for a moment, I cringed because I knew that he was looking at me beneath my character. And then there are times when you just have to let it go; it's not up to you to fight every battle. There are times that I don't have the time to explain all of this, so I walk away knowing that someone is looking at me beneath my character. So thanks, rap music, I appreciate that. [Laughs.]

On the song "U Mean I'm Not," you guys parodied the gangsta rap movement of the time. Now here we are almost 20 years later, and even some of the so-called backpack rappers are rapping about guns and cocaine. What are your thoughts on that, and do you think this trend is ever going to end?

I think it's starting to die down, to be honest with you, even though anyone and their mom may speak about cocaine and guns. It's kind of bizarre, but who's to say that a backpack kid doesn't come into contact with cocaine or a gun? They probably do, if we're going to be honest about it. But it's twofold. It's them trying to play the game, and the game kind of playing them. And just because you speak about one thing doesn't mean you can't speak about another. That person may be looking at things like, "Damn, I thought there would be more options for me out here." It's unfortunate, but it may be their reality. You know, "I'm having to play this game musically, but I'm also having to play this game in reality." They might be selling themselves short, but that may well be their reality. "Damn, I went to school, but now I've got this cocaine and I'm trying to get some money to feed my kids." I think it depends on how the artist presents it as to how justifiable that kind of subject matter is. There's a whole gamut of songs that can be made—even if it's them speaking on a gun or cocaine. But as an artist, I would like to think that there are records that can be made outside that box.

How did Black Sheep come to be involved with the Native Tongues?
It was really a situation where Lawnge introduced me to them. I had met Lawnge in North Carolina, and we both wound up moving back to New York. We happened to bump into each other on the street in Manhattan, and he was kind of in between spots to live. I had a two bedroom that I had just gotten into. He was a cool dude that I had met down south, and I was like, "Yo, you can crash with me." This was before I even knew anything that was going on musically. He was just a guy that I was fond of. So he comes up and brings his records and equipment to his room, and he sets it up. And then he starts explaining how he's been coming up, and how he's hooked up with Red Alert, who had him in the studio with the Jungle Brothers while they were recording their first album. He had all kinds of stories about these cats that Red Alert had put him onto. So, slowly but surely, I met Red, and then I started meeting everyone around Red, which was Jungle Brothers, De La Soul, Tribe Called Quest . . . We just kind of hit it off with all these cats, and we found ourselves hanging out with them all the time.

Lawnge and I had started rhyming together back in North Carolina, so we used his equipment to kind of put some stuff together. I started seeing that this really could work, so we put our money together and made a demo. Once we presented it to Red and his management office, they made some calls to labels on our behalf. They set up a few meetings, and that was it. We were off and running.

Last year, your single "The Choice Is Yours" was listed at number 73 on VH1's list of the 100 greatest hip-hop songs of all time. What are your thoughts on that?
I am so grateful that "The Choice Is Yours" has stood the test of time. That is such a dope thing. I mean, I don't really care about VH1's list, but on the other hand, to be in the company of 100 great records . . . I appreciate that. That's love. It's definitely a cool thing.

A funny thing about that list . . . When they interviewed me for that, their list was different from what ended up appearing on that program. On the original list, we were number nine; it was the number nine record. Then, when they wound up airing the program, it was number 73 or whatever. [Chuckles.] And that was great, but nine would have been really dope. I was already making plans based on its being number nine, but shit happens.

When you have a legendary song like "The Choice Is Yours," does that make you step up your game on future songs? Do you ever think, there's a bar there, and I have to make this song as good as that one?
I think you just try to be dope, period. There's definitely some pressure there . . . There's a bar, and I think everyone should set a bar by which to measure their successes. You have to be honest with yourself—does this new song reach up to that bar? It's not necessarily that it has to be better than that previous record, but you want it to reach that bar regarding the caliber of work that you do. And if it doesn't, you have to be honest. I think a lot of people get disillusioned and start to believe that everything they make is dope. I think some of these cats need to humble themselves a little bit and understand that that's not necessarily the case. Some days, you can write something that's great, and on other days, you can write something, and when you look at it, you can tell that something was on your mind. You might even say, "What the hell is this?" Everything you write or record is not going to be a classic, and you have to understand that and be able to differentiate between the good and the bad.

On your first album in particular, you guys used a lot of really great samples, from the Bar-Kays to Herb Alpert. A lot of people outside hip-hop believe that sampling isn't really creative. They think it's lazy. What are your thoughts on sampling?
Sampling is dope, especially when it's done where I come from, and that's when you take a snippet—something that by itself may not even be recognizable—and alter that by changing speeds or chopping it. I'm talking about a one or two bar loop, which is maybe only four or five seconds, and is from a song that has long since been forgotten. But there were artists who saw the business mechanic of it . . . You know, if you take something that was very popular and put something—anything—over it, it will create nostalgia, and it will be listened to. It's simple mathematics; it will be listened to, and if you promote it, it can become something huge once again. Then there were groups like Black Sheep and De La Soul and Tribe Called Quest who were trying to take sampling to the next level in regards to the art form of it. It became a thing where, ultimately, there was so much money

being made off the lazy man sampling that anyone using any sample from the music has to pay so much money that it becomes cost prohibitive. The original artists see a possibility of a big payday and ask for way too much money now—especially for someone like me who isn't trying to build his entire song around that one sample. In the way we did it, we took a small snippet and changed it to the point where it was unrecognizable and it then became something of your own. But yes, sampling was definitely abused a little bit early in the game, and as a result, cats now want astronomical amounts of money for even the tiniest sample.

DISCOGRAPHY

1. *A Wolf in Sheep's Clothing* (1991) [as Black Sheep]
2. *Non-Fiction* (1994) [as Black Sheep]
3. *Sure Shot Redemption* (1999)
4. *Redlight, Greenlight* (2002) [as Black Sheep]
5. *8 W/M/Novakane* (2006)
6. *From the Black Pool of Genius* (2009)

CHIP FU
Emcee

East Flatbush, Brooklyn trio the Fu-Schnickens was comprised of Chip Fu, Moc Fu, and Poc Fu. The three talented lyricists gained attention after performing at an event at Howard University and were quickly signed to Jive Records. The Fu-Schnickens' 1992 debut single "Ring the Alarm" was an instant hit, creating anticipation for the group's debut album *F.U. Don't Take It Personal.* The album soon spawned two more hit singles in "La Schmoove" (featuring Tribe Called Quest's Phife Dawg) and "True Fu-Schnick." The album reached the Top 20 on *Billboard* magazine's Top R&B/Hip-Hop Albums chart, and was certified gold.

In 1993, the group recorded the song "What's Up Doc? (Can We Rock)" with NBA basketball sensation Shaquille O'Neal (as "Shaq Fu"). The song became a Top 40 hit and made the group even bigger stars. The following year, the Fu-Schnickens released their second album, *Nervous Breakdown.* Although the album was not as successful as their first, it did spawn another hit song, "Breakdown." As the musical landscape of hip-hop was changing after the recent release of albums by newcomers Wu-Tang Clan and Black Moon, Chip Fu urged his fellow group members to change their style and adapt to the new sounds of the genre. This led to inner turmoil within the group, and this, coupled with Jive Records' insistence that they create more mainstream music, led the group to disband.

In 1995, the label released a greatest hits collection which contained four previously unreleased tracks, but the Fu-Schnickens were finished as a group. After remaining relatively silent for nearly a decade, Chip Fu reemerged in 2004 on Ali Shaheed Muhammad's solo debut, *Shaheedullah and Stereotype*. In 2007, Chip Fu was asked to appear on the remix of Nas' "Where Are They Now?" That same year, Chip Fu released the popular underground single "Love Mi Sensi." He then appeared alongside Zhane's Renee Neufville on the track "Ready fi War" on Pete Rock's *NYC's Finest* album. Chip Fu released the underground mixtape *Stop Playing* in 2009, and the EP *War Paint* in 2010.

What does hip-hop mean to you?
When I think of hip-hop, I think of lifesaving. Growing up in Brooklyn, I think a lot of people weren't as open to as many things as other people are. I say lifesaving because there are probably a lot of worse things that some of us would have been doing if there was no hip-hop.

What are some of your earliest hip-hop-related memories?
For my brother's 13th birthday party, I wanted to give him a gift. There was this crew in the neighborhood called the Jam-a-Lot Crew, which consisted of Educated Rapper and Doctor Ice, who later made it big as part of UTFO. The Jam-a-Lot Crew played at my brother's 13th birthday party, and I actually wrote a rhyme for my brother. I kicked this rhyme for my brother, and Educated Rapper came over to me and said, "Keep that up. You could be good at this someday." I was like, "Cool. All right." And then years later, I found out that the guy who told me that was Educated Rapper. That blew my mind. For him and I to meet and actually talk about it later was kind of funny.

Was there a specific moment when you knew you wanted to be an emcee?
I think the moment I knew I wanted to be an emcee was when I heard "Eric B. Is President." When I heard that, I looked at things differently. Rakim changed the way in which you maneuvered your pen on paper. There was no more cat/rat/bat rhyming. I was attracted to that, and I said, "That's what I want to be. I want to be an emcee of that caliber." I didn't want to emulate his style, but I wanted to be able to move people with the things I said.

Around 1989 you were involved in quite a few emcee battles. Is that right?
Yeah. It was kind of strange because I wasn't used to that. What gave me the push to actually do it was Busta Rhymes, because we went to high school together. There was this place called Woody's in Manhattan, and we both went there. KRS-One was there in the crowd. He was like, "Yo,

you should get on stage and show these people what you've got and just let them know how nice you are. You should just tear these emcees down." And I did just that. And from there, I battled at every club that had an emcee battle. There was one battle that was billed Hip-Hop vs. Reggae, and I actually signed up on both lists. And I won both battles.

How were the Fu-Schnickens formed?
Moc Fu and Poc Fu had already started the group. I was a solo artist, and I was looking for something to get into. They were like, "Yo, you should come down to one of our practices." I went down there and tore it up and they were like, "You need to be part of the group." That was actually right before I started doing the emcee battles. I kind of did those just to get the name of the group out there. I did my thing, and everything happened from that point. Poc Fu and I actually grew up on the same block. His grandfather and my father were friends. Then Poc Fu met Moc Fu in high school and they formed the group, so I didn't really know Moc Fu at the time.

Was the group already called Fu-Schnickens when you came on board?
Yeah, they already had the name. I was like, "Are you serious? All right. Why?" Then we gave the name meanings, like "For Unity." But at the time it didn't really mean anything. They just wanted to come up with a name that would stand out from the rest of the groups out there.

A lot of your rhymes back then were influenced by cartoons. I'm not really sure if you could do that today, as hip-hop takes itself so seriously now. Why do you think that is?
I think hip-hop is so serious today basically because of the change in climate regarding politics, things that are happening in the streets, people passing away. So now a lot of people want to be taken seriously. Back then, things were happening, yes, but not to the level that they are happening now. I think people get sucked up into the way the media portrays hip-hop music now, and they get lost, and it's terrible. It's like you have to be a certain way in hip-hop—you have to be angry, you have to lash out at people. To get respect, they feel like you have to get arrested, you have to sell drugs. It wasn't like that when we were coming up.

It seems like that element of fun is missing today.
Right now it's more about being serious, but I think there has to be a lot more balance. I think that's what's missing in hip-hop, period. I should be

able to hear a Drake record, and then a Redman record right after that. There's no reason why I can't. Again, it's all about the change in climate. I do think there are some underground acts coming up now who are trying to bring it back to that point where it was more fun, which should at least balance it out a little bit.

You guys worked a lot with Tribe Called Quest at the height of their powers. What was that like?
It was crazy. The energy was crazy. Watching Ali [Shaheed Muhammad] take nothing and make something out of it . . . He knew what he was doing before the track was made. That kind of shocked me. When it came to creating music, it was really easy for him. It wasn't like how some of the producers are fighting to come up with beats. He knew what he was doing. Phife came in and dropped his verse . . . Everyone was just very focused at that time. We were focused on winning.

You're working with Ali Shaheed Muhammad on your new album. Has he changed the way he works, or is it pretty much the same as it was back then?
It's sort of the same. The only thing that's different is that we're a lot older [laughs], and our approach is different. He'll say something like, "Chip, you can't make a record like this." We've already made several records together, and sometimes he'd say, "What you're doing is hot, but nah." It's kind of cool now because we understand each other from all the work we've done together in the past, so the stuff we're doing now is incredible. The stuff he's producing is incredible. The record he just did for me is called "This Is Ska," and it's a ska record. You would never think that Ali would produce a ska record. You just wouldn't expect that.

The Fu-Schnickens introduced Shaquille O'Neal as the unofficial fourth member on the song "What's Up Doc?" How did that collaboration come about?
The whole thing came about when our record label informed us that Shaq was a big fan of our music. We were his favorite emcees, and he used to mimic my verses. So Jive Records flew us out to an Orlando Magic game. I don't really watch basketball, so I didn't know who he was at the time. But the other group members were telling me all about him. "He's a first-round draft pick." So Shaq said he had lyrics, and he set up some studio time.

Instead of creating a new song, we rerecorded "What's Up Doc?," which we had already recorded some time before that. The thing was, the original version had a sample of Bugs Bunny in its chorus, and we couldn't get the sample cleared, so we'd had to shelve the song. So we decided to just take the sample out of the song and just say the line ourselves. We did that and then put him on the song, and he just took off from there.

A lot of people have complained that actors and athletes rapping hurt the integrity of hip-hop. What are your thoughts on that?
People need to understand the dynamic at play here. A lot of emcees always dreamed of being athletes. You could hand them a football or a basketball, and they'll tear it up. It's the same thing with athletes—a lot of them dreamed of being rappers. It's sort of the way some actors feel about rappers acting—they don't like it. But then if you take someone like Mos Def, who studied acting but chose music . . . You can't say that he's not a good actor just because he's also a rapper. You don't always know the path that some of these people took to get where they are. Having said that, I can understand why some emcees feel that way toward athletes and actors rhyming, because they haven't paid their dues; they haven't been out there battle rhyming and chewing other emcees up. Athletes and actors who have money can just jump right in and record their own albums without doing those things. But you can't really say that some of these guys didn't already have that dream of being an emcee. Look at Nelly—if he wasn't making music, he'd be playing football. When you see him on those MTV football specials, he's tearing it up out there. And that's what he did in high school.

The Fu-Schnickens had the opportunity to perform alongside groups like KRS-One and the Wu-Tang Clan on the final episode of *The Arsenio Hall Show*. What was that experience like?
It was crazy to have all those guys in one room. We all knew we were there for one thing, and that was to make sure this closing show was a good one. There were no egos. Everyone got along with everyone else. We practiced for hours to get the show the way it was. I think, for me, that was one of the best days for hip-hop. There were certain people I had never met, and to be able to be around them and to create with them was amazing. To be able to create with Ol' Dirty Bastard and Method Man and the entire Wu-Tang Clan, as well as MC Lyte, and Yo-Yo, and CL Smooth, and Das-EFX, and Guru . . . It was just incredible.

Sometimes when you create a song with someone else of that caliber, it tends to make you elevate your game. Did you find that to be the case in that particular instance?

I don't think it was a competitive thing for anybody that day. I think that day it was more about knowing that we were chosen to do the show. I mean, out of all the groups in hip-hop, they chose Naughty by Nature, they chose Das-EFX, they chose the Fu-Schnickens. They chose the groups at the time that were making noise and had people following them. It made me feel good to know that someone said, "Yo, you gotta add the Fu-Schnickens to that roster."

What are some other moments from your time with the Fu-Schnickens that stand out in your mind?

Me, personally, I was the guy who kind of stayed in the booth. I mainly just wrote and recorded. The only other thing that really stands out was when we went overseas to other countries and the audiences were reciting my verses word for word. It was crazy to go to places like France or Japan and see people kicking my verses. I was like, "This is crazy that they bought the album and actually practiced how to kick the verses." The creative side of everything was crazy, too; the way we went into the studio and received beats from Ali, and received beats from Diamond D, and K-Cut, and everybody else. Those producers came and dropped their beats and they never left the studio. It's not like it is today where you purchase a beat from a producer and it's all about him getting his money. Back then the producers sat there and oversaw everything to make sure that the song was hot—because his name was on it also. I enjoyed working with the producers. The producer would give you a bare track, and he'd make sure you put the song together correctly. Then he would add horns or maybe a harder snare, you know what I mean?

I understand that contractual difficulties kept you out of the music scene for a long time. What exactly happened?

More than anything else, Jive Records wanted the Fu-Schnickens to be another DJ Jazzy Jeff and the Fresh Prince. I understand where they were coming from, but I couldn't do those kinds of things. Music was changing, and people were still gravitating toward us after "Breakdown." That was the direction I wanted to see the group go, because no one expected us to come up with a song like "Breakdown." I felt like we needed to continue to think outside the box. I thought we needed to think bigger. We had just done the record with Shaq, and we had to come with more hot shit. And Jive was trying to make us go in a direction that we were not happy with. In order for us to get out of our contract, we had to break up as a group. So we broke up, and we kind of realized that the whole Fu-Schnickens thing was not going to work with us coming back together because we all had creative differences. I really wanted the group to get into a creative zone before anything else, and take the time to listen to what was out there first before trying to put out a record just to be in the marketplace. It didn't make any sense. Just making a record like that probably would have been a waste of time. So I kind of made up my mind that I would just go to school and do what I had to do until the contractual issues sort of died down. I just waited it out. When I finally got the paperwork saying I was out of the contract, which was years later, I started putting out my own music. But I was always recording, even when no one was hearing it.

In 2007, you made an appearance on the remix of Nas' "Where Are They Now?" That must have been another big moment in your career.
The craziest thing was that Nas' people called me and I hung up the phone on them. Twice. They said, "This is such and such calling from Ill Will Records, and we want you to be on this Nas remix." I have friends who do a lot of phone pranks, and I was like, "Stop messing around" and hung up the phone. Then when I checked my e-mail, I had a couple of messages from the same people. They were like, "Just lay your verse and send it in." I laid the verse on Friday, and on Monday it was all over the Internet. People were like, "Dang, Chip tore the song down," or whatever. And I thought, man, I thought they were playing. That's when it hit me that it was a real song. When they sent me the beat, it didn't have Nas on it. I was like, "I need to do my verse. You never know, it might be real, and I don't want to miss out."

You're back in the studio now working on a new solo album. In what ways has the rap game changed while you were away?
The difference for me is that I can go into the booth and try a whole bunch of things without messing anything up. Back when we did everything on tape, that was a lot harder. If you messed up, or you kept messing up, you'd have to cut the tape. When it came to drops, you'd have to have two people at the board to push buttons. But today, everything is digital. It's more

fun for me because everything I used to do in the past, I can apply to now and it's better. When I step in the recording booth now, I'm stepping into the booth in my house. Then I can record what I want and just e-mail it to the producer and he can say, "Just change this up," or whatever. I really like that. But what I don't like is the approach that other people are taking. They're like, "I'm gonna go into the booth and just kick a bunch of nonsense and put it out there." I mean, it's good that you can put your music out there with no middle man, but just make sure that what you're putting out there is palatable. You can't just say you're going to do some hip-hop, and then go and do some foolishness.

Tell me about your alter-ego, Jungle Rock Jr.

I had an idea when Pete Rock, myself, and Renee Neufville from Zhane did that song for his album called "Ready fi War." That's a big reggae song, huge overseas. So I said, "Why don't we get together and do a collective thing?" It was going to be called Jungle Rock International. The idea was that Pete Rock could deejay, and Renee could sing, and I'd just wild out, basically. We thought about it, but we ultimately left it alone. So I thought, I'll just put out a bunch of records under the name Jungle Rock Jr., which is ultimately the other side of me with the singing of the reggae and all the other stuff that I was not able to do on the Fu-Schnicken albums. And I'm happy that people are gravitating to it. Now they know what to expect from me. They're like, "Well, I know Chip is crazy is with the rhymes, but he also does this reggae shit. What's next from him?" I like that it's working because it keeps people in tune to what I'm doing.

What are some other steps that you've taken to stay current? I mean, a lot of emcees come back from a hiatus and their music sounds corny and stale, but your new music sounds very contemporary.

The main thing is that I never stopped writing new material. I always compared my music to what's out there. I was real hard on myself. If it sounded like it couldn't compare or it couldn't compete in the marketplace, I didn't put it out there. But then it got to a point where I started hearing certain emcees step their game up. I've got to give credit to Eminem, I've got to give it to Royce the 5'9 . . . I've got to give it to a lot of emcees. I can actually say that emcees like that brought me back to the mic. Listening to them and getting serious about my craft, I just stay in the booth. No one knew that I did; the only person who knew I was recording all this stuff was

Ali. I did the majority of my recordings at his house. I learned all the Pro Tools and stuff from him, and it was over.

Nas said hip-hop is dead. What are your thoughts on the current state of hip-hop?
Hip-hop in the way that we knew it is dead, and that's understandable. The state of hip-hop is going through its changes. Do I like it? Well, I respect it. I respect the fact that guys are getting their money. I don't respect what they're trying to push off on the kids, because I have a child of my own. There are certain emcees in the game that I do respect, because they're serious about their craft and they're trying to think outside the box. Then there are other emcees that I don't respect. At this particular point in time, I'm just going to watch the game. I'm not going to dictate what people are going to like or they're not going to like. This is where hip-hop is right now, and I've got to respect that. I mean, it's going to make me work even harder, but trust me, I've got something for the game.

DISCOGRAPHY

1. *F.U. Don't Take It Personal* (1992) [as Fu-Schnickens]
2. *Nervous Breakdown* (1994) [as Fu-Schnickens]
3. *Greatest Hits* (1995) [as Fu-Schnickens]
4. *War Paint* (2010)

CHUCK D
Emcee/Producer

L ong Island native Chuck D formed the musical group Spectrum City in the early 1980s. After hearing a couple of the group's underground singles, noted producer and Def Jam cofounder Rick Rubin convinced them to sign to the label in 1986. Chuck D and company then recruited Flavor Flav and Terminator X to the group and rechristened the collective Public Enemy. The following year the group released their groundbreaking debut album *Yo! Bum Rush the Show*. The album featured innovative production from in-house producers the Bomb Squad, as well as potent political commentary from Chuck D. Today the album is hailed as a bonafide classic and is considered one of the most influential albums in the history of hip-hop. It has been named one of the top 100 hip-hop albums by *The Source* and one of the 500 greatest albums ever recorded (in any genre) by *Rolling Stone*. Interestingly, Public Enemy's second album, 1988's *It Takes a Nation of Millions to Hold Us Back*, would also be considered a seminal album and would once again make both prestigious lists. *It Takes a Nation* was also named Album of the Year by *The Village Voice*, making it the first hip-hop album to receive this honor from a predominantly rock publication.

In 1990, Public Enemy released *Fear of a Black Planet* and sold more than a million copies of the album the first week. The album, which displayed a significant maturation from its predecessors, would ultimately be named (once again) to both the *Source* and *Rolling Stone* lists of the greatest albums ever recorded. It has also been chosen by the Library of Congress for inclusion to the National Recording Registry. The group continued their winning ways in 1991 with their fourth album, *Apocalypse 91 . . . The Enemy Strikes Black*. This time out, however, the group changed their musical direction with an album produced by newcomers the Imperial Grand Ministers of Funk. On the strength of successful singles like "Can't Truss It," "Shut 'Em Down," and a remix of "Bring the Noise" (with rockers Anthrax), the album once again went platinum.

The prolific Public Enemy have continued to crank out one innovative album after another, with no two projects sounding alike. Their subsequent releases include *Greatest Misses*, *He Got Game*, and *Revolverlution*. In 2004, *Rolling Stone* ranked Public Enemy at number 44 on their list of the 100 Greatest Artists of All-Time. Public Enemy is recognized today as one of the foremost groups of the "golden era" of hip-hop. Having influenced everyone from Ice Cube to Immortal Technique, the group is significant because it paved the way for political, social, and culturally conscious hip-hop. The group also broke down numerous barriers and were recognized in a way that no hip-hop act before them had been.

In addition to his work with Public Enemy, Chuck D has released two solo albums, *The Autobiography of Mistachuck* and *I Don't Rhyme for the Sake of Riddlin'*. In 2000, Chuck D, Professor Griff, and Kyle Jason combined forces to establish the rock/rap hybrid group Confrontation Camp.

Chuck D is one of the greatest and most accomplished emcees ever to rock a microphone. His importance to hip-hop cannot be overstated. Quite simply, the man is a living legend.

What does hip-hop mean to you?
It's a culture of creativity, spawned by black people who have always been creative for various reasons; especially in this hemisphere. It was our expression and it has come down through all forms of art, music, fashion, and style, but it has been the term of creativity for the last 40 years. We've always been a creative people, so hip-hop doesn't begin and end with our existence. It's a term for the latter day originality and creativity.

Before you made your first album, did you ever rap about other things, or did you always have an understanding of what your message and your purpose was?
I grew up in a time when songs had to come from something to mean something. When I grew up with James Brown and Bob Dylan and the

Beatles on the other ends of things, a song actually had to do more because it was an audible offering and a world of very little visuals. You couldn't take visual components of art around with you as much, if at all. So a song had to *mean* something to you; whether you had a transistor radio or a Walkman or a box, words had to do that much more.

You've influenced legions of emcees. Who do you consider your biggest influences?

In rap it started out with people like Melle Mel, Kool Moe Dee, Run-DMC, Eric B. & Rakim, KRS-One . . . the legends. Then later on the contemporaries were Ice Cube and Big Daddy Kane. And there were so many others, but that kind of started it off right there. James Brown was an influence both musically and lyrically. Sly and the Family Stone, Aretha Franklin, Gladys Knight.

Flavor Flav and yourself seem radically different. How did you two hook up?

We both came from the same hometown. We wanted to show people that black people are just as diverse as anyone else, and that happened to be a shock to white people. [Laughs.] But I don't see, when people start looking at each other as human beings, why you would have to explain why two different personalities happen to be friends. Flavor Flav and I are amongst a bunch of black men who are different and diverse. A lot of times people kind of hold it to Flav's and my relationship, but there are a lot of people who are in that mix, as well.

Your styles seem radically different, but they complement each other and come together to create art.

In a black household you could have somebody who's a lawyer and then someone who's been convicted living under the same roof. [Laughs again.] So I think it works well together because we both know where we come from and who we are.

How did you land your first deal with Def Jam?

Rick Rubin tried to get me to record for his new label for about a year. And then we found a way to bring everybody in, as opposed to my coming in alone as a solo rapper with Def Jam. That's how we came up with *Yo! Bum Rush the Show*; it was an onslaught of many diverse characters embedded in the realm of paying homage to hip-hop. Before I became a professional, we were definitely public servants to a whole bunch of aspects of hip-hop music.

In "Fight the Power" you guys took Elvis Presley to task for stealing black culture. What are your thoughts on white emcees like Eminem?
Well, I wasn't so much taking Elvis to task as I was the whole Americanization of rock and roll just being exclusively white American and dominant. And it's the same thing with Eminem. I have respect for Eminem as an artist, and I have respect for Eminem in regards to what he had to study to come in, because he's a human being. But then when the masses of people connect somebody's skin color to being dominant at something in America by American rules, then that's something you should always attack. No offense to Elvis and Eminem, two icons whose names begin with "E."

I remember once reading an article in *The Source* about 3rd Bass where it was stated that roughly three-fourths of your fan base is white. Considering the messages that you're trying to convey, did you ever find that statistic disappointing?
No, because I understood the people where I come from, and that basically the music was going to come through a company, and it's going to reach out across America. Thank God for *Yo! MTV Raps* for reaching out across America and giving exposure to rap music. And I know that if I did a concert for black folks, it would be for two dollars or it would be for free, and everybody would show up. But you know, once you start getting into the realm of charging people this and charging people that, it enters the realm of business. Sometimes people bug me out. They say things like, "Yo, you went to Iowa. There are a lot of white people there." And I say, "Yeah, but if I was playing in Nigeria, there would be a lot of Nigerians there." [Chuckles.] So there you have it. I played in front of 50,000 black people in the middle of Ghana. You know, the message is going to reach wherever. If we're going to be anywhere, it's because it's reached that demographic wherever it's at.

One thing that has always impressed me about your discography is that no two of your projects ever has the same sound.
That's something we set out to do. But, you know, there are a lot of people in rap music and hip-hop that don't understand that. But I felt that in hip-hop and black music we are always trying to please. And we were like, no, this is how we are, and we're going to hold to that and never

repeat ourselves twice. You have to stand up for something or you'll fall for anything.

The Notorious B.I.G. sampled your vocals from "Shut 'Em Down" in the hook of his song "Ten Crack Commandments," which thematically goes against everything you've spent your entire career promoting—
It's their right to actually have a differing point of view, but you have to call me on it first if you're going to use my voice.

What was your initial reaction to the song the first time you heard it?
I thought nothing of it. My fellow songwriters kept pulling my coattails. "Yo, man, this is what is being done here. This is who these people are, and we need to also get paid as your fellow songwriters. [Laughs.] I tried to get them to just forget it, but . . . As you know, when you collaborate with people it's not always that easy. So it was really a thing of big business. It was a Def Jam and BMG discussion that led to [the lawsuit]. It's unfortunate because I thought Biggie was the type of artist—as was DJ Premier, who produced the song—who was able to cut across and just be able to make a difference. But, you know, the companies to which all of these things are connected can make people say, "Okay, you guys are okay. How about me?" And then I had to look at it as, well, you used it for this type of song, you should have called me. But in all due respect, Puffy called me when he was getting involved with another Public Enemy record [for his song "P.E. 2000"]. He showed the utmost respect by calling me, and I respected that, and I respect him to this day for a lot of the things he's done.

Public Enemy was one of the first hip-hop groups to touch upon social and political issues, and now, sadly, seems to be one of the last groups to do so. What are your thoughts on this?
There's a big world out there, and a lot of things are happening around the world. Maybe the United States seems to be experiencing a lull, but I think when it comes down to the basics of what rap music and hip-hop is about, other places adhere to them a little bit better. You've gotta pay attention to what's going on around the planet, as opposed to this one little spot. Things move, the world moves, and culture moves, too. There's no given reason why the United States should lead the world in culture. That's not supposed to be an automatic given.

At the height of Public Enemy's popularity, mainstream audiences embraced politically charged songs like "Fight the Power" and "By the Time I Get to Arizona." Today it seems like audiences would rather hear empty dance tunes. Do you think we'll ever see a day when politically themed songs will be as accepted as they once were?

I don't know. I think the United States has things that come and go. Political records are the rage in other parts of the world. Sometimes you've got to leave your home to figure out what's going on somewhere else. Look at Brazil; as much party and dance music as they've got going on, they've got a lot of political issues that need to be addressed, and they do it.

I think it's really impressive to think that such important records were ever so universally embraced in the first place, and I think a lot of that speaks to the talents of you guys as messengers.

You've only got X amount of time in your life to make statements, and timing is everything. And even when you do something like that, you can't take credit for it; you have to thank the people and circumstances which made it possible for you to do that. You can't ever really get full of yourself.

This year you spoke out against a law in Arizona which essentially makes racial profiling legal with your song "Tear Down That Wall." How did that song come about?

The song came about because I saw the treatment of the people along the Texas, New Mexico, Arizona, and California borders. What I saw was a growing schism of racist overtones just to get people voted in and out of office. And a lot of money that this nation claims it's short of has been put into this wall and this emphasis on immigration, and at the end of the day it's just for somebody's office seat or whatever so they can just sit and gouge themselves. That's what made me write the song.

What would you like to see Public Enemy's legacy be?

I'd like to see Public Enemy recognized as the Rolling Stones of rap, just like Run-DMC is recognized as the Beatles of rap. I'd like rap music to be looked at as being as legitimate as rock and roll.

DISCOGRAPHY

1. *Yo! Bum Rush the Show* (1987) [as Public Enemy]
2. *It Takes a Nation of Millions to Hold Us Back* (1988) [as Public Enemy]

3. *Fear of a Black Planet* (1990) [as Public Enemy]
4. *Apocalypse 91 . . . The Enemy Strikes Black* (1991) [as Public Enemy]
5. *Greatest Misses* (1992) [as Public Enemy]
6. *Muse Sick-n-Hour Mess Age* (1994) [as Public Enemy]
7. *Autobiography of Mistachuck* (1996)
8. *He Got Game* (1998) [as Public Enemy]
9. *There's a Poison Goin' On* (1999) [as Public Enemy]
10. *Objects in the Mirror Are Closer Than They Appear* (2000) [as Confrontation Camp]
11. *The Best of Public Enemy* (2001) [as Public Enemy]
12. *Revolverlution* (2002) [as Public Enemy]
13. *The Revolverlution Tour Live* (2002) [as Public Enemy]
14. *New Whirl Odor* (2005) [as Public Enemy]
15. *Power to the People & the Beats* (2005) [as Public Enemy]
16. *Rebirth of a Nation* (2006) [as Public Enemy] [w/ Paris]
17. *Bring That Beat Back* (2006) [as Public Enemy]
18. *How You Sell Soul to a Soulless People Who Sold Their Soul?* (2007) [as Public Enemy]
19. *Fight the Power: Greatest Hits Live* (2007) [as Public Enemy]
20. *Remix of a Nation* (2008) [as Public Enemy] [w/ Paris]
21. *I Don't Rhyme for the Sake of Riddlin'* (2010)

CHAPTER SEVEN
MICHAEL CIRELLI
Poet/Author

Michael Cirelli discovered hip-hop at a young age while growing up in Providence, Rhode Island. He later attended college at the University of Vermont. During a hiatus from college, Cirelli volunteered for a year and a half at a halfway house in England. He then spent another two years living in a Tibetan Buddhist colony. He also lived for several months at the famed French monastery of Vietnamese monk Thich Nhat Hanh in Plum Village. Cirelli then returned to the States and enrolled in college at San Francisco State. He lived in Oakland, California for six years, where he became heavily immersed in the local slam poetry scene. As a rookie, Cirelli placed fifth at the National Poetry Slam Individual Finals. Cirelli would ultimately serve two years on the Oakland slam poetry team, and another two years on the Long Beach, California poetry team. In 2001, he became the first person ever to make all three Bay Area teams—Oakland, San Francisco, and Berkeley—in a single year. In 2004, he made a memorable appearance on HBO's *Russell Simmons Presents Def Poetry*, performing his popular poem "A Love Letter to Kelis."

That same year saw the release of the book *Hip-Hop Poetry and the Classics*, which he coauthored with Allan Lawrence Sitomer. The tome—one of the first to offer a high school curriculum which compared the works of classic poets to contemporary emcees—was a huge hit and even gained the attention of Kanye West, who championed the book. Cirelli has since relocated to New York City, where he pursued his MFA in poetry at the New School. After graduating, he became the executive director at

Urban Word, an organization which presents literary arts education and youth development programs in the areas of creative writing, journalism, college prep, and hip-hop. In 2008, Cirelli released his first collection of hip-hop-themed poetry, *Lobster with Old Dirty Bastard*, to critical acclaim. A self-proclaimed hip-hop head, Cirelli says he penned the book with the intention of introducing hip-hop into the academic poetry arena.

What does hip-hop mean to you?
As a poet, hip-hop is language, is swagger, style, youthfulness, the evolution of literature. As a hip-hop head, it is energy, culture, it is mine and it is not mine. As an educator, hip-hop is a bridge, a continent, a way for us to all engage, reflect, and respect a culture, hopefully in an authentic way that will be different for each person if they retain accountability to themselves and to hip-hop.

When did you first become aware of hip-hop?
My earliest reminiscences of hip-hop are living in Providence. I kind of grew up with hip-hop. It was a music that was accepted in my neighborhood, and it was a music and culture that was kind of breathing itself into the city at that time. Breakdancing was very popular. This was in the eighties, and as a child, I was breakdancing. I think my first hip-hop cassette was Run-DMC's *Raising Hell* in 1986. I think I got that in my Christmas stocking, which was interesting. I had two fathers, because my parents divorced when I was three or four years old. My mother was remarried when I was five, so I was raised by my mom and my stepdad, who was also Italian-American. Then I still had my real father's side of the family, which was an old Italian family in Providence. My real father was kind of a hustler. He had a very unscrupulous lifestyle. He never really had a job. So I had the blue collar upbringing in my home, and then I had my father who was getting me the Sergio Valente pinstriped jeans, the Pro Keds with the fat shoelaces, and the name buckles. He would get linoleum from the linoleum shop around the corner from his house for me to breakdance on with my friends. But it was interesting because my parents—my mom and my stepdad—put Run-DMC's *Raising Hell* in my stocking because they knew I liked rap music. So I guess it was never a threatening music or culture to my family, and I think it was—and is—seen as a threatening kind of movement or culture to a lot of suburban white folks because of all the racism in American culture. So those are my earliest memories.

Then, when I got into high school, I got into alternative music like the Smiths and the Cure. I went to an all-boys Catholic school, and I was a jock; I played ice hockey. I kind of had a hiatus from hip-hop, but luckily found my way back to it around '92 and '93, which was kind of the golden era of the music. By the time I went to college I was fully immersed as a hip-hop head all over again. It was interesting, because I went to the University of Vermont, where everyone was into Phish and the Grateful Dead, and I had found my love for hip-hop again. This was around the time that *Stakes Is High* by De La Soul came out, and that is, to this day, my favorite hip-hop album of all time. I had a little bit of a hiatus, but hip-hop was always in my bloodstream. As I developed into a writer and a poet, I was able to appreciate hip-hop in a much more profound way through the lyrics. I've never been a person who is into producers and the musicality of it, although I do love good beats and great music. I've always approached the music through the lyrical content and quality. And as I've gotten older and my own academic sensibilities around the word heightened, I was able to look at it in a whole new way and really see the connections between the lyricality of hip-hop music and things that I was excited about as a writer. As I got into the slam poetry scene, I was actually more inspired by emcees than I was by poets. As a result, my poetry back then had a lot more rhythm to it. It wasn't overly rhyming, but it was rhyming. It really excited me. I just saw hip-hop as the evolution of poetry and the evolution of language.

Did you ever write rap lyrics in addition to your poetry?
I never really wrote rap lyrics, to be honest with you. I always had this thing where deep down inside, when you really love something, you wish you could do it . . . But I never really did it, or even felt like I really needed to. I guess I wanted to be a fan. I thought about that a couple of years ago when I was writing my book, and I guess I just really liked the thought of being a real fan and not feeling like I have to have a stake in it. I guess I do have a stake in hip-hop culture, more from an educational standpoint, but as far as actually emceeing . . . I just like being an incredibly huge fan of emcees and breakdancers and graffiti artists, and kind of just soaking those things in and finding my own inspiration within them. I'm able to champion it through my poetry.

I've heard people refer to me as a hip-hop poet, which I think is interesting. I don't know what a hip-hop poet is, but I don't write poems that rhyme anymore. I don't write bars. When you think of hip-hop, you think of different elements such as musicality and rhyming, but my poetry doesn't really have much of that in it. I think it definitely embraces the energy of hip-hop, but I find it interesting that a lot of people from the academic poetry community call me a hip-hop poet. I guess it's because I write about hip-hop culture and iconography. In much the same way that jazz iconography and culture became prevalent in more academic poetry in the late seventies and eighties, I wanted to include hip-hop culture and iconography in the academic poetry conversation. I had found when I was in grad school that anytime you mentioned hip-hop, it had this sort of negative connotation to it; it was seen as lowbrow art. Anytime you talked about spoken word, it was seen as lowbrow art. All the poets in the MFA program looked at *Def Poetry* like it was just bad, terrible poetry. They looked at hip-hop like it was the bane of literature, if one was to put it into a literary context. So my goal was to talk about the complexities and the dynamics of hip-hop in a context that they could understand. I wrote all the poems in my first book as 14-line quasi-sonnets, and then I also placed the figures into situations that you wouldn't normally associate with them. For instance, the title of the book is *Lobster with Old Dirty Bastard*. That poem is about Old Dirty Bastard going to Randazzo's Clam Bar in Sheepshead Bay and having dinner with his 13 kids, and the ruckus that happens during that dinner. I would learn a piece of truth about these icons and then create the story around it. Talib Kweli, I learned, had been expelled from Brooklyn Tech. So I then wrote a poem about what happened when he got expelled.

I just kind of flipped the script a little bit in regards to how we can look at these people, and I kind of placed them into situations that anyone can understand. My idea was to sort of straddle both worlds in a lot of ways. The hip-hop heads are obviously going to be into it, but the academics can also get into it and sort of see that there's more to hip-hop culture than what's heard on the radio.

What emcees and poets have most influenced you, and in what ways?
Again my favorite emcees are the ones that have really strong lyrical qualities. I would say that right now my favorite emcee is Lupe Fiasco because of the density of his lyrics and the poetry in his work. To me, Lupe Fiasco is so much more evolved lyrically than 95 percent of the emcees out there.

You can just take a verse and break it down in a million different ways. He's using double and triple entendres. He just really blows me away. I find it really, really inspiring. I want to write that, but I don't want to do what he's doing; I want to write something that speaks to how talented he is.

I also love the more obvious folks like Talib Qweli and Mos Def. I love De La Soul—especially Trugoy. Then my poetic sensibilities are different. One of my favorite poets is a guy named Jack Gilbert, who is just an old white guy who writes very quiet poems that are set in Japan or Greece. He's kind of a reclusive poet who puts out a book, and then doesn't put out anything else for another 15 years. I also love a lot of contemporary writers. One of my favorite writers out right now is a guy named Terrance Hayes. I also like a lot of my friends—folks who have come from, and evolved through, the performance spoken word scene. There are poets like Willie Perdomo and Rachel McKibbens that I like immensely. I like to try to find the balance between reading as much poetry as I can and listening to hip-hop and the new voices that are out. There's a guy named Blu out of California who's really talented. Then there are guys like Wale . . . It's interesting to see how new people are doing it and changing it and evolving it.

What inspired you to write *Hip-Hop Poetry and the Classics*?

The way that a lot of poets get involved in teaching is by being on a stage somewhere performing and reciting our poetry, and there was a teacher in the audience. And the teacher says, "Hey, you should come to my classroom and do a poetry workshop with my students." Or maybe they're a part of an organization that sends poets into the classroom. Within the last 10 years, folks have realized that spoken word artists reach the young people a little bit easier than the traditional poets, so there has been a whole movement of organizations such as Urban Word that champion this art form as a way to teach writing and literacy in the classroom. So when I got into the classroom—this white guy from Providence in South Central, teaching 30 kids poetry—I immediately thought of who was the most representative emcee from that geographical area that these kids would be into. I had already acknowledged and realized the poetics of rap lyrics. There was never a differentiation to me. So I just started bringing lyrics to the classroom. Then, in order to teach literary devices, I would just pull out the literary devices in the lyrics and let the students identify them and find ways to learn them and find elements of writing and literacy through those lyrics. If you go into a classroom and ask students who their favorite poets are, they might have some answers. But if you go in and ask who their favorite rapper is, you could have the conversation for an hour. From there you can evolve that to the things they're talking about and the politics that are invested in their lyrics. So *Hip-Hop Poetry and the Classics* came out of that using hip-hop in the classroom as a tool and as a subject of its own discourse and study, and then connecting that to what the students have to do in the classroom—the standards-based curriculum that they have to follow.

So when I met up with this teacher—an amazing teacher—who was a multiple California Teacher of the Year and has about four young adult fiction books out, he was completely impressed with the methodology that I was using. I'm not formally taught; I was just kind of going from the heart, which is kind of the best teaching methodology anyway. So we just started putting it all down. We tried to find culturally relevant poetry that we could connect with the hip-hop lyrics. I think if we just did hip-hop to teach literary devices, it wouldn't have as much weight in the Department of Education as it did when we connected a poem by Sojourner Truth with a lyric by Talib Kweli and then connected that with a literary device that was being used in both. We were writing it for about four or five months, and then I got into grad school and knew that I had a short window of time that I would still be living in L.A. So we cranked it out that summer. A small educational publisher called Milk Mug put it out, and it became a huge hit. It was crazy how it blew up, and I was meeting teachers from all over the country who were using the book. I'm seeing it in libraries like my own hometown. It was actually one of the first curriculums of its kind that used hip-hop in the classroom. And since then, there have been some really great ones. It really broke ground in that way, even though it was very conservative and user friendly and very simple in a lot of ways. But we found that that simplicity was really helpful to a lot of teachers. A lot of the more politically oriented stuff got cut out of the final draft, which kind of bummed me out a little bit. But at the end of the day, it served its purpose, and I think it opened up some doors for other folks who are continuing to do the work. There were hundreds, maybe thousands, of teachers at the time who were using hip-hop in the class, but we were lucky enough to be able to put it into book form and put it into a format that teachers across the country with no hip-hop background could use and benefit from.

Which emcees' styles have you found to be the most similar to classical poetry in terms of style and structure?

A lot of the early emcees with the A-B rhyme schemes—those are all connected back to the Romantics and all of the classical poetry that has come out of Western literature; even blank verse, which is unrhymed iambic pentameter derived back from Shakespearian poetry. I would say that as hip-hop lyrics have evolved, it has started to take new shape. Now you have folks like Aesop Rock, who can do a whole verse that doesn't even really rhyme, but it sounds like it rhymes. But still the elements of internal rhyme, the elements of A-B-C-D, A-B-C-D-B-A, all those different meters are found still to this day. Method Man does some really cool, kind of classic rhyme schemes, where he'll rhyme a couplet, then end a line with a word, then rhyme another two couplets, and then end a line with the C rhyme that was two bars before that. Those are all found in Old English poetry.

Poets such as yourself have expanded the boundaries of poetry by studying the lyrics of emcees. Do you believe emcees could—and should— push the boundaries of their art form by studying classical poetry?

Yes. I think a lot of them probably do. It's evident when you listen to guys like Lupe or Black Thought. The Roots' album titles are taken from books: *The Tipping Point* and *Things Fall Apart*. "Pushing pen like Chinua Achebe . . . " Kanye West is dropping names of the Last Poets. Nas had Abiodun Oyewole from the Last Poets on his album. They're definitely entrenched in these literary movements. Like myself, I'm not so interested with old poetry. [Laughs.] It's just too antiquated and dry. I can appreciate the ability to create these poems with these strict forms, but I think that emcees are doing that today, and they're doing it in a language that I can understand. For them to be able to create these amazing verses that all follow the same rhythm meter and rhyme scheme is pretty much just as complicated as troubadour poets writing villanelles and sestinas.

WRITINGS

1. *Hip-Hop Poetry and the Classics* (2004) [w/ Allan Lawrence Sitomer]
2. *Lobster with Old Dirty Bastard* (2008)
3. *Vacations on the Black Star Line* (2009)
4. *The Poetry Jam* (2010)

CHAPTER EIGHT
DADDY-O
Emcee/Producer

B rooklyn-bred emcee Daddy-O co-founded the seminal hip-hop
group Stetsasonic in 1982. The group, which was comprised of members Daddy-O, Prince Paul, Wise, DBC, Delite, Bobby Simmons,
and Frukwan, is significant because it was one of the first hip-hop groups to
utilize a live band. With their positive and inspirational lyrics, Stetsasonic
served as a precursor to the alternative hip-hop movement of the early 1990s.
In 1986, the group released their debut album *On Fire*. The album rose to
number 32 on the R&B/hip-hop album chart and would later be named as
one of *The Source* magazine's top 100 hip-hop albums of all time. In 1988,
the band released their sophomore album *In Full Gear*. The album produced
three solid singles, "Sally," "Talkin' All That Jazz," and "Float On" and received critical acclaim. (The album would later be re-released in 2001 with
three bonus tracks.) In 1991, the group released their third album, *Blood,
Sweat & No Tears*, which once again received critical praise.

After the release of *Blood, Sweat & No Tears*, the group decided to take
time off to work on other projects. Prince Paul would ultimately become
one of the most accomplished producers in hip-hop, and he and Frukwan
went on to become a part of the "horrorcore" group Gravediggaz. In 1993,
Daddy-O released his solo debut *You Can Be a Daddy but Never Daddy-O*
on Island/Polygram Records. The album spawned the successful single
"Brooklyn Bounce," and kept Daddy-O in the public eye.

Daddy-O has since enjoyed a prolific career behind the mixing boards,
producing and remixing songs by artists such as Mary J. Blige, Big Daddy

Kane, Red Hot Chili Peppers, Queen Latifah, Lil Kim, Jeffrey Osborne, and the B-52s. In addition, he worked with Puff Daddy and the Notorious B.I.G. to form the group Junior Mafia. Daddy-O spent four years as a Senior Director for MCA Records. He then went on to work for Motown Records, and later as an A&R Director for Kedar Records. In 2008, Daddy-O and the members of Stetsasonic reunited for several concert dates and there has since been talk of a new album.

What does hip-hop mean to you?
Definitely expression; expression of urban youth that started in the seventies, and musically born out of the bowels of disco. That's something that most people don't say, but it's the truth. In most cases, disco is the mother of hip-hop. I always say there were two discos: the disco of John Travolta and those guys, and then there's the disco that we listened to in Alabama Park and East New York and Brooklyn. I'm talking about stuff like C.J. & Company and First Choice—the funky stuff that we started the breakbeats with, and then we expanded from there. Hip-hop is style and expression, and it definitely comes out of the Bronx, which was prone to violence. They were tired of seeing violence, so they said, "Hey, we're going to dance against each other . . . Hey, let's go out and paint these trains. Let's pick up these mics, let's learn how to scratch." Grand Wizzard Theodore created the scratch, but after that we learned how to scratch and cut. It was a way to get rid of all the bad things we had been seeing, which is a big contrast to what we have now; today you have guys who think there's some fallacy of street credibility and that it's all about being tough. That's exactly the opposite of the roots of hip-hop. We had already been tough, and tough gets you killed. This was a way to get away from that and do something different.

When did you know that you wanted to be an emcee?
Probably about 1980. I heard it first in 1979 on what was called an "uptown tape," which was from Grandmaster Flash and the Furious Five. This was actually a tape that wasn't performed in a club. It was actually performed in Flash's bedroom, but all five emcees were on the mic. We used to always love those tapes, and they were really clear. I didn't understand what I was listening to; it was poetry—I understood that—but it was in rhythm to beats. I thought, I wanna do that! And that was when I started my journey.

What was the hip-hop scene like when you first established Stetsasonic in 1982?

There were little or no records. In the beginning, making records was wack. You know, that was actually recording what you did. We used to come out and plug into street lamps and perform in the street every night. It was about being fresh every night. A lot of the music was uptown, and it hadn't really shifted down to Brooklyn yet. It was underground. It was a bunch of young guys like me who were underage trying to sneak into clubs. This was a new sound. DJs played records with the labels whited out so you didn't really know what the records were. Everyone was searching for breakbeats, even if you were just a fan. You tried to figure out what records were "Keep Your Distance" or "Big Beat" by Billy Squire. It was a really exciting time. I think one of the most notable things was that people didn't look at this as leaving their regular life to the side; they just looked at hip-hop as something that we did. It's very interesting. I think of Datarock saying a rhyme that he used to have; he'd say, "Can't see Kool Herc/can't go to work/can't hang out with the fellas so you got a sad smirk . . . " The most important thing is that when you heard a lot of those rhymes, you'd hear people talking about going to work. It was kind of an extension of the sandboxes, if I see it correctly. Everyone's minds were not focused on making millions of dollars. It was just "we're gonna get pretty good with this, and just do what we can with this craft."

I'm fascinated by that sense of maintaining your integrity by not getting a record deal.

We were just like, "What the heck is a record? If we put this on a record, we're wack!" Because now—after everyone's got records—you hear the same routines over and over again. Even Flash and them—and I love them—caught a lot of street flack because those first records they put out on Enjoy Records were just stuff they used to say at parties. Flash and them were the best and the worst in all areas . . . I mean, you can hear Melle Mel saying the same rhyme on three different records. And that's what we were all afraid of—that we would wind up repeating all that stuff . . . For Stetsasonic, it wasn't until we heard the Fearless Four do "It's Magic" that we realized that there was a way to make records and not be wack. Well, it was between the Fearless Four and the Treacherous Three, because Treacherous Three had the record thing down pat.

How did Stetsasonic land their record deal?
Mr. Magic and WBLS were running a citywide contest, so we entered the contest and beat everybody. We actually won first, second, and third prize. What I mean by this is, first, second, and third prize were all record deals, and all three of those labels wanted to sign us. We chose Tommy Boy Records, which was actually the second place prize. Sugar Hill Records was first prize, and Pop Art Records was third prize. We decided to go with Tommy Boy because Afrika Bambaataa was with Tommy Boy.

Would you have ever imagined that hip-hop would grow to the point where it is today?
Absolutely not. I mean, we wanted to be national and international voices, true. But in terms of the magnitude it's achieved, none of us could have seen that.

Today hip-hop songs are featured in commercials for everything from detergent to soft drinks. Do you believe this universal acceptance of hip-hop music is a good or bad thing?
I think it's good and bad. The one thing I do say when it comes down to the ad world is that I would rather see Jay-Z in an HP commercial than some wack rapper rapping about Kool Aid. And I don't agree with people who are not from the craft doing it. I mean, if I was going to go out and make a basketball commercial, I'd have to go out and get someone who was at least as good as someone in the Rucker League. If I had a choice I'd grab Michael Jordan or Kobe Bryant, because it's basketball and that is their craft. What I don't like is to see people actually disrespect the craft by getting the guy from the mailroom to do a rap.

What do you think when you see these celebrities or athletes trying to rap? I mean, even David Hasselhoff is making a so-called hip-hop album now.
I don't like it, but here's one of the lessons I learned from Delite coming up. I just wasn't smart enough to not hate on people and not to be egotistical, and Delite would always calm me down. We formed Stetsasonic together, and without him, Stetsasonic just never would have gone on to become a real group . . . I just would have been a hothead and made everything explode. The one thing that Delite always said to me whenever I would complain about cats is, "Do it better, man. Why are you complaining about

them? Just do it better. If they're going to be better than you, then there's no reason for you to keep complaining." I think there's a responsibility there for artists to see things that other people do and say, "I can't do that." When people look at what Denzel Washington does, they say, "I can't do that." What I don't agree with is artists endorsing these fools. It needs to come across: "This is my lane. I don't try to come across into your lane. I'm not trying out for the NBA." I think that's our responsibility as artists. When you look back at the "golden era" of hip-hop, nobody tried to follow Run-DMC or Big Daddy Kane. They didn't look at it as "I can do that." You can call these guys simplistic rappers or whatever, but whatever you say, just let some fool try to remake "Darryl and Joe." You can't do it. That level of excellence is what I would desire to see, even if only to stop some of these people who are not in the craft from trying to come in. I think if there was that high degree of craftsmanship, integrity, and excellence, less people would believe they could do it.

What are some of your fondest memories with Stetsasonic?
At the top and pinnacle of that list is playing Madison Square Garden. I'm a Brooklyn boy, and I'll never forget playing the garden—and almost falling off the stage—and standing at the very tip of the stage in the garden and saying, "Brooklyn, make some noise!" It just sounded like an earthquake. Then we played for 90,000 people in Senegal, which is just ridiculous. We played for another 30 or 40,000 at Wembley, which was ridiculous. My fondest memories really are the performances. We were a performance band first—we didn't even know we were going to make records—and we always knew we wanted to do shows.

I believe your solo album *You Can Be a Daddy but Never Daddy-O* personifies everything that was great about the golden age of hip-hop. However, the album was not a huge success. Why do you think that is?
I think, at that particular point, as far as my status and general public reputation, most people looked at it like I had arrived. I always think about music people and the way we were set up at the labels. There was always a television there playing the video stations. For people to look up from their desks and see me on a motorcycle rapping, I think people thought, He's kind of graduated a bit. But you could blame a little bit of the sales on the promotion of the record. The thing about making music that you really have to understand is that you're just not everybody's cup of tea. That's probably just what it was. It

wasn't really that people hated me or anything, but that just wasn't what they really wanted to hear at that time. The thing with music is that we stay out there; we are archived and we continue to exist out there. It could be another three or four years, and anything could happen. That album could resurge as long as it's out there. So I don't look at it in any kind of negative way at all. I had a good run. I had a number one single with "Brooklyn Bounce" in a bunch of territories in the U.S. I got to tour.

The one thing that I did learn is that I really didn't really want to be a solo artist. I went on tour, and from my first show I was just choking. I mean, I did well, but I was like, "Man, where are my guys?" I was so used to doing routines and stage antics with them. To try and hold that all together by myself . . . I developed a whole new respect for solo artists. I thought, Man, I don't know how in the hell LL [Cool J] and [Big Daddy] Kane do this.

You're also an accomplished producer, having produced everyone from Big Daddy Kane to Mary J. Blige. What are some things that you've learned as a producer that have made you a better emcee?
You know, this is the first time that I've ever been asked that question, and I'm not really sure . . . Being a producer, I did learn a bit more about music. I learned more about beat placement and where things are going to go on the track. In a way, I think that gives you a cheat card as an emcee. If you think about me in the studio making the Daddy-O solo record, I'm laying it all out for myself. So if you take the title track . . . I'm the producer, so I know I'm going to play the first couple of bars really raw and put nothing on it and just make it sound really warm. Then I'm going to do the old Jamaican wheel and let the record go back and then bring the record back in full. I could never have thought about that kind of thing if I was only an emcee, but as the producer I get to think about intros, outros, segues—all those things that as an emcee I would not really have thought about. When you're only an emcee, someone just kind of hands you the beat and you try to figure out what you're going to do with it. But when you're making it, you can say, "Man, I hear an airplane up under that snare," and you can just put it up underneath there. So I think that being a producer gave me an emcee cheat sheet.

What are some of your favorite memories from behind the boards?
Working with the Red Hot Chili Peppers is one of my favorite memories. Meeting them was incredible, and then Flea actually played some extra things for me in the version I did of "Higher Ground." It was kind of interesting to

see how these guys were so heavily into James Brown and George Clinton, which totally blew me away. So that's a great memory. Then I wrote and produced a song for Jeffrey Osborne, and I cried because he did the most incredible single take that you could ever hope to see in your life. He just went through it, and it was awesome. He just had that great voice, and those were the words—*my words*—that I had written in my bedroom. It was just amazing. And then any of the work I did with Puff [Daddy] and Mary [J. Blige] and those guys . . . It was just such a heyday for Puff. We championed him to be this young up-and-coming mogul. Just making those records, going in the studio and doing the "Real Love" remix—all of those things were very dear to me.

You've also worked as an A&R representative. What are some things you learned working in that capacity?
It was a blessing and a curse. It's not about the check alone, but it's completely beneficial. You're talking about checks, expense accounts, a lot of traveling. I originally went to work for a record company just to learn about the inner workings of a record company. Standing on the outside and looking in, we used to always say, "They're jerking people; they're putting people's albums on the shelf." You know, I kind of came to a doubtful place where I said, "I don't really believe that they're doing those things. Maybe artists are doing this to themselves." So I went to work at a record company to try and find out if some of that stuff was true. A lot of it was true, sad to say.

I learned the music promotion game. I learned what it means to get your record on the radio. I learned quite a bit about retail, and a lot about publicity. But I also learned that I didn't believe that music had a place in corporations. I never liked that idea of big corporate music. My philosophy is that all great music is made for five blocks. Maybe those five blocks are proverbial, but when you talk about real life, Bruce Springsteen is making music for Asbury Park; Jay-Z is making music for Marcy; Stetsasonic is making music for East New York; Hammer is making music for the people in Oakland. That's what happens, and then it usually spreads out and then people [from other places] start listening to it. So that concept of big corporate music, that's a little weird.

Most aficionados agree that something is missing from hip-hop today. What do you think that is?
Us. I don't think that we—my generation of artists—took enough initiative to be mentors. I could sit here and talk about these kids until I'm blue in

the face, but if I wasn't in there teaching them how to do it, then I have no right to complain about what they're doing. I see some similar things about the generation from before us, as well. Just the other day I was listening to an interview that we did right after "Talkin' All That Jazz." And one of the things we talked about in that interview was that at that time a lot of musicians would not even work with us. I think that they should have been bullish about being mentors—these same guys who were saying, "All this rap stuff is just a fad . . . " And that was Van Gibbs' position in this interview. He said, "I think you sample because it's easy. And because it's cheaper." And I made this argument with him that it was not cheaper; I was paying more to clear that sample than it would have cost to have anybody come in here and play a guitar. I think they didn't take the initiative to mentor us, and I think we've ultimately done that, as well. So when you ask me what's missing, I think it's us. I have to put the blame on me. I can't put it on this young dude. Who knows more—me or him? So it's kind of senseless when you see Ice T talking about Soulja Boy. Ice T is my man, but that's a bunch of bullshit. Ice, you've already done it all. Why can't you go and talk to this young brother? For you to sit and talk about how wack he is is just bullshit.

DISCOGRAPHY

1. *On Fire* (1986) [as Stetsasonic]
2. *In Full Gear* (1988) [as Stetsasonic]
3. *Blood, Sweat & No Tears* (1991) [as Stetsasonic]
4. *You Can Be a Daddy, but Never Daddy-O* (1993)

CHAPTER NINE
DJ JS-1
DJ/Producer/Graffiti Artist

Born and raised in Queens, New York, DJ JS-1 began working as a graffiti artist and as a DJ during the "golden age" of hip-hop in the late 1980s. He then spent most of the 1990s honing his craft, battling (and defeating) local DJs in battles and appearing on Bomb Records' *Return of the DJ* album series. During this period, he also started dabbling in production. In 1999, DJ JS-1 was asked by DJ Skribble to appear on the MTV show *Deejay Day* during their high-profile "Hip-Hop Week." While taping the show, he met former Roots beatboxer Rahzel, and the two have since joined forces and become musical partners. MTV soon asked DJ JS-1 to come back and spin during their *Campus Invasion '99* show. In 2002, DJ JS-1 was initiated into the world famous collective the Rock Steady Crew, which is one of the ultimate honors in hip-hop.

In 2003, DJ JS-1 released his first album, *Ground Original*, which featured a virtual who's who of hip-hop. He has since released three more albums, *Claimstake*, *Audio Technician*, and *Ground Original 2: No Sell Out*. As with the first *Ground Original* album, these subsequent LPs featured many of hip-hop's most talented emcees spitting over JS-1's original productions. JS-1 has produced such hip-hop heavyweights as KRS-One, Ultramagnetic MCs, La Coka Nostra, Big Daddy Kane, Sadat X, Common, EMC, Masta Ace, Kool G. Rap, OC, Everlast, RZA, Evidence of Dilated Peoples, Jeru Da Damaja, Casual, Craig G, and many more. In addition to producing his own albums, DJ JS-1 has also crafted a number of scratch albums, as well as a handful of popular mixtapes.

What does hip-hop mean to you?
When I think of hip-hop, the main thing that comes to mind is making something from nothing. The creation of hip-hop music came from taking a bunch of different genres of music and repeating the breaks. Graffiti evolved from people putting up their names and the names of their streets into an art form. Hip-hop came from a community that didn't have anything, and it's making a whole lot of something out of nothing. That's how I look at it—it's creating.

What are some of your earliest hip-hop-related memories?
When I was growing up in Queens, hip-hop was everywhere. Everyone was trying to breakdance or rhyme or do graffiti. I just remember riding my big wheel outside my grandmother's house when I was about five years old. This would have been around 1979 or 1980. I remember seeing people with the cardboard out, trying to breakdance. I remember seeing them painting murals on the pizzeria around the corner. That was like the first real thing that stood out in my mind. I was like, what is that? Here I was, five or six, and they had told me to stay away from those guys, so I wanted to know exactly what that was.

Which came first for you—deejaying or graffiti?
Definitely graffiti. From an early age, even before graffiti, I would just sit and draw. And then I started seeing these guys doing graffiti right around the corner. There was this one wall that they would always do murals on, and I would just watch those guys. You know, it was really popular in the mid-'80s. Graffiti was all over the place, and the mayor of New York City was always on TV talking about trying to get rid of it. Living right here by the seven trains, you just saw that stuff all the time. I was always trying to draw from the third grade or so. Then, around the eighth grade, I went out and started trying to bomb. That just led to my doing tons of pieces, and I was very heavily into that all the way through the '90s. I was always deejaying on the side, but then I started making money deejaying, so I kind of left the graffiti thing alone to pursue that.

When did you know you wanted to be a DJ?
A couple of things that stand out to me were seeing Jam Master Jay and seeing Grandmaster DST when he did those scratches for "Rockit" live on the American Music Awards. Being a little kid, those guys just looked so

cool up there with the turntables. Everything seemed to kind of revolve around them. I just kind of always took to that and liked that, and I sort of always knew that this is what I wanted to do. Then, in the mid-'90s, people started to give me recognition for some of the mixtapes and skills stuff and just sort of seeing what I was doing. I guess once I got guys like KRS-One to record with me, and I started touring with Rahzel in the late '90s, I knew that I could really do this. I felt like if these guys—some of the most talented in the world—were taking me seriously, then I figured maybe I had a real shot at this. That was when I really knew that this was what I was going to do. I mean, this was always my thing, but I went to college and all that so I would have a backup plan. You can't really count on something like this making you a living.

How did you come up with your moniker, DJ JS-1?
That's basically from the graffiti stuff. I wrote "JERMS" in the beginning. This was back when I was doing the Wild Style pieces, and I always liked the five-letter tags. Back then I always wrote JERMS on my work. Then, when I started to bomb the highways and streets, I basically shortened it down to JS. The one was a graffiti thing. You would put that at the end to signify that you were the first person to write that. It began as JERMS-1, and then I just shortened it to JS, and kept the one at the end. And everybody would see those more because unless you were a graffiti writer, you really wouldn't go to the Graffiti Hall of Fame. So everybody else would see the JS-1s on the highway, and that was sort of my name at that point because everybody knew me from that. When I started to DJ or do parties and it came time to put my name on a flyer, I figured I might as well keep the same name everybody knew me as. There was no sense in having four different names.

How did your first official album, *Ground Original*, come about?
In the whole time I was deejaying and collecting records from the late '80s, I was also trying to produce. I always had cheap samplers and a four-track or an eight-track or the digital recorder when they came out and Pro Tools . . . I was just always into that side of things. I guess in terms of the business side of it and just something I always wanted to do, I knew I had to separate myself from the pack. There are a billion people who can scratch really well, and they're out there doing what they do. I figured it was time for me to try to showcase some of my production work. I just basically did demos with my friends and doing local stuff. So I started using my connections

and reached out to these people I grew up around, whom I had been seeing at shows for years. So I reached out to KRS-One and Big Daddy Kane and all those types of people. They know what I'm about, and that I'm trying to do some real hip-hop stuff. I guess they liked what I was doing. It was a big thing for me to separate myself from the rest of the turntablist crowd. I can say, "Look, I also have production on these albums."

One of the things I really like about your albums is that you're making an effort to bring back the scratch hook. That really seems to have died out over the past decade. Why do you think that is?
There are a million reasons. The first reason, and the most obvious one, is that the sample clearance thing kind of killed it. It also killed a lot of the kind of music that I love, like the Large Professor and Diamond D stuff. I mean, if you look at a guy like DJ Premier, his first three Gang Starr albums were built on loops. And then he started chopping everything to try and get around sample clearance. He sort of invented his own style of sampling just to try to get around sample clearance stuff. And the same thing happened with the scratch hooks. To me, it's mostly rumors; not too many people really get sued. I think Premier told me he only got sued once for scratching something in the hook, and they don't clear all of the stuff he scratches in the hooks. I think it's just a rumor that gets around and people get nervous, so they stop trying to use it. The big name acts don't really want to use that style. And a lot of them—and this is sad—don't want to use scratch hooks because they look at it as old school. It's not current; it doesn't sound like a Lil Wayne song. It doesn't fit into the format of what everyone else is doing. I had this weird theory that all the stuff that I like—stuff like Gang Starr and the early Common—died out because it's middle-of-the-road hip-hop. What I mean by that is that it's not commercial—it's not Lil' Wayne or Nelly, so those people are going to hate it—and it's not underground enough to fit in with the crowd that likes Atmosphere and those kinds of groups. I think that type of music just gets lost in the mix. Dilated Peoples still does it, but it's because they have DJ Babu. The disappearance of that stuff sucks, but it's definitely because of sample clearance and people thinking that it sounds too 1990s. A lot of people can't do it the right way. A lot of people are trying to use scratch hooks, but most of them just sound like they're trying to be DJ Revolution, and he's a hard act to follow.

You use more scratch samples than most DJs who do scratch hooks. That must be ridiculously costly when you're recording for a small label and the profits aren't really that big to begin with.

No. Honestly, I've never cleared a sample in my life. I figure if someone ever sues me, then great—that means they listened to my record! [Laughs.] I don't even pay attention to that stuff. As for the reasons I use so many scratch samples, I look at it as that's my part to talk on the song. Through those samples, I get to say some of the things that I feel. The guy making the song can control the vibe of the song, the mood, the title, the beat, but sometimes you have some stuff that you want to say. So it's a way for me to speak. And I just always loved that. Growing up and buying hip-hop records, my friends and I would always go through a new album and try to see what Pete Rock or Dre used to scratch in the background on those NWA albums. We would hear Premier or Lord Finesse scratch something, and we'd say, "Wow, this is where he got this sample . . . " I just enjoy doing that. I collect acapella versions of songs just to find stuff to scratch into songs. It's difficult, too, because it's tricky in that the pool of stuff you can use is kind of limited; there are only a certain amount of hip-hop acapellas available. There are only a certain amount of lines that are going to work properly in the songs. When you start using multiple phrases on songs and you do multiple albums, it's limited. Like Premier, he's constantly on the prowl looking for new phrases because he's used so many. It does become more difficult with each song you do, but I love it. That's part of the fun in making it.

Because you make the same style of music, I would guess that you're a big DJ Premier fan.

Of course. He's the man. The thing is, I've learned so much just from listening to his music. There's an art to it, there's a way to do it properly. He's just so good at what he does and the way he composes his stuff. The reason that Premier is my favorite guy isn't even the music so much as it is just the way he is. If you meet him and talk to him, he's just a regular cool dude. He'll just sit and *want* to talk with you about hip-hop. He's really passionate about wanting to preserve good hip-hop, and he's just dead serious. I remember being at a studio one time and Dr. Dre was in another room of the studio. There was this security that was there, and they wouldn't even let me go to the bathroom while he was in the building. So you have to love a guy like Premier who'll just invite you over to his house. That's why I love that dude. Obviously the music he's made is just amazing. I mean, shit, if he wasn't around I can't imagine how little music I would have had to listen to in the past 15 years. [Chuckles.]

You produced and scratched on Sadat X's last album, *Brand New Bein'*. How did you hook up with Sadat, and what was it like working on that album?

I met Sadat through my friend JW. They're friends, and Sadat was always hanging out with us. He was talking about wanting to put together a new project. We were just kicking around ideas for the name of an album, and he really liked the title *Brand New Bein'*. He was like, "That would be cool." And we were just like, "Since we're hanging around each other so much, why don't we just knock out a song or two every time we're together." Over a few months we knocked out a song here and there, and then all of a sudden we had the entire project pretty much together. We called in a few guests to rhyme on it, and all of a sudden we were like, "Oh, look, we've got an album."

The song "Gamer" from that album is one of the most innovative hip-hop tracks I've heard in a long time. Building a beat out of samples from old video games was a really interesting idea.

I'm not even going to lie, I forget what games I took some of those samples from. Rahzel is on there beatboxing, doing some of the drum effects. I had that track sitting around for a while. Actually, C-Rayz Walz did his verse first, quite a while back. We were just kind of considering what we should do with it. We were like, "Who are we going to add on it? What are we going to do with it?" One day I was talking with Sadat about video games, and we were reminiscing about all the old game consoles. I was like, "You've got to do this." And we just put it together. I'm a video game freak. When you called, I was just sitting here playing *Assassin's Creed II*. [Laughs.]

What are some of the most memorable moments of your career thus far?

Definitely recording with KRS-One, and doing some shows with him. Really, recording with all the guys I've got to record with has been amazing—guys like Pharoahe Monch and Kool G. Rap. Another one is the first time I got to do stuff on stage together with Mix Master Mike. That was really cool for me. I was like, "Wow. I'm deejaying with a guy that I really

71

look up to." There have been many moments that have been amazing for me. You know, being on stage with someone like a DJ Premier or Q-Bert or Afrikka Bambaata. Just all of that stuff in general has been incredible. Honestly, I've gotten to a point where literally once a month I'm having a moment where I think to myself, Wow, *this* is the greatest moment of my career. I'm lucky to get to be around a lot of cool people and things.

Your latest album, *No Sell Out*, features more than 40 artists. It must have been difficult to coordinate that many schedules.
Most of us make our money by touring and doing as many shows as possible, so that makes it very difficult trying to link up with people, schedule studio time, know who's available when . . . It gets very difficult when you have multiple emcees on songs, and they aren't even in the same part of the country. I mean, the artists always want to hear what the other guy's going to do and see the direction of the song. That's why with this album I really kind of took everything in my own hands and orchestrated every detail of everything myself. That made it flow a little bit easier than leaving things up to the artists, because it would have been very difficult to sort of piece things together. Everyone would have just sort of gone in their own directions, and it wouldn't have been cohesive. It's definitely a headache, but this is what I do, and honestly I kind of enjoy it. Once the project is finished and I sit back and listen to it all together, I'm like, "Wow. This is so cool." The kind of albums that I make, and the way I make them, it doesn't really matter when you get it or when you hear it; anyone who would like that style of music is going to like it the same if they get the album the day it comes out or three years after the fact. It's not going to make a difference. It's difficult, but it's so rewarding when I think about who I get to work with and what I get to do. It's a really cool opportunity for me.

You do a lot of performance work. What is your favorite part of performing in front of a live crowd?
My favorite part is when people who've never seen what we do come out. We're kind of pigeonholed into the underground hip-hop scene and the turntablism crowd, so it's usually the same fans who come out to our shows. So anytime I get to be in front of a different crowd, I love it. When we get to perform at these European festivals and there are 15,000 people there . . . I love doing what I love and scratching over the old breakbeats, and being able to bring that to those people. That's my favorite part. To

be honest with you, even some of my favorite guys, the guys who used to do that, aren't doing that anymore. Now it's like straight Crooklyn clan electro dance mash-ups all night long until your head falls off. Now that everybody's doing that, my favorite thing about deejaying is *not* doing that.

Sadat told me the European hip-hop crowd is terrific. I keep hearing that the energy there is like what it was here 20 years ago.

It's getting worse around the world as time goes on, but for the most part, it is really, really good. I think the reason is because they didn't have the MTV and major radio presence pushing the commercial stuff down their throat. They didn't have all that marketing. They do now, but they didn't used to. When you would show up there, these kids would know about you just through word of mouth, the Internet, or from going to a show. And a lot of the horrible groups that we don't like didn't tour in those places. The good groups—the real hip-hop groups—would be out there touring, getting the word out. There would be a Gang Starr tour, and that would help spread the word that me and Rahzel would be there. I think they appreciate it more there because they don't get those artists very often. In New York, there are 25 shows a night with everyone coming through. You become spoiled. Over there they just appreciate it so much more. Jeru Da Damaja shows up and those kids are jumping through the roof, thrilled that he came. But if he does a show over here in Brooklyn, some of the kids are like, "Oh, that's cool. Jeru again." [Laughs.] In Europe they're more open minded as far as music goes. What I like about it is that they'll mix; you'll have people who like rock and dance music and old school hip-hop and house all hanging out in the same place. Over here you don't really see that. It's kind of segregated in terms of what people listen to.

There has been a lot of debate since Nas first proclaimed that hip-hop was dead. In your mind, is hip-hop dead?

I always tell people that as long as I'm alive that shit ain't dead. [Laughs.] I mean, what the hell am I doing? It's not dead. It's just that the style of hip-hop that we all grew up with and loved is no longer the style that's in. It's not what's making the big bucks. Everyone is just scared. That's the big overall problem. There's no room for that stuff anymore. Now everyone is doing the Lady Gaga dance electro stuff. It's not really dead. People keep saying it goes in cycles and it'll come back around, but I don't really see Public Enemy/Gang Starr–type hip-hop becoming really popular again in the mainstream. That style of music is still out there and millions of kids around the world still love it, so it's not dead. I see that when I'm somewhere like Montreal doing a show with Rahzel and Premier. It's still alive, it's just not thriving like it once did. It's not in the mainstream. It's sort of out of the public eye now.

Most of the disgruntled hip-hop fans are people from our generation. Sometimes I wonder if it's just us not wanting to grow with the music. I wonder if it's some sort of deficiency on our part that we're not able to respect the style of music that these new kids are doing now.
When you look at a lot of the music that's out there now, the content level is so low. If you look back at a group like Naughty by Nature, who was commercial at the time, their music had content. There was a concept there, and they were talking about something. You could listen to the words and maybe gain something from that. Never mind the beats—I'm not really into this style of beats either—but if you break it down as a song and you listen to what they're saying, there aren't many songs on the radio that you can listen to without feeling like a moron for having listened to them.

DISCOGRAPHY

1. *Ground Original* (2003)
2. *Claimstake* (2004)
3. *Audio Technician* (2004)
4. *Ground Original 2: No Sell Out* (2009)

CHAPTER TEN

ERIC B.
DJ/Producer/Emcee

L ong Island duo Eric B & Rakim broke onto the scene in 1985 with the single "Eric B. Is President," quickly establishing themselves as one of the hottest and most influential acts in hip-hop. Two years later, they released their debut album *Paid in Full*. The album immediately climbed into the Top 10 R&B chart. This masterpiece—considered by many to be the single greatest hip-hop album ever made—established Eric B. & Rakim as a cutting-edge duo. Eric B's powerful production broke new ground, with some songs containing as many as ten different samples layered together. Eric B's extensive sampling of James Brown also led to an era in which the singer's catalog would be heavily sampled and interpolated by just about every producer in hip-hop. Rakim's clever wordplay, internal rhyme schemes, and skillful delivery proved to be far more advanced than anything which had preceded it, and the duo quickly became one of the most respected and imitated groups around. *Paid in Full*, which ultimately went platinum, represents a clear shift in the artistic direction of hip-hop music. In 1987, Eric B. & Rakim's song "Paid in Full" was remixed by production team Coldcut and released on the soundtrack for the film *Colors*. The remix, which became a hit single in the U.K. and a staple in dance clubs everywhere, is now recognized as a hip-hop milestone.

Eric B. & Rakim's second offering, *Follow the Leader*, was released the following year. On their second outing, both Eric B. and Rakim stepped up their respective games. While *Follow the Leader* may not be as widely recognized as *Paid in Full*, it represented clear growth in terms of production and lyricism and is an undeniable second masterpiece. The album produced four solid singles, including the title track "Follow the Leader," which peaked at number five on the Hot Dance Music chart and number 16 on the R&B chart. The album would ultimately attain gold status. In 1989, Eric B. & Rakim appeared on Jody Watley's hit song "Friends." The song, which peaked at number nine on the *Billboard* Hot 100, is significant because it was one of the earliest instances in which rap artists appeared on an R&B single.

By the time Eric B. & Rakim's third album, *Let the Rhythm Hit 'Em*, was released, the musical landscape of hip-hop had changed dramatically. NWA and front man Eazy-E had completely changed the direction of hip-hop with a new subgenre known as "gangsta rap." Adding to this, groups like Tribe Called Quest and De La Soul had emerged, introducing the world to alternative hip-hop. These new trends coupled with the group's determination to maintain artistic integrity led to somewhat diminished sales and a difficulty in finding a mainstream audience. Nevertheless, the album still managed to go gold and was once again hailed as a masterpiece, becoming one of the first albums to receive *The Source* magazine's coveted five-mic rating. After making notable contributions to the soundtracks of the films *House Party 2* ("What's on Your Mind?") and *Juice* ("Know the Ledge"), Eric B. & Rakim released their fourth and final album, *Don't Sweat the Technique*. The album, like their three previous outings, reached the Top 10 on the R&B/hip-hop chart. Shortly after the release of the album, Eric B. & Rakim disbanded and went their separate ways.

Three years later, Eric B. released a self-titled solo album on which he tried his hand at rapping. In 1996, Eric B. was hired by Suge Knight as head of the Death Row East label. Displaying an uncanny business sense, Eric B. has since diversified. "Anybody can be an artist, but not everyone can be a businessman," he has said. "A businessman will always outlast the talent, because the talent comes and goes." Aside from owning more than a few restaurants, three successful music studios, and establishing his own line of energy drinks, Eric B. also manages a stable of boxers that includes Floyd Mayweather, Riddick Bowe, and Oliver McCall. In 2008, Eric B. joined forces with a newcomer and established the group Eric B. & Avion, releasing the single "Get on the Floor."

What does hip-hop mean to you?
For me, it's a lifestyle. It's everything that I do.

What are your earliest hip-hop-related memories?
Just being in the park . . . learning music, carrying records, understanding music and the turntables, and just the business itself.

How did you get into deejaying?
Back in the early eighties, there was a group called King Charles. They had a big sound system and they used to play in the park in Queens. The DJ's name was Vernon. He was the DJ, but the system was owned by a guy named Charles. I started carrying records for them as a kid. I learned the business from those guys.

How did you meet Rakim?
I was a mobile DJ for a radio station in New York called WBLS. I started out on one of the first street teams ever. I was out playing music in Long Island, and I met this guy named Alvin Toney. He said there were a couple of guys out there who rapped really well, and that I should meet them. One was Freddie Foxxx, and the other was Rakim. So I went to meet with them, and then we went from there and started doing music.

What are your favorite Eric B. & Rakim memories?
Being able to play at the Apollo. That was a big moment for us. We played Madison Square Garden. Those are the kinds of things that really stick out in my mind.

I know you met just about everyone in the business at that time. Was there anyone who gave you advice coming up?
Rick James was definitely a guy who taught us all how to live. You could ask Eddie Murphy and Mike Tyson and all those guys. Rick James was the one who made us realize that we were making real money—that we should come out of the shadows and not be afraid to make money and spend money. We came from an era in which we were told that you shouldn't do this and you shouldn't do that. And Rick James said, "You only live one life. Don't let anyone else live your life for you." And that made me buy my first car; the first car I ever owned in my life was a Rolls-Royce.

You were known as the first man in hip-hop to own a Rolls.
You know, I had a lot of firsts. But I try to teach people about the holes that I myself fell into. I don't want other people falling into those holes. Those accomplishments are great, but some of my greatest accomplishments are

being able to sit down with people and say, "Hey, don't make this mistake, don't make that mistake . . . "

What are some of the pitfalls that you try to help people avoid?
Just business stuff. I tell them to make it business, not personal. I tell them in everything they do they should make business decisions rather than personal ones. It has to make business sense to make money. At the end of the day, all these conversations about "I like this" or "I don't like that"—you have to forget those things. At the end of the day, it has to be about business. You don't have to go home and sleep with these people. Just get your money and keep on moving.

You guys recorded *Paid in Full* in a week. Is that right?
You know what it really was? If you put all the time together that we spent . . . You know, we spent a day here on this record, and a day here on that record. When you put it all together and you look at the actual running time, it probably took us about a week to put that album together.

I understand both Marley Marl and MC Shan were involved with the making of that album.
When we first started, I went out to Long Island. Rakim's brother worked at a place where they pressed records. They had a pressing plant. So every breakbeat you could imagine, every record you could imagine, they pressed out of this bootleg pressing plant. So I got the records from him, and Marley Marl knew how to use the equipment. I wasn't an engineer at the time, so I paid Marley Marl to be the engineer. I gave him the records that I wanted to use—the beats and the sounds that I wanted—and told him exactly what I wanted put together. And the reason that MC Shan was involved is because, at the time, Marley Marl didn't want to do the mixes; he was in the room with this chick and he didn't want to do the mixes, so me and Shan sat there at the board and did all the mixing for the single.

You've had a couple of instances where producers have tried to claim work that had your name on it. What are your thoughts on that today?
That's what they all do until you go back and go over the timeline . . . When we started Eric B. & Rakim, we started it as a mom-and-pop business. And then it turned into a corporation. So with everything that was successful, people want to say that they did this, that, and that. If you listen to people, they'll tell you that Marley Marl produced the records and that all this stuff

supposedly happened, but if you asked Marley where he came up with the records he wouldn't be able to tell you. I tell people, if you think Marley Marl produced the record, look at the record and you'll see that Marley Marl doesn't get any credit for production. He doesn't get any of the publishing money either. And he's never gotten any royalties from the record. And look, Marley Marl sued Cold Chillin' Records to get all of his money back, and he never sued us. Why are we so special? I'll tell you why: because he didn't produce the record. If someone wants to take credit, that's fine and fantastic. That doesn't bother me at all. At the end of the day, I know who's getting paid and who's not. All these guys who said that they did this and did that, they still have the right to sue, and they haven't sued yet. Hey, if you did it, you'd sue and you'd say, "I did this and I did that." You would have gotten paid, but here we are 23 years later, and no lawsuits have emerged. So what does that tell you? It's all conversations to make those people feel good.

I understand Doug E. Fresh was involved in a small way—
No, no. Doug E. Fresh was involved in a *big* way. Doug E. Fresh was my mentor. He was the guy that I took the records to so I could bounce them off him. At that time, Doug E. Fresh was on fire with "La-Di-Da-Di" and "The Show." Those were two of the biggest records of that time. They were on an independent label out of California, and they just sort of took on a life of their own. The record just grew and grew, and it's still growing. Doug was touring the world and playing these big stages, and I used to go to Doug's house . . . I'd do a record in the studio, and then I'd come and play it for Doug. And he would sit there like my professor and say, "Eric, let me ask you a question: how did you come to this record and this sound and this sound?" I would say, "Well, Doug, I was at a party and I heard this record, and I did this, this, and that." And Doug would sit there and look at me. "You know, Eric, that's pretty interesting. How did you come up with this 'Eric B. Is President' record?" And I'd tell him, and he said, "You know, Eric, nobody's ever done anything like this before. That's pretty interesting." And you know, all the records I did, I bounced them off Doug E. Fresh.

I came in on such a high level having a guy like Doug, who was one of the greatest entertainers in rap music, actually sit there and listen to my records. That was an honor for me. So when people say he was involved in a little way, I say that's not true. He's really the guy responsible for guiding us with the songs that now appear on the *Paid in Full* album.

The DJ is often the unsung hero. Did you ever feel that you were working in Rakim's shadow?

No. You know what? I got into this business to make money. I didn't get into this business to become a star or to get recognition. Pay me and I'll go off into the sunset. My thing was and still is that I'm doing this to make money. This is a business. It's not a vanity issue for me. It's not for me to be on the cover of a magazine and say, "I, I, I, and me, me, me." Pay me and let me go about my way. So that never affected me, and anyone who knows will tell you that I put in the effort to do everything. But at the end of the day it's a group effort and a family business, so it didn't bother me. And it still doesn't bother me. Show me the money and I'll get out of the way. I could still be appearing in every magazine, but I don't do them because it doesn't make any money. And I'm not trying to impress anybody. I got into this business to get out of the streets and to make money.

What happened to Eric B. & Rakim? Why did you break up?

Nothing happened, really. I just woke up one day and decided I didn't want to do it anymore. I had a great run with it, and it just got to a point where it had become a pain in the ass, and I just wanted to do other things. When you have disagreements with people, it's usually over either money or over women. Me and Rakim, from dollar one, from the very first money we made, which was $1,500 for a show on Long Island—we split it all 50/50. And we still continue to split the money 50/50 today. Second of all, the name of the group was made up by Rakim. And third, we never slept with the same women. So we don't have an issue.

A lot of people have pushed Rakim to say stupid shit, but at the end of the day, if nobody stole our money and nobody slept with anybody else's woman, then there is no issue. That's my take on it. I got tired and said enough was enough, and I walked away from it.

Of what accomplishment are you the most proud?

The accomplishment I'm most proud of is my publishing deal and my music deal. I was the first person in hip-hop to ever get a million dollars to do a record. I was the first person to ever receive $2 million for publishing. And the first person to get $2 million to make a record. Even with the boundaries that I broke down 23 years ago, people are still yelling at the record companies to give them a million dollars. I think it's pretty funny. Back then I got a chance to learn and understand business. We were at

Island and 4th and Broadway Records, and we had sold over a million records. Yet they didn't even want to buy us t-shirts. They didn't want to do anything to promote the record. We had sold maybe three million records, and then U2 came out the door with a big giant video. They did posters and advertisements everywhere. And I said look, *Paid in Full* cost them less than $7,000 to make. It might have been $5,000, and even that's probably pushing it. "We're at two or three million records, and you didn't spend any money to promote it." And they looked at me like I was crazy, and I said, "Let's do basic math. Basic math doesn't change. I don't care who's doing the accounting, basic math doesn't change." So I sat down and did the math and said, "Hold up, there's something wrong here." They did no promotions at all for the *Paid in Full* album, and we were selling records just based on word of mouth. For U2's record they were out doing radio, television, posters, a promotional tour . . . We never even did a promotional tour. Our promotional tour was our paid gigs and going to the radio station. So I said, "If we can't make the lion's share of the money, then we shouldn't even be doing this."

They wanted us to sign up. They wanted to give us $450,000 to come back. Our manager Russell Simmons was like, "Oh, Eric, you should take the deal. That's more than Run-DMC has ever gotten." And I said, "Russell, if I don't get the $450,000 today I'm fine with it because it's more money than I had before anyway." He looked at me like . . . I think if he thought for even a second that he could have beaten me, he would have started swinging. He was upset that I didn't settle for the $450,000. Then I ran into a guy named Michael Haley who worked for MCA Records. I was at a party that Prince had thrown, and I bumped into Michael Haley. He came up to me and said, "Eric, what are you doing?" And I told him that we were supposed to sign with Island the following day, and that they wanted to pay us $450,000. Michael Haley said, "Yo, come to MCA. We can double their offer." So I tell Russell, and he says, "See, Eric, there you go again, always trying to do business. You have to let me take care of the business." And Russell went on and on. So the next day we're on a plane flying first class. It was Lyor Cohen, Rakim, and myself, flying on a plane to meet in a hotel. Then it became a bidding war, and Warner Bros. jumped in and threw their money on the table. Being able to spearhead my own business and break down those barriers—saying that we should get the money we deserve for the things we were doing—is, I think, my greatest accomplishment. Being able to go out and get $2 million for publishing is still a great accomplishment, and this was back in 1988!

What are your thoughts on the current state of hip-hop?
I think the problem with the current state of hip-hop is that everyone has an opinion. Instead of just enjoying it, they have to complain about it. It's just like when you go to a basketball game—you enjoy the game, you don't criticize the players. Everybody has to pick everything apart. "Soulja Boy is this, and that person is that . . . " Enjoy the music! If you don't like it, turn it off and find something that you do like. Everybody's a critic today. Instead of just embracing the music and being thankful for new music, you want to be a critic. I don't care what the record is, there's someone who's going to like it. We have to get this thing back to where it's entertainment and fun again. It's gotten so critical now. There are blogs and everybody wants to rip the artists apart.

I laugh when I hear silly stuff like people saying that Jay-Z's new album is the worst shit they've ever heard. Are you kidding me, man? Jay-Z, to me, is the Roy Jones Jr. of rap. We've asked more of Roy Jones in boxing than we have of any other boxer in history. Roy Jones went all the way up to the heavyweight division and won a title in every division on the way up. And Jay-Z is the same way . . . He continues to do it, and we continue to ask more of him and press the issue. He's delivered time and time again. Ten number one albums, on his way to 11 . . . You know, enough is enough. Instead of embracing him and enjoying his music, everyone wants to criticize him. When I came up, everyone was so excited about the music and the infusion of new songs and new people, and it was a great time. But now everyone is a critic.

DISCOGRAPHY

1. *Paid in Full* (1987) [as Eric B. & Rakim]
2. *Follow the Leader* (1988) [as Eric B. & Rakim]
3. *Let the Rhythm Hit 'Em* (1990) [as Eric B. & Rakim]
4. *Don't Sweat the Technique* (1992) [as Eric B. & Rakim]
5. *Eric B.* (1995)
6. *The Best of Eric B. & Rakim* (2001) [as Eric B. & Rakim]
7. *Classic* (2003) [as Eric B. & Rakim]
8. *Gold* (2005) [as Eric B. & Rakim]

CHAPTER ELEVEN
DREAM HAMPTON
Journalist

Hip-hop journalist dream hampton (she publishes her name in lowercase letters as a nod to feminist author bell hooks) was born in Detroit, Michigan in 1972. At the age of 18 she relocated to New York City, where she attended NYU's Tisch School of the Arts. During this period she went to work at *The Source* magazine, where she became the first female editor to be employed there. She soon became close friends with an up-and-coming emcee known as Biggie Smalls (later redubbed the Notorious B.I.G.), and even convinced him to appear as the subject of a short film she made for her documentary class. Although she was only employed at *The Source* for 18 months, hampton wrote many notable pieces which pushed the boundaries of hip-hop journalism. Her essays on police brutality, the politics of the music industry, and the (then-) escalating misogyny found within the realm of hip-hop featured a literary style and depth that had been sorely lacking in much of the hip-hop journalism preceding her. With a style that was as equally informed by literature, poetry, and even documentary filmmaking as it was by her contemporary music writers, hampton provided a dimension and shading to profiles of artists like Snoop Doggy Dogg and Tupac Shakur that was so detailed that it can be said to have been transcendent.

She then took her formidable talents to the newly established *Rap Pages* magazine, where she continued to cover the hip-hop world as the publication's editor-in-chief. She also penned a number of memorable articles and artist profiles, from Jay-Z to Mary J. Blige, as a contributing writer at Quincy Jones' *Vibe*. Her writings have also graced the pages of such noted publications as *The Village Voice, Spin, Harper's Bazaar, Essence,* and *Parenting*. Her essays and articles have appeared in numerous collections including *And It Don't Stop: The Best Hip-Hop Journalism of the Last 25 Years, The Vibe History of Hip-Hop,* and *Born to Use Mics: A Reading of Nas' Illmatic.*

In 2003, hampton collaborated with Jay-Z on his memoir *The Black Book*. However, when the book was completed the following year, Jay-Z opted not to publish it because he felt its contents were too personal. Seven years later hampton and Jay-Z collaborated on a second offering, *Decoded*. In addition to this, hampton also served as coauthor of Kamal "Q-Tip" Fareed's 2011 memoir *Industry Rules*.

Besides being an accomplished writer, hampton has also found success in filmmaking. Her narrative short film *I Am Ali* was an official entry at the 2002 Sundance Film Festival and won the award for Best Short Film at *Vanity Fair*'s Newport Film Festival. She was an associate producer of the Emmy-winning VH1 *Behind the Music: Notorious B.I.G.* and co-producer of the Peter Spier–helmed B.I.G. documentary *Bigger Than Life*. In 2010, hampton made her feature directorial debut with the acclaimed concert film *Black August*, which features performances by Mos Def, Common, Talib Kweli, Dead Prez, and the Roots.

What does hip-hop mean to you?

The first thing I think of, if we were playing that word-association game, is rock and roll. What I mean is, I just think of how transgressive rock was; even as it played on certain traditions like the blues, it was so loud and so bold and so irreverent that it created its own space; it looked like something completely different from that which preceded it, even if it was just an extension of that.

Also, I've always argued that hip-hop is a generational schism that we, as black people, experienced in the late 1980s and early nineties, when hip-hop really began to define itself. Of course you had Sam Cooke and all these people struggling with secular music versus gospel, but the secular music that Sam Cooke was singing wasn't so different from what Mahalia Jackson was doing that it was unrecognizable. So I think that what hip-hop became in black households was unrecognizable to the parents, and while that had happened a generation before with white kids listening to black rock, it hadn't happened in our own community. Music had always been very much unified in black households, so that hadn't occurred in the black community until hip-hop. At *The Source* we had that whole idea of the hip-hop *nation*, which I never really liked . . . And I understand that that's a way of being more inclusive, and I don't think you can exclude people of other races like the Puerto Rican b-boys or the white Jewish people like Charlie Ahearn or even Dave Mays and Jon Schecter, right? But essentially this is a black youth phenomenon, so I would say that that inter-generational schism coincides completely with the billion dollar crack industry. As then in the late eighties when hip-hop becomes more in the tradition of a Richard Wright autobiographical narrative, there are these things going on in the streets that are also, on a practical level, dividing the black community along generational lines.

What are your earliest hip-hop-related memories?
There was a tape that a girl on my block possessed. Her mom had a boyfriend who would go to New York and get those Korean bootleg Gucci bags, and then come back and sell them. And he brought home a battle tape with Roxanne Shante and the Real Roxanne, and on that tape they were being so violent with one another—verbally; everything, like "Your pussy is a cesspool." Of course there were other experiences, like we were skaters here—we don't breakdance and all that shit here in Detroit . . . We used to do stuff at the skating rink, and I remember Soulsonic Force and "Planet Rock" and all of that. But in terms of a narrative kind of gripping me, it was definitely that battle between Roxanne Shante and the Real Roxanne.

When did you first begin thinking about combining your passions for writing and hip-hop music?
Well, I never really did. It just sort of happened. There has never been a point where I've identified myself as a hip-hop journalist. I think at best, I write, but I'm certainly not a reporter. I don't even ask people as many questions as you've asked me, and you've only gotten in like three so far. When I was with Tupac, I didn't even have a tape recorder, because I think people lie when you turn on the tape recorder. I'm not a reporter. I don't get second and supporting facts and stuff like that. But there was a time when I realized, okay, I'm doing this, so I went back and read Norman Mailer's profile of Marilyn Monroe, and then it got to the point

where I was defending myself for knowing cats who lived in my neighborhood. People used to be like, "Well, I like dream hampton, but what about *this* aspect of her work?" And sometimes it was rooted in sexism, like she must be sleeping with them to get this kind of access, but other times it was just a very valid criticism, like "How can you know the people you're writing about?" And that's when I went back and read people like Gay Talese and [about] his relationship with Floyd Patterson. That's when I started reading a certain kind of journalism that gave me permission to do what I did. I just didn't think I could be the first person to know the people I was writing about! [Laughs.] I mean, Floyd Patterson lived on Gay Talese's couch, and yet he wrote three dozen pieces on him for *Esquire*. But, of course, Floyd Patterson didn't have a vagina, so that was never questioned.

So there was never a time when I really considered myself a hip-hop journalist. I've always been a hip-hop *fan*, but I've never been like, "I'm a hip-hop journalist." I'm far less prolific than a lot of people that I consider my colleagues. And those guys pitch stories. You know, I've never pitched a story—*ever*. I told *The Source* that I wanted to cover Tupac, and no one else wanted to do it. They definitely weren't going to make it a cover story. They were like, "The 'Brenda's Got a Baby' nigga? Whatever. Have fun." [Laughs again.] So maybe that's the closest I've come to a pitch.

A lot of the so-called hip-hop writers are far less eloquent or literary than you are. When you're writing about hip-hop, you almost seem to transcend the genre, for lack of a better phrase . . .
Thank you. I'm a reader! I'm a far more prolific reader than I am a writer. I have something due right now, and I'm reading *Just Kids* by Patti Smith, about her and Robert Mapplethorpe! [Laughs.] I'm on deadline. Why am I up at night reading this book?

I get the feeling that some hip-hop-themed writers are not reading as much extra-curricular material as you do. It feels like many of them are writing in a vacuum.
I don't get the sense that Jim Daly—the news reporter who wrote all of that Son of Sam stuff—is just sitting around reading Philip Roth! I think that journalists tend to be short readers. Having said that, I think that Daniel Smith reads as much as me. Kevin Powell reads as much or more than I do. I don't know . . . I don't really think that's fair.

Maybe I'm looking back through rose-colored glasses, but it seems to me that the writing was a lot stronger around the time when you were writing for *The Source.*

I don't necessarily think that's true. From where I stand—and I was never a big reader of *The Source*, even when I was there—I would say that Selwyn Hinds' period seemed pretty together, when he was the editor-in-chief. I think it's easy to make statements like that, but I don't really think that would bear out if we were to sit down and look through all the issues. It's like when people say that a certain era in hip-hop was the golden period. But then if we were to really just Google every record that was released that year, from the Skinny Boys to Young Black Teenagers, we would find that there were really only four or five great albums. And then if you were to do the same thing with the year 2006, we would find that there were another four or five great albums. I mean, I love sweeping generalizations, but they don't usually tend to be true. [Chuckles.] If we were to sit down with a bunch of issues of *The Source*, I think you'd probably find that even after Dave Mays and all his stupid bullshit he pulled with Almighty RSO, that Selwyn was probably a much better editor-in-chief than Jon Schecter was. But you know, I made that whole rock and roll analogy earlier . . . Well, there were like entire decades of *Rolling Stone* when the magazine was almost unreadable, and you can't just blame it on hair bands. Hunter Thompson was still writing, but he was doing a parody of himself.

I understand that you wrote a scathing review of NWA's album, which resulted in Eazy-E's writing you a letter—

No, no, no—he sent me a *threat*. He just said, "I'm gonna kill that bitch dream." I forget now who gave me the message. I don't know; I've gotten so many threats that I really can't remember them all. It seems like maybe the message just came through to *The Source*. Back then rappers would just call us up and curse us out. [Laughs.] I remember Eric B. calling us and cursing us out, and we put him on the speaker phone, and we were all honored.

Wasn't that over a story *The Source* was doing on MC Hammer?

Yes! Cheo Coker has a better record of all this shit than I do, because he actually wrote a big piece that may have wound up getting killed for *Spin*. It was like a 12,000 word essay . . . I was only there for 18 months, but yes, Eazy-E threatened me. I think the thing that offended him the most was that I attacked their sexiness; I said they looked like extras in a porn flick. And I guess by his estimation, they were the *stars* in a porn flick! [Laughs.]

You were good friends with the Notorious B.I.G. Could you tell me a little bit about how you met him, and about the evolution of your friendship?
Because we had been riding him about it, Matty C. opened up the "Unsigned Hype" column for a little bit more of a democratic process. That involved us sitting around after office hours, getting high and listening to demo tapes, and voting on them. So that's how I first heard Big. Later Puff got promoted to the V.P. of A&R, and he was like, "Yo, I gotta get some new shit. Who do I need to talk to?" "You need to talk to Matty." Puff then called Matty, and then Matty gave Puff Biggie's demo.

Now in terms of me actually meeting Big . . . Puff moves fast. He's like a fast slow person; he'll move quick to make the deal, but then it'll take forever for the album to come out. But he immediately got on the thing with Big. So I would say in between me hearing the tape and me actually meeting Big might have been four or five weeks. But by the time I met Biggie, it was with Puff. I met him in the basement of Daddy-O's house, and Biggie was doing his first ever professional recording, which was his rhyme for the "Real Love" remix. He really never unlocked his eyes from his Tims; he was incredibly shy. It wasn't even like Puff was saying, "Come with me and meet the dude you've been telling me about." It was more like, "Yo, I'm in Brooklyn. Come over to Daddy-O's with me." I lived around the corner from Daddy-O, and around the corner from Biggie; we all lived in a three block radius. So Puff picked me up and we literally went around the corner to Daddy-O's, and there was Biggie.

But after that, I would see Biggie on Fulton on my way to NYU and it was like the difference between being a commuter in a neighborhood, or basically a gentrifier. Here I am this NYU student, who comes from a way worse neighborhood in Detroit, but whatever . . . I knew that there were kids on the street, but I had already left my hood, and I didn't want to meet a whole new hood. [Laughs.] That's not what I'm in New York for. But from that point on, Big went from being invisible to visible to me. So every time I'd walk down the street he'd be like, "Yo!" And then eventually he was like, "Nobody fuck with dream. This is my girl." And then I got to know everyone on the block, and then the next thing you know he's coming to classes with me. I'm like, "What the fuck are you doing? You just going to stay in here with me?" And he was like, "Yeah, what else am I going to do?" [Laughs again.] So I'm like, "Come to class with me. We're screening *The Cabinet of Dr. Caligari* today. You'll like it." So that's literally how we became friends. We got high and then went to school and sat through *Battleship Potemkin* together.

You also spent something like six months with Tupac. What was that experience like?

We were both in the same movement. When I first came to New York, I hooked up with my best friend, Monifa, whom I had met in Atlanta, and we co-founded a chapter of a national organization; so we co-founded the New York chapter of the Malcolm X Grassroots Movement. And we were kind of charged with our elders and mentors—old Black Liberation Army and old Panther people, but mostly BLA and Republican New Africa alumni—to raise awareness about political prisoners in the United States, and to use hip-hop to do that. So we basically ended up coming up with the Black August concert series years later. But at the time we were doing little spotty shows. And obviously Mutulu Shakur is one of the ex–Black Liberation Army people that we identify as a political prisoner; someone who declared war on the American government and is imprisoned because of his politics and a series of trumped-up charges. One of the very first fundraisers we did for Mutulu was in Brooklyn, and Biggie performed. He was *really* drunk, and my best friend Monifa was very mad at him. [Chuckles.] But Biggie didn't know who Tupac was, and probably didn't remember who Mutulu was. He was just performing as a favor to me, and we might have raised like $600. We were—and are—very much a grassroots organization. Even now, if we do the Black August concert, we net about $6,000 and that money literally goes on the books of the people we work with: Mutulu Shakur, his co-defendant, Sekou Odinga, people like that.

You asked me about the cover story for *The Source*, but Tupac and I met way before that . . . We met because of the work I was doing on his stepdad's campaign, and then later, when I left *The Source*, it was because Latifah offered me a job as A&R at Flavor Unit Records; this was when she was turning her management company into a record label. So I wound up working as A&R on Naughty by Nature's second album, and Apache's first album. Naughty by Nature did a song on the *Juice* soundtrack called "Uptown Anthem," and Tupac was in the video. So on the video set, that was my first time actually meeting 'Pac. I remember he said something flirty to me, and I was like, "I'm glad I ran into you; I need $300 for posters for this fundraiser for Mutulu." And he was like, "Aw, man, you're one of them activist chicks . . ." [Laughs.] So he *never* flirted with me ever again after that. *Ever.*

So the six months we spent together for that cover piece . . . I know that I got on his nerves sometimes. Even you now, you spend time doing these interviews and you have no idea what's going to happen to them, but it's not like going on TV and having the sense that even if you get edited, it's still going to be you. I don't know right now if you're using a tape recorder or if you're taking notes, how good you are at taking notes; I've certainly been misquoted, and it'll be a small misquote but it'll change the entire meaning of what I was saying. Well, it's really annoying for artists. I mean, publicists are artist's least favorite people at the magazines and at their labels. They don't see how, as opposed to the promotions department, which sends them to radio stations where they try to charm a DJ, which then in turn equals spins, which, in their mind equals money, sitting with a writer for an hour or two is going to equal money; particularly back then. And that's an hour, let alone six months . . . It was a test of whatever acquaintance we already had. We didn't have it easy like me and Big; Big and I had a very easy and great friendship. I wanted to talk to him every day, he wanted to talk to me every day. Me and 'Pac didn't necessarily have that; we argued a lot. We got kicked out of a restaurant for arguing at the top of our lungs about his rape case.

You worked with Jay-Z on his unpublished memoir, *The Black Book*. What was that experience like?
I didn't know him because he was my neighbor. I met Jay because he thought I was a man and he wanted to thank me for a very understanding review of *Reasonable Doubt*. Coming from Detroit, if there was one thing I knew it was drug dealers. In the *Village Voice*'s mind, *Reasonable Doubt* wasn't a big enough album to get its own review, so they made me do a double review of Nas' *It Was Written* and *Reasonable Doubt*. Jay was doing an interview with a good friend of mine for what was probably his first cover at *XXL* in its earliest incarnation. My friend Darryl Dawsey was writing that article, and he put me on the phone with Jay. I guess he had mentioned me and Jay was like, "I love that article that he did on me." And Darryl

was like, "Oh, no, dream is actually a girl. I just missed her call, so let me return her call while you're here." So Jay got on his phone and thanked me, which I thought was nice. Because you never hear when people *like* stuff. I thought that was not only very professional, but quite kind. And then later, when I was an editor-in-chief at *Rap Pages,* I'd written a cover piece of Mary J. Blige for *Vibe.* I had written the piece, and then by the time it had come out, I was editor-in-chief at *Rap Pages.* So I'm doing some after-hours shit at *Rap Pages,* working, and I get a call on my office phone and I answer it on the speaker, and he says, "Yo, this is Jay-Z. Can you pick up? I'm shy." And then he was like, "I really like that piece you did on Mary." And now I was like, Oh, you're just fucking weird! [Laughs.] You're calling me about another artist. Most artists only read about themselves, and they only commented when they hated it, and you're calling to tell me that you liked a piece of writing I did? I thought he was hilarious, and we just became friends after that. And he turned out to be a word nerd, so we would just call each other with words. Or he would be like, "What does this word mean?" We just had that kind of fun. And then I think we really became good friends after Biggie died. I had conversations with him . . . Puffy is a lot more closed. I've known Puffy longer than Biggie, Jay, or any of these guys, but he's a really private person, so he wasn't really someone I could talk to after Big died. And Jay turned out to be someone that I could. I say all of this to say that we had a history going into the book; one where he felt comfortable talking to me, which is really important for him, because Jay is actually private, too. He's like that drug dealer paranoid/private. So we wrote the book, and then it didn't come out, but we're doing another book right now, which should be released next year.

What were some of the factors that went into Jay's decision not to publish *The Black Book?*
It took me a year and a half to write it, when we had initially thought it would take six weeks. I had never written a book before, so I just thought it would be like a long article. [Laughs.] I didn't know that it wasn't. In some ways I think that if I had had that book done in six weeks and it had been ready when *The Black Album* was ready, it might have gotten published. But that's just me imagining shit. I believe Jay when he said that I had been sending him chapters, and he was fine with that, but then when he had the whole book in his hand, he almost passed out. He said, "I couldn't

imagine somebody holding my life in their hands." That's what he told *Rolling Stone*, which was more than he told me at the time. He felt really bad as a friend, knowing that I had put all this work into that, so there were definitely a couple of months where he was just avoiding me. I just had to get real Zen about it; you know, it's the journey and not the destination.

And you learn things when someone writes a book about you. I don't know how much you know about your parents' marriage, but he didn't know a lot of the details, just like I don't. And I think that some of those interviews . . . *changed* him in a way, and it was good. So overall the book was a success, but just maybe between something like four people—me, Jay, his mom, and his dad.

WRITINGS

1. *The Black Book* [unpublished] [w/ Jay-Z]
2. *Decoded* (2010) [w/ Jay-Z]
3. *Industry Rules* (2011) [w/ Q-Tip]

CHAPTER TWELVE
KOKANE
Emcee/Singer

omona, California emcee/singer Kokane grew up around music. His father, Jerry B. Long, Sr., was a noted composer and arranger for Motown Records, whose most famous arrangements include the Temptations' "Just My Imagination" and "Ball of Confusion." In addition to this, his cousin was Cold 187um, a producer and emcee from the group Above the Law. Kokane's affiliation with Cold 187um helped him land a recording deal with Epic Records through Eric "Eazy-E" Wright. In 1991, Kokane released his debut album *Addictive Hip Hop Muzick* under the *nom de plume* Who Am I? Kokane then appeared on the classic NWA album *Niggaz4life*, also co-writing the hit single "Appetite for Destruction." During this time he also appeared on and helped arrange tracks for Above the Law's 1993 album *Black Mafia Life*. The following year Kokane released his second album, *Funk Upon a Rhyme*. The album is notable for its single "Slow Burnin' 22.5 Degrees Farenheit," as well as the diss song "Don't Bite Da Funk," which was recorded at the height of the infamous Ruthless Records/Death Row beef.

That same year Kokane contributed heavily to Above the Law's album *Uncle Sam's Curse*, appearing on six of the album's 12 songs. Kokane left Ruthless Records in 1996 following the untimely death of Eazy-E. In 1999, Kokane released his Battlecat-produced third album, *They Call Me Mr. Kane*, on Eureka Records. In 2000, Kokane reconnected with Snoop Dogg and went to work as an in-house singer for his Doggystyle Records. This union led to Kokane's contributing heavily to Snoop's album *The Last*

Meal, appearing on eight songs. He also made an appearance on Dr. Dre's classic album *The Chronic 2001*, trading verses with the likes of Xzibit, MC Ren, and Defari on the song "Some LA Niggaz."

Kokane has since made appearances in the motion pictures *The Wash* and *Old School*, and has continued working steadily making his own albums and appearing on other artists' songs. His subsequent albums include *Don't Bite the Funk Vol. 1*, *Mr. Kane Part 2*, and *Back 2 tha Clap*. He has also recorded albums with the groups the Hood Mob and Raine N Lane. In 2010, Kokane returned with the album *Gimme All Mine* and a mixtape with DJ Crazy Toones titled *On the Backstreets*, which featured appearances by Ice Cube, WC, Above the Law, and Snoop Dogg.

What does hip-hop mean to you?
Culture. The struggle. Diversity. Something that changes according to the times. Funk. It's the essence of an entire culture, so it's deeper than just putting a sound down. It's deep.

You father was a composer for Motown. What are some of your earliest musical memories?
I remember being about five years old and going to the studio with my pops. I remember that the mixing board looked like . . . space. It was huge. I thought it was a U.F.O., you know what I mean? [Laughs.] I remember going into those old studios, which were popular in the 1970s. And there was always music playing around the household—everything from the stuff my dad recorded with the Temptations all the way to Marvin Gaye, Roy Ayres, Donnie Hathaway, George Clinton and Parliament. Once that stuff got into my eardrums and kind of settled there, music just became second nature to me.

When did you first discover hip-hop?
Ah, man, Grandmaster Flash! All of those folks back then . . . I was born in New York, but I moved to California when I was four, and I can remember the hip-hop element even back then. It was that whole New York anointing, so to speak. It was already upon me before I even came to California, you know what I'm saying?

Your first deal was with Ruthless Records in 1991—
Actually, I signed my record deal in 1990 with Epic. I was going to come out with a record under the name Kokane, spelled with a "K." It was Kokane because I had the dope lyrics; it was a play on words. And when I got

signed with Epic Records, they were afraid of the negative connotations of the name, so they renamed me Who Am I? The name was the holdup there . . . The Kokane record was supposed to come out in 1990, but it didn't. Instead, they released this Who Am I? record, and people didn't know who that was. People were going to the record store and asking for Kokane, and they were like "Who the fuck are *you?*" [Laughs.]

How did you hook up with Eazy-E?

I hooked up with Eazy through my cousin, Cold187um, who was in a group called Above the Law. They had hooked up with Eazy back in 1989 through a cat named Larry Goodman, which is the real name of Laylaw, who was a contributing factor to NWA. He hooked up that situation over there, and I was always bustin' rhymes and doing talent shows in Pomona and things like that. After we recorded a three-song demo, which was produced by Cold187um of Above the Law, it was given to Laylaw. As a result of this, we finally sat down at a roundtable conference with Eazy. When Eazy heard the three songs I had made, he said, "I've got my George Clinton." Back then I was on the hip-hop tip—you know, I never really left the b-boy thing alone—but I was also doing all kinds of other different things, as well. And that meeting started my business relationship with Eric "Eazy-E" Wright.

What was Eazy-E like in real life?

He was one of a kind. No one can really judge anyone else because at the end of the day you don't know what anyone does behind closed doors. He was a walking persona of that oppression that we came from; you know, he was the good, the bad, and the ugly all rolled up in one. But the one thing that made his steps beautiful, in my opinion, was the fact that he was a giver at the same time. He gave a lot of folks opportunities when it was much more difficult to find opportunities to play this genre of music, which would ultimately become known as g-funk. Eazy allowed us to shine, and he said, "Don't compromise the integrity of who and what you are, and what you want your artistry to be." Behind closed doors, Eazy helped a lot of kids. If there had been no Eazy-E at the time that I was at that fork in the road and trying to make it into this music industry, I would never have come this far. Here I am 21 years later, and look at where I am today.

There was nobody like Eazy-E. He always had his Compton hat on, Levis, a t-shirt . . . But the man also knew how to get suited and booted and talk about mechanicals and structure and business. There was an intelligence about that brother that led to the establishment of a lot of artists, such as Dr. Dre to Snoop to Eminem to Ice Cube. That's why I always give big ups to that brother, because you can't respect the future if you don't respect the past. And it's our job to educate the young ones, because this music is a part of our history.

You worked on NWA's classic album *Niggaz4life*. What was that experience like?
Ah, that was cool, man. Watching them make those NWA records was really something. Dre is a phenomenal dude. All of those collective people made those projects all the way down to the bass player . . . You had to be there to really understand what that magic was all about. It was amazing to witness that sort of energy at a time when it was still fresh like the Beatles had once been. It was mass mania, man! I mean, it was bananas, homie. It was a really good thing for me. They invited me on, and they accepted me as a different kind of artist. I have to give big ups to Eazy and Dre, as well as my cousin Cold187um, for getting me on a record that big at that time. That record was a classic, and it's gone down in history as one of the NWA greats. There will never be another NWA in the same way that there will never be another Tupac; there will never be another Eazy. That experience was something else, man, and I carry that same legacy with me today.

Your singing style is very reminiscent of that employed by George Clinton in Parliament. Having worked with both George Clinton and Bootsy Collins, what was their reaction to you?
Oh, man, I got my funk card! [Chuckles.] You do a lot of things because you're passionate about this music . . . I did a lot of songs with different cats, feeling their different musical vibes. But this was a case of me as a child patterning myself after those guys and their techniques; I took some of their spirit, but didn't emulate them. I patterned things after those guys and then changed and incorporated them into my own style. Well, whenever you have *those* cats validating your style . . . It changes you and the way that you put down your music, and it also lets you know that you were doing it right all that time. I sat up with George Clinton and Bootsy Collins and they told me that it took them 17 years for audiences to understand their style—their "cosmic slop," so to speak. And for me, it was the same thing! My style and their styles are different, but they understood the science of it—that we're still funkin'! They sat me down and they validated me

and they said, "You got it, Koke!" I mean, I even had George Clinton come in one day—and this is a blessing, and I'm humbled by this—and he heard a track I had just done and asked, *"When did I do those vocals?"* And it was *me* on there! So it's definitely a blessing to see that type of reward because it encourages you to continue on, because you're never too old—unless you say you're too old. So even though I've been in the game a certain number of years, I got a fresh new wind.

Your album *Funk Upon a Rhyme* is a definite West Coast classic, yet the sales were rather disappointing. Why do you think that is?
Well, part of it was probably the name. And you have to remember that at that time it was Ruthless versus Death Row, and with that there were a lot of things happening that were political. There were a lot of things going on, and it was all a pot of gumbo that was boiling over and leading up to that whole Ruthless versus Death Row thing, and Eric dying . . . Then once that happened, we were over there at Relativity Records, and shit was going haywire. I suppose it was inevitable for it to happen like that, but you know, the record did something like 175,000 to 200,000 in sales. And you have to realize that I had videos out there, but I didn't get the kind of marketing push that Snoop and those guys got. And I was selling those same types of records.

I've always felt that your album was ahead of its time, which may have been part of the problem.
Yeah, yeah! God bless you, man, thanks.

I know there's some controversy about this, but I have to ask: Who do you feel created the g-funk sound?
No doubt. It's undisputed. Cold187um, and then it trickled down to me. So really, Above the Law were the originators of g-funk, plain and simple. Cold187um used to bring that type of soulful sound that Dre campaigned as being his own style. He brought a lot of that source music to Dr. Dre. I think it's a shame, because a lot of times Cold187um doesn't get the kind of props he deserves. A lot of stuff was taken from him. We're grown men now, so it's water under the bridge . . . The thing of it is, though, the truth is the truth, and the truth is that Cold187um was responsible for the music that came to be known as g-funk. I guarantee you that if you go look up that information and you listen to those songs, it all backs up exactly what we've been saying all this time. I feel that it's important for everybody to know that.

You guys dissed Snoop, Dre, and the Dogg Pound on your song "Don't Bite Da Funk." How did that song come about?
Again, this was Ruthless versus Death Row, and there were a lot of negative forces on both sides. At that time we felt like Snoop, Dr. Dre, and the Dogg Pound had taken our essence, which we called g-funk. There were several beefs with them at that time. Then they had dissed me on a song called "Blunts and Tanqueray." We heard that and we were like, okay . . . Because Snoop used to be over there with us. Truthfully, Above the Law was about to put out a record with Snoop Dogg. Before all this other stuff happened, Above the Law was working on their music and I was working on mine. And Snoop and them couldn't wait, so Warren G. took Snoop Dogg over to Death Row. At that time, even in 1991, when NWA's *Niggaz4life* came out, there was an internal battle regarding the business side of things. So Dre was thinking about leaving Ruthless, and Above the Law and Kokane were thinking about leaving, too. At that time Suge [Knight] was doing some managing work for both myself and Above the Law. So Eazy arranged a meeting, and Dr. Dre never showed up. We showed up and rekindled the business side of things with Eazy, but by this time Dre was already set on leaving. So he and Suge did their business to get Death Row started up. And at that time, Snoop was over there with us! So Snoop couldn't wait around until we finished putting together my album, so Warren G. took him over there to Death Row, and that's what started the whole thing. There was beef between both sides for months and months and months, and we felt like, *dang*, Snoop was around us—*him and Warren G.!* And we felt like they took our whole sound and our whole essence. I mean, if you listen to Above the Law's *Black Mafia Life*, Dr. Dre's *The Chronic* sounds just like it—except *Black Mafia Life* was finished before *The Chronic*.

The thing I find fascinating is that you later wound up working with all of those guys—a lot. Considering all the beef that you had behind you, how did you guys wind up collaborating again?
Because at the end of the day we're all grown men. Me and Snoop were friends back then. I mean way before any of our albums took off real big, we were all friends. We all used to go to those studios in Torrance where Donovan was. I remember all of them hanging out with us—Warren G., Nate Dogg, Snoop . . . I was hanging around one of Snoop's friends from Long Beach named Half Dead, and Half Dead used to come to the studio

that we had down the street in Claremont. So Snoop shot a kite to me, and I shot a kite right back, and then we hooked up and we said, "We're gonna squash this shit." You know, I was a fan. At the same time we were beefing with them, I still liked their music. And at the same time they were beefing with me, they still liked my music. That was the conversation between Snoop and I. So we squashed the beef and he said, "I'd like you to sing on a couple of things." So I did, and things just got comfortable between us and he started coming back around. And those records are classic, too, and it turned out that two grown-ass men, Snoop and Kokane—Calvin and Jerry—really had respect for each other.

In the past you've commented that you feel that a lot of the positive messages are missing from today's hip-hop. What did you mean by that?
Well, it's plain and simple. Just listen to the radio. As technology was ushered in, the music started to change. If you look at the music from the eighties or the nineties, there was substance to that music; they were talking about socially conscious things. From Public Enemy to X-Clan . . . Even when NWA was saying, "Fuck the Police," there was a reason behind it. Demographically speaking, those records were more than just fun, they were a part of our lives, our everyday struggles. And today's hip-hop doesn't have any of that anymore. People today would rather dance, and there's nothing wrong with that, but today, in this generation, they don't even incorporate real instrumentation into the music anymore. There used to be a substance that made black radio black radio. Today there's really no black radio. And you can't knock what's selling right now, but I'm from an era where musicianship was something to be respected, and they made music that helped people and made their lives better. There were guys like Gil Scott-Heron, and even Marvin Gaye, to some degree . . . You don't see India.Arie get played more than Lady Gaga, and I'm not knocking her hustle at all, but come on . . . I mean, you turn on the radio and you hear this music and you know there's a person deep down inside there who's been passionate about music, yet this whole music game is in the Twilight Zone right about now.

DISCOGRAPHY

1. *Addictive Hip-Hop Music* (1991) [as Who Am I?]
2. *Funk Upon a Rhyme* (1994)

3. *They Call Me Mr. Kane* (1999)
4. *Gangstarock* (2002) [w/ Gentry]
5. *Don't Bite the Funk Vol. 1* (2004)
6. *Mr. Kane, Pt. 2* (2005)
7. *Back 2 tha Clap* (2006)
8. *Pain Killerz* (2006)
9. *The Hood Mob* (2006) [as the Hood Mob]
10. *The Album* (2008) [w/ Raine N Lane]
11. *Gimme All Mine* (2010)

CHAPTER THIRTEEN
KOOL KEITH
Emcee/Producer

Kool Keith, Ced G, TR Love, and Moe Love established the seminal hip-hop group the Ultramagnetic MCs in 1984. Although their first single was 1985's "To Give You Love," it was the classic 1986 single "Ego Trippin'" that made them stars. The group released two more singles, "Traveling at the Speed of Thought" b/w "MCs Ultra" and "Funky" b/w "Mentally Mad," before finally releasing their critically acclaimed debut album *Critical Beatdown* in 1988. The album, widely considered a classic, was significant because of Ced G's progressive production as it was one of the first utilizations of "chopped" samples. (This means that samples were rearranged and reedited rather than simply looped.) The group then disappeared from the scene for a while before returning in 1992 with their sophomore album *Funk Your Head Up*. Due largely to a dramatic change in production sound, reactions to the album were mixed. However, a Beatminerz remix of the song "Poppa Large" would prove to be another hit for the Ultramagnetic MCs. The group's third studio album, *The Four Horsemen*, would prove to be as cutting edge as its predecessors.

After *The Four Horsemen*, the Ultramagnetic MCs disbanded, and Kool Keith went solo. One of hip-hop's most unpredictable and groundbreaking artists, he has since recorded more than 40 albums—many of which were concept albums—under a variety of aliases. His 1995 album *The Octagonecologyst*, recorded under the alias Dr. Octagon, remains the most commercial of these releases. Kool Keith is also known as the voice on the Prodigy's 1997 hit dance single "Smack My Bitch Up." The prolific emcee has made collaborative albums with the likes of Ice T and Tim Dog, and reunited with the Ultramagnetic MCs for the 2007 reunion album *The Best Kept Secret*. Notable albums recorded by Kool Keith include *Sex Style* (1996), *Black Elvis/Lost in Space* (1999), and *Ultra-Octa-Doom* (2007).

What does hip-hop mean to you?
The first thing I think about when I think of hip-hop is me. But you know, there are different types of hip-hop. It's hard to think of hip-hop now. Today, they call commercial music hip-hop. They call pop music hip-hop. Then you've got original hip-hop. You've got the original uptown Bronx hip-hop like Grandmaster Flash and Kurtis Blow. Then you've got Run-DMC hip-hop, Whodini . . . Right now they claim that M.I.A. is hip-hop. You've got turntable hip-hop and fat beats hip-hop. I'm confused right now regarding what is really hip-hop. It's weird.

You're one of the most consistently creative artists in hip-hop. Today it seems like there isn't as much creativity in the music as there once was. What is your take on the current hip-hop scene?
The current hip-hop scene is stuck. They're mostly rhyming about wealth right now. Everybody's rhyming about what they have, what they own. We seem to be stuck in that genre of the music right now, and we've been seeing this type of hip-hop for the last 10 years. You know, it's cool to rap about money, but after a while, it becomes monotonous. That seems to be the subject that's attracting everybody right now. You know, that's why I like a group like the Black Eyed Peas. They used to open up for me at shows. I think will.i.am is so humble. I've known the whole group since way before they had Fergie, and they've remained true to themselves throughout all of this. They came out and did what they are doing, and I think people probably doubted it for a minute, but they actually broke through, and I'm happy for them. They're one of the only groups out there that are basically anti-stereotypical rap. They're cool because they're not saying, "I murdered your mom, I'll run up in your house, I'll kill the police . . . " After a while of hearing that type of stuff, a group like the Black Eyed Peas becomes a refreshingly welcome thing to the ear. I'd rather listen to someone like them because I feel like they're a relief from the normal tired story. You know, that "I grew up in the streets, life is hard" stuff. After a while, all of that grows monotonous. Everybody grew up in the streets. I grew up in the streets. I grew up in the ghetto. Everybody lived in the projects. Everybody lived around crackheads and drug

dealers. After a while, hearing all of that gets old. Right now there are 50 million groups out there, all telling that same old tired story.

Today it seems like you're miles ahead of most of these emcees conceptually. You're very innovative. Can you still relate to these kinds of groups?
I do, because I'm a very innovative guy. I create music in a different way. I stay ahead of the game. I make music that is so far ahead of the times . . .

But do you still listen to much of the contemporary hip-hop?
I don't feel that I have to listen to that type of stuff. I don't have to bank my whole life on that. I have a different style of my own. Some rappers have their own niche, and I'm thankful to say that I'm one of them.

In hip-hop, a lot of artists fade away after a couple of albums. Most of the biggest artists only have 10 or so albums, and that's considered longevity. Yet you've recorded about 50 albums.
I did a lot of solo albums. I did a lot of albums that were basically albums of my own, and then I got caught up in a lot of concept albums that people were kind of into.

What's the secret to your longevity and continued success?
I like to do shows and come out and meet the fans. I travel around the world and meet my fans. I don't try to live through the Internet like a lot of the artists do today to try and relate to their fans. I don't do all of that. I don't hide behind the computer. I think I'm a more accessible artist than a lot of others are. I try to travel and go around and shake hands with people—say hi and sit down and talk with people. I try to be a real person for my fans. I want them to say, "You know, he came to my city and he shook my hand and talked to me about this song or that." I travel all the time.

What are some of your fondest memories of your career?
My fondest memories are doing shows and discovering people there that I would never have expected. You know, Trent Reznor has come to my show. It's the people that you would never think would know you. My fondest memories include things like touring with rock bands that are completely separate from hip-hop; guys I would never think would know me. You know, sitting around with guys like Dave Grohl or Anthony Keidis and the Red Hot Chili Peppers. It's crazy to learn that these people have listened to my music.

CHAPTER THIRTEEN

As we discussed earlier, you're extremely prolific. How often do you record, and how many unreleased songs do you have lying around?
I record a lot of songs. My whole thing is that I've given so much music to the world that there's a time I need my music just for myself. I've sacrificed myself, cut my skin and given my own blood, and given people so much music. I did a lot of projects for myself, but also for my audience. I enjoyed making those projects, but sometimes I save some of the music for myself; music that is free, that isn't confined or restricted to any certain subject or genre. I've made a lot of songs that I knew I would never release. I just did those for myself. Those songs are a special treasure for my own ear, where I can rhyme the way I want to rhyme to the kinds of beats that I want to make.

You do most of your own production now. What do you bring to the table for your projects that other producers can't?
When you listen to the music industry today, everybody has a standard sound that they conform to. They all use the basic sound and structure that radio looks for. When you turn on the radio, all of the beats and all of the choruses sound the same. I pick out some beats from producers, but a lot of producers are just so set in their ways and happy with their own production styles that they don't really focus on the artists. They just make generic beats that will fit anyone. The beats they show me are the same ones that they're going to show the next rapper or singer. Anyone can use it. They don't design their beats exclusively for the artist. So there are times when I like to make unique tracks for myself that better fit the intensity of the story I'm trying to tell. And everything I do is distinctive and different. There are a few producers out there who make distinctive cutting-edge music; people like the Neptunes and Timbaland. I think a lot of producers are stuck in a time warp in terms of production. A lot of producers are stuck in the sampling stuff, which is cool. But for me, the sampling thing is old. We did that with Ultramagnetic a long time ago, but I've since jumped the gun and started trying to make new tracks and creating something different. Why should I go out and steal other people's music and rap on tracks that were made by other people? Why should I pay some guy on the publishing for some song that he made a long time ago when there are millions of keyboards and sounds out there that I can use? I try to make music that actually fits the song that I'm making. I have a darker side than most rappers, so I try to make music that's as intense as the story I'm telling. I'm

like Cameo when they came out. They had their own sound. Slave had their own sound. Those groups didn't have a bunch of different producers producing records for them. Barry White didn't have twenty producers. The Gap Band didn't have twenty producers.

It seems like everyone's afraid to take artistic chances these days.
They're just using the same keyboard the next guy is using. Everyone's got the same band structure. "I've got a keyboard player, I've got a drummer . . . " People are scared to hit a certain note. Everyone is scared to make a certain type of record. I personally get off on making something brand new that I can't even understand myself. You know, "This shit is going to be hot in 2020." I get off on making records that sound like they're from the year 2030.

DISCOGRAPHY

1. *Critical Beatdown* (1988) [as Ultramagnetic MCs]
2. *Funk Your Head Up* (1992) [as Ultramagnetic MCs]
3. *The Four Horsemen* (1993) [as Ultramagnetic MCs]
4. *The Basement Tapes* (1994) [as Ultramagnetic MCs]
5. *Big Willie Smith* (1995)
6. *Sex Style* (1996)
7. *Cenobites* (1996) [w/ Godfather Don]
8. *New York What Is Funky* (1996) [as Ultramagnetic MCs]
9. *Brooklyn to Brixton* (1996) [as Ultramagnetic MCs]
10. *Dr. Octagonecologyst* (1996) [as Dr. Octagon]
11. *Dr. Octagonecologyst 2* (1996) [as Dr. Octagon]
12. *Big Time* (1996) [as Ultra]
13. *The B-Sides Companion* (1997) [as Ultramagnetic MCs]
14. *Smack My Bitch Up* (1998) [as Ultramagnetic MCs]
15. *First Come, First Served* (1999) [as Dr. Dooom]
16. *Black Elvis/Lost in Space* (1999)
17. *I Don't Believe You* (2000)
18. *Matthew* (2000)
19. *Pimp to Eat (2000)* [as Analog Brothers]
20. *Masters of Illusion* (2001) [w/ Motion Man]
21. *Spankmaster* (2001)

22. *Game* (2002) [w/ H Bomb and Marc Live]
23. *Freaks* (2003)
24. *Diesel Truckers* (2004) [w/ Kutmasta Kurt]
25. *Official Space Tape* (2004)
26. *Clayborne Family* (2004) [w/ Jacky Jasper and Marc Live]
27. *The Personal Album* (2004)
28. *Confidence* (2005)
29. *Execution One* (2005)
30. *7th Veil* (2005)
31. *Nogatco Rd.* (2006)
32. *Project Polaroid* (2006) [w/ TOMC3]
33. *Serving Your Area* (2006) [as Randolf Lift with Kool Keith]
34. *Collabs Tape* (2006)
35. *The Commi$$ioner* (2006)
36. *The Commi$$ioner 2* (2006)
37. *The Return of Dr. Octagon* (2007) [as Dr. Octagon]
38. *The Best Kept Secret* (2007) [as Ultramagnetic MCs]
39. *Sex Style: The Unreleased Archives* (2007)
40. *Ultra-Octa-Doom* (2007)
41. *Dr. Dooom 2* (2008)
42. *7th Veil: Stoned* (2008) [w/ H Bomb]
43. *Down on Land* (2008) [as Randolf Lift with Kool Keith]
44. *The Undertakerz* (2008)
45. *Tashan Dorsett* (2009)
46. *Bikinis-N-Thongs* (2009) [w/ Denis Deft and Yeti Beats]
47. *Lost Masters Collection* (2009)
48. *Tim Dog & Kool Keith* (2009) [w/ Tim Dog]
49. *Idea of a Master Piece* (2009) [w/ 54-71]

KOOL ROCK SKI
Emcee

I n the early 1980s, three portly emcees (Prince Markie Dee, Kool Rock Ski, and Buff Love) established the legendary hip-hop group the Fat Boys. In 1984, the Fat Boys released their self-titled debut album, which is widely considered to be a classic LP. Riding on the success of the single "Fat Boys," which remained in the Top 15 for an impressive 18 weeks, the album ultimately went gold. This is significant as it was one of the earliest hip-hop albums to accomplish this feat. The following year, the Fat Boys became one of the very first hip-hop acts to appear in a major motion picture (*Krush Groove*). The Fat Boys are also notable for being one of the first hip-hop groups to land a number of lucrative endorsement deals, including Mountain Dew, Pepsi, Sbarro, and Swatch. That same year, the Fat Boys joined the likes of U2, Run-DMC, Pete Townshend, Ringo Starr, Bruce Springsteen, and many others for the anti-apartheid single "Sun City." Along with LL Cool J, Run-DMC, and Whodini, the Fat Boys then embarked on the first major hip-hop tour, The Swatch Fresh Fest. The group became so popular at the time that another group released an album under the name the Skinny Boys in the hopes of emulating their success.

The Fat Boys subsequently released two more gold albums, *The Fat Boys Are Back!* and *Big & Beautiful*, before breaking out with the 1987 platinum release *Crushin'*. This album spawned the Top 10 single "Wipeout," which featured the Beach Boys singing backup vocals. That same year, the group starred in their second major motion picture, *Disorderlies*. During this period, the Fat Boys also released a hits collection entitled *The Best Part of The Fat Boys*, becoming the first hip-hop group to release a greatest hits collection. In 1988, the Fat Boys scored another hit with their cover of Chubby Checker's tune "The Twist," featuring Checker himself singing backup vocals.

In 1990, Prince Markie Dee left the group to pursue other interests. The two remaining members would then record one more Fat Boys album, *Mack Daddy*, before disbanding in 1991. Sadly, Buff Love passed away in 1995 at the age of 28, weighing nearly 450 pounds.

In 2009, a skinnier Kool Rock Ski, now simply known as "Kool Rock," reemerged with an EP titled *Party Time*. Kool Rock and Prince Markie Dee are also planning a Fat Boys reunion album.

What does hip-hop mean to you?
Hip-hop is not just the music, although that's usually what people think of. It's really a culture: the clothing, the style, the vibe. As you can see, most of the commercials that are done today are created around the hip-hop generation. The rock and roll generation is pretty much gone, and now we've moved on to the hip-hop generation. Once the hip-hop generation came in, people had no choice but to go with the flow. Most of the people who were living in the rock and roll generation have no idea that they're living in a hip-hop generation. [Laughs.] They're still caught up in the past. The same way that rock and roll changed the course of America, hip-hop changed the course of America. Barack Obama and Bill Clinton are perfect examples of what the hip-hop generation is all about; it was our generation that voted them into office.

It's amazing to think that we have a president now who admits that he listens to people like Jay-Z and Ludacris.
It is amazing, but I always knew the day would come. I don't want to sound like a prophet or something, but I knew it was going to happen one day. One day soon; not one day after I leave this earth, but one day *soon*. And it was time for a change anyway—not for a change of color, but a change in the way people act toward one another—especially as races. When you're walking down the street, as a black man, people of other races stop and kind of stare at you like you're an alien or something. [Laughs again.] I think it was time for a change in regards to the way we look and act toward one

another. And I think that's what Obama meant when he said it was time for a change.

When the Fat Boys first got together, you were called the Disco 3. How did the Disco 3 get together?

We grew up in the same blocks. I met Mark [Morales] first, and me and Mark became best friends. Then Buff moved in around the block when Mark and I were in our preteens. Then me and Buff became close, and we went from junior high to high school together. Me and Buff went to one high school, and Mark went to another. Over time, we really got into football. Everything we did was about football; we ate, drank, and slept football. During this time we were always rapping, so when our football plans fell through . . . We were doing talent shows and little parties here and there. We heard about this talent contest, and we entered it. We won the day we entered, and then we won the semi-finals. Then the finals were held the next week, and we won the finals. The guy who put the contest together was Charlie Stetler, who then became our manager.

I remember reading that you guys weren't really interested in winning the recording contract, and that you were actually more interested in winning stereo equipment.

[Chuckles.] We were young back then, and we were like, "Let's go for the stereo equipment!" We were kind of led in the right direction. "You don't want to win the stereo equipment, you want that record contract." We were just too young to know any better.

Daddy-O explained to me that in the early days of hip-hop a lot of groups were afraid to get recording contracts because they thought it might damage their credibility. You guys were one of the first groups to appear in movies. Did you guys have any fear of losing credibility by appearing in films?

No. We kind of looked at it like Run-DMC, Kurtis Blow, LL Cool J, the Beastie Boys, and New Edition were all in the movie, too, so it couldn't be too bad. There were so many people that we came up with that we didn't really look at it that way. We didn't look at it that way until after *Disorderlies* came out. [Laughs.] Once we saw the finished cut, we were like, "Wow, this is not really a hip-hop movie." But I think that just shows how much we extended our horizons as far as the music. We were no longer just a hip-hop group or a rap act. We were getting worldwide recognition. As far as the early days people not wanting to record or make movies, that's cool, but let's face it: everyone does this to make money. Of course you love the music, but the love kind of leaves you after a while. You do it for love, don't get me wrong, but once that money comes into play, you still want to see that money being generated and going into your pocket. People have been rapping about money for a long time. I mean, you look at Big Bank Hank from the Sugarhill Gang, and he was rapping about money and how he had all these cars . . . He didn't actually have these things, but he was rapping in the hopes that one day he might get them.

When you guys found success, you got really big really fast. How did life change for you?
One day you're just growing up, walking the streets with Mark and Buff, with nothing in your pockets. You know, if you've got $10 in your pocket you're doing pretty good. Then the next week you've got $2,000 in your pocket, and then that grows into $60 or $70,000. And this is overnight, and you're like, what the hell? The people around you change, but we never changed. We were the same guys who wore jeans and sneakers. We didn't run out and buy $4,000 gator boots and stuff like that. Of course you're gonna buy a car and take care of your family, because that's the kind of background we came from; you take care of your family first, and you help your friends out. But then after a while, your friends start to look at you kind of differently. "You changed, man, you don't come around and hang out no more." Well, you know, I don't wanna have a damn .45 to my head at two o'clock in the morning [laughs] with someone wanting to blow out my brains to take my money. "That's why I don't hang out on the old block anymore." But you don't forget about the guys from the old block, you just kind of pick them up and take them somewhere else to hang out.

The Fat Boys appeared on the song "Sun City." How did that song come about, and what was that experience like?
Steven Van Zandt approached our manager with the idea. He was a fan of ours, and one thing that still bugs me out is that he said, "Bruce Springsteen is a big fan of you guys' music." I was like, *"Bruce Springsteen?"* He was like, "Yeah, Bruce loves you guys." And Michael Jackson said the same thing to us when we met him at the 1986 Grammys. So we went to do the "Sun City" thing, and it was late at night. We shot the video from about

five o'clock in the afternoon until about six in the morning. Melle Mel was there. I saw Bruce Springsteen just sitting on the curb by the street. I walked by him and said, "How are you doing?" And he said, "Oh, hey, how are you doing, man?" And we started talking! [Laughs.] I mean, here's a guy who's coming off just selling damn near 30 million records, and he was just really down to earth. He was just one of the guys. So we did the project, and we had a lot of fun doing it. It was a notch in our belt, and it was for a good cause, which was fighting apartheid.

We also did the Mandela concert at Wembley Stadium in 1988. It was us and Salt-N-Pepa representing the hip-hop community.

What are some of your fondest memories with the Fat Boys?
Just sitting up late at night with Buff, just talking. We would just talk about how we could get better at what we do, and we talked a lot about where we came from. A lot of people think our success was an overnight thing, but it was a lot of hard work to get to where we were at. We just sat there, and we couldn't really believe what was happening at the time. Buff and I would just be sitting there talking, and then Mark would bust through the door. We would just sit there until four or five in the morning, and Buff would be falling asleep. Then we would move from Buff's room to my room, and Mark and I would just sit there and talk. It was a special time, just hanging out with the friends that I had grown up with. We were just bugging out and having fun, because after a while, it got to the point where we couldn't even walk out on the streets anymore. You couldn't just go to the mall or take a female acquaintance out to dinner, because you would have a line of people standing at your dinner table waiting for an autograph. I mean, you appreciate that they like your work, but when you're that young, that doesn't really register in your head. You just want to be left alone.

When you guys left the hip-hop game after your last album, some of that attention and autograph seeking had to have died down. At the end of the day, did you miss that attention?
To be honest with you, I didn't miss it at all. I was always one of the guys. I could just hang out with any group and fit in with them. That was me. You could ask anyone who knows me, and they'd tell you that. And that was all three of us, really. But anyone who knows me would be like, "That's just Kool Rock." People walk up to me and ask me questions and I just talk with

them and answer them. Then when they leave, they'll say, "He's a cool cat." But I don't really need all the fanfare and accolades that come with being a big star. Sometimes people don't know how to make that transition, but I've found no problem with it.

You guys recorded hit singles with the Beach Boys and Chubby Checker. What were those experiences like?

If we would have stopped after the Beach Boys song, we would have been satisfied with it. And this is not to take anything away from Chubby Checker, but as far as us being a hip-hop act, I think we should have stopped after the Beach Boys song. But, of course, our record company and management, after seeing the popularity of that first song, wanted to keep on with the novelty of teaming us up with an old group or solo act.

I think we met the Beach Boys around 1986 on the set of *Disorderlies*. They were in the last part of the movie. Our management had said, "The Beach Boys have agreed to do a cameo in the movie." We were like, "Okay, that's cool, but who the hell are the Beach Boys?" [Chuckles.] I mean, we didn't grow up listening to that music. So they came to the set and did their part. And they kept popping up everywhere we went; we did this TV show for Disney, and they were there at the same time. Our road manager suggested that it might be nice to do a record together; not necessarily to put out, but just to see how it sounds. But our manager was like, "We're not going to do a song just to see how it sounds. We're going to do a song and put it out." So "Wipeout" came out, and it got accepted. It went over very well, and I think it peaked at number four on the Top 100. The song went platinum-plus. So we were like, okay, we'll just leave it at that. Run-DMC had done "Walk This Way," so this will be okay. But then they were like, "Let's bring in Chubby Checker next!" [Laughs.]

I have nothing against the record companies and the managers for doing what they do, because that's their job. And we had one of the best managers in the music industry at that time. Charlie Stetler could pretty much have sold sand to a beach! He was that good. But at the same time, he was taking us down this road where we had no chance of getting back to our core audience. And by the time we wanted to get back to our core audience, they had pretty much drifted on to somebody else. NWA was coming out, Public Enemy was doing their thing. It was kind of like the Fat Boys got pushed back to the side.

Your sound changed a lot on your last album, *Mack Daddy*. You didn't sound as comfortable. What happened?

The album was rushed. We got a boatload of money put in our pocket. We had just come off the breakup—Mark had just left the group. One night Buff came to my house and said, "Someone wants to invest in us to put out a new album." I said, "What company?" And he said, "No, it's independent." I said, "Cool, I could go independent. Then we won't have an overhead or anyone looking over our shoulder." So the next day, Buff brings me this big envelope with stacks and stacks of hundreds in it. He was like, "Yo, that's for you." I'm like, "What is this for?" And he says, "We've got to do an album." "Are you serious? Where are the contracts?" [Laughs again.] And he was like, "Don't worry about it, I got it." So I'm like, whatever.

So we had no direction on the album. We were running around like chickens with our heads cut off. I mean, we had *no* direction. Buff was over here buying every kind of car he could find, and I was over here just dating different girls . . . It was all chaos. So by the time we got into the studio, that's how the sound was—chaos. There was nothing structured. And to this day, that album still pisses me off because I'm like, man, it could have been so much better. We should have taken advantage of the opportunity that we had, but we didn't. Instead we lollygagged and just threw songs together in one hour. We would just go in there and say some shit and then it was, "Okay, see you tomorrow." [Chuckles.] We had had money before, but we had never had money and this kind of freedom where no one was telling us what to do with it. Now it was being pushed at us and we would say shit like, "I'm gonna go buy me a Mercedes tomorrow!" That's how it was, and that's why the album came out the way that it did. It was real half-assed. I mean, it charted at like number eighty-one on the charts with absolutely no promotion.

It was fun making that album, but again there was no structure and we had no management. We were just managing ourselves.

I always thought that album sounded a lot different from your previous efforts.

We would sit down and say, we're not going to sound like the Fat Boys anymore. Let's sound like NWA or Ice Cube! So we were rapping songs in a way that people had never heard us before. Everyone who had grown up a Fat Boys fan was like, "What happened? Why are you guys so hard now?"

First of all, we called the album *Mack Daddy,* and that was hard enough. "Why are you moving away from what you do?" At the same time, we *had* to get away from what we had done previously. We couldn't go into the studio at that time and rap about "give me some hot macaroni and cheese." We had to try something different, but we could have done something better than what we did. But, you know, you live and you learn.

In 1995, Buff Love passed away. That must have been a very difficult time.
Buff was the heart of the group. A lot of times they made me the captain as far as putting things into place and sitting down with the manager, but when it came down to who the fans wanted to see, it was Buff. He was just an ordinary 'round-the-way guy. He loved the finer things in life, but at the same time, he didn't turn his nose up at people. People knew that he was down to earth. He was my best friend. Mark is my best friend, too, but Buff and I just had this camaraderie. We just knew what the other one was going to say or think next. Once he passed, it just kind of messed me up. I mean, we grew up together. There were periods where we would go three or four months and not see each other maybe one day. We would spend months together on tour, and then we'd get off the plane and get into the limousine and go home. Within an hour, this guy would be at my house! I'd be like, "What are you doing here? I just saw you for three months straight. I don't want to see you anymore." [Laughs.] He'd say, "Let's hang out," and I'd say, "All right, let's go." He was just all about having fun, and keeping the people around him laughing.

You just recorded your solo EP, *Party Time*. In what ways had the recording aspect of making music changed since you had recorded with the Fat Boys?
It was a lot quicker. Instead of working on a forty-eight-track board, you just open a laptop and everything is right there. Everything was really quick. When we did this project, we did it a different way this time. We didn't just go in there and complete one song. We did like eight songs in one day! The process has changed. This time I thought of wittier things to say, too. Instead of just going in and saying anything, my producer told me I had to step it up. He said, "You got kids out here who are like eighteen years old who will eat your ass up! You have to step up your lyrics." We concentrated more, and we stripped the beats down to make it sound more hip-hop. "Let's make it more street, let's make it more New York." It's just

a pure New York sound, and a lot of DJs told me, "This is just raw." We did do some autotune stuff because we wanted to keep up with the times, but I can see now that people are starting to back away from autotune since Jay-Z dropped "D.O.A. (Death of Autotune)."

I was impressed with your flow on this project. Was that flow always there, or did you have to consciously work to sound more contemporary this time out?

I did a lot of writing over the years. You know what's weird? I do a lot of battle rhyming, for some odd reason. I write a lot of battle rhymes. It's like, well, who the hell am I going to battle? [Chuckles.] But you've got to keep yourself relevant. There are a lot of street corner cats out there who will put you in your place, so you've got to have something for them. And not just in the streets, but also in the studio. What if somebody comes into the studio and says something subliminal about me? Then I've got to say something subliminal back. That's just a part of hip-hop. That's just the competitive aspect of hip-hop. It's not about somebody trying to disrespect you as a person, it's just a competition. They want that notch on their belt. They want to say, "Yeah, I destroyed that cat from the Fat Boys!" You don't want to get put into that category. I've just been a competitor and I've gotten better through the years. I'm taking the craft a lot more seriously, and I'm loving what I'm doing.

DISCOGRAPHY

1. *The Fat Boys* (1984) [as the Fat Boys]
2. *The Fat Boys Are Back!* (1985) [as the Fat Boys]
3. *Big & Beautiful* (1986) [as the Fat Boys]
4. *Crushin'* (1987) [as the Fat Boys]
5. *The Best Part of the Fat Boys* (1987) [as the Fat Boys]
6. *Coming Back Hard Again* (1988) [as the Fat Boys]
7. *On and On* (1989) [as the Fat Boys]
8. *Mack Daddy* (1990) [as the Fat Boys]
9. *All Meat, No Filler* (1997) [as the Fat Boys]
10. *Party Time* (2009)

KEITH MURRAY
Emcee

L
ong Island emcee Keith Murray began battle rhyming at the age of 13 under the moniker MC Do Damage. The young Murray won many battles, and even famously attempted to battle legendary emcee Big Daddy Kane. In the early 1990s, Murray was introduced to EPMD's Erick Sermon, who instantly recognized his potential and eventually got him signed to Jive Records. Murray soon made a thunderous entrance into the rap game when he appeared on Sermon's 1993 single "Hostile." The following year Murray released his own debut album, *The Most Beautifullest Thing in This World*. Buoyed by two hit singles—the title track and its follow-up "Get Lifted"—the album quickly went gold.

In 1996, Murray released his sophomore effort, *Enigma*. The critically acclaimed album reached number six on *Billboard*'s Hip-Hop/R&B chart. Murray was then imprisoned for 33 months after being convicted of second-degree assault. Murray has repeatedly insisted that he was innocent, and celebrities like Britney Spears and LL Cool J came to his defense. Murray's third album, *It's a Beautiful Thing*, would be released in 1999 while the emcee was still imprisoned. He soon dropped his fourth album, *He's Keith Murray*. However, it was his fifth album, *Rap-Murr-Phobia (The Fear of Real Hip-Hop)*, that brought him back to the public eye.

In addition to his work as a solo artist, Murray has also recorded albums with the "super groups" Def Squad (with Sermon and Redman) and the Undergodz (with Canibis). He has also appeared as a featured artist on a number of hit singles, including LL Cool J's "I Shot Ya," Boyz II Men's "Vibin'," Mary J. Blige's "Be Happy," and Total's "Can't You See."

What does hip-hop mean to you?
Hip-hop means a lot of things to me. Culture; life; unity; youth; money; communication; bringing different cultures together; intelligence; fun times; seriousness; originality. Those things are what hip-hop means to me.

I understand your uncle was an emcee when you were growing up. Tell me about that.
My uncle is the original b-boy T-Roy. I first became aware of what he was doing in the early 1980s. That was when I first became aware of hip-hop. He used to walk around the house like a rappin' jack; all day, everything he said was a rhyme. Any situation he encountered, there was a rhyme. He was a true b-boy with the Kangol and the permanent-pressed Lee jeans. He had the movement of his hands, his head was moving, and he just knew how to put words together. He never really wrote rhymes, but he always rhymed and he came up with creative stuff. This was intriguing to me. I was like, "Yo, what is this?" He said, "All you have to do is put words together that make sense and rhyme." He gave me my first hip-hop tape; it was *The Great Adventures of Grand Master Flash and the Furious Five.* Then he gave me the Fatback Band record. And from there, I just fell in love with hip-hop music. I just emulated him and started putting my own rhymes together. I had my own style, though. That was one thing he taught me: "You don't want to sound like anyone else. You have to have your own original flavor."

I've been told that you battled Big Daddy Kane when you were only twelve or thirteen. What happened?
I had an uncle named Born True who was Big Daddy Kane's bodyguard. He used to take me all over Brooklyn to all the projects, battling everybody. Battling, battling . . . This was the kind of scenario where you never said the same rhyme twice. You had a million rhymes, and you were always coming off the top of your head. That was what hip-hop was.

Then my uncle invited me to the video shoot for "Long Live the Kane." If you look at that video, you can see me. There's a guy with a sky blue hat on, and that was me, but all you could see was the back of my hoodie! [Laughs.] Being there with such high-caliber talent made me realize that hey, I was in the same cypher as Big Daddy Kane! I realized that I could do this on a professional level.

I had never really hung around Kane. I was at the house with him one time, and then one time we were on 42nd Street—the Deuce—drinking forties and shit. And Kane was like, "I'm gonna tell your uncle," and I was like, "No, don't do that!" [Chuckles.] Then I was there on his birthday. They had a concert at Nassau Coliseum with the entire Juice Crew. So my uncle Born brought my cousin and me to the show. I was only thirteen. I never thought I would be the next generation of what these guys were doing. Big Daddy Kane ripped it at the show. You know, he was rocking the flat-top and the four-finger rings. So later, we were all sitting at the table after the show, and my uncle said, "Yo, Keith, I got somebody for you to battle. Go get 'em!" So I went to the other end of the table and kicked the rhymes I had, and then Kane kicked his. Of course he dominated the situation, because he was Big Daddy Kane, at the peak of his career. I was nervous and shy, but I wasn't shy when it came to rhyming. So I just kicked a few verses back and forth with Kane, and he said, "Yo, shorty, how old are you?" I said I was thirteen and he said, "Yeah, you're gonna be nice." And ever since then, I just kept rhyming. I never stopped. I was just relentless.

It wasn't really a battle, though. I just had the opportunity to rhyme for the greatest emcee at the time, next to Rakim. It was a real transformation for me; that day I became a real emcee.

At 35, do you still battle?
There have been a few instances where I had to dominate individuals, but I don't really tangle with niggas if I can keep from doing so. But once in a while I've had to shut a nigga down with a few bars here and there. I'm still ferocious at 35. I've got a battle mentality, and I'm ready at any time for a nigga to open his mouth so I can make an example out of him.

You were a protégé of EPMD's Erick Sermon. How did you meet him, and what was that meeting like?
I'm from Long Island, where De La Soul, Biz Markie, Public Enemy, Rakim, EPMD, K-Solo, and Prince Paul all come from. I lived on Carlton Avenue. I knew K-Solo. He was older than I was, but he used to come to my high school sometimes. And I had a friend named Mark D who knew him. Then Solo started coming around us. My main man Wink knew Solo, so whenever Solo would come around, Wink would talk to him. Then one

day I learned that Erick Sermon had moved into my hood. K-Solo came up to the store where we used to be hustlers committing petty crimes, and I said, "Solo, take me to Erick's house." And he said all right. He told me to meet him there at a certain time. I went to the house, Solo went up and knocked on the door, and E answered and said, "What up?" And that was the first time I met Erick Sermon, the Green-Eyed Bandit. I was like, "Oh shit, that's Erick Sermon." Then we went downstairs and I started reciting my rhymes for him, and basically, I never left that basement.

As everyone knows, Erick and Parrish [of EPMD] had a nasty breakup in the early 1990s. How awkward was it for you to be a member of that camp when all that went down?
It wasn't awkward for me at all. It was actually better for me. Remember, I went to Erick's house. I didn't know Parrish at all. I didn't know Das-EFX at all. It was just me and Erick hanging out every day. He would tell me to come over at a certain time. He lived five minutes from me. I would go sell drugs on the corner, run with L.O.D. [Murray's clique, the Legion of Doom] and cause havoc, and then go back to Erick's house. This was around the time I got out of jail and was going back to college at New York Tech. I was actually doing my first year of college, but I would come home and go to the block. One time I was on the tour bus and I saw Parrish Smith and Das-EFX, but I didn't know them. Then they came to Erick's house like, "What up?" And then I heard that EPMD got into some bullshit, and I was actually in the basement when the detectives came to question Erick [about a possible hit contract on Parrish Smith]. They took E to the station, and I was like, "What is this?" So I went back to the block. Then, the next thing I knew, the whole EPMD thing blew up. Then Erick moved to Atlanta, and I didn't see him for an entire year. Niggas on the block were like, "What happened? I thought Erick was gonna sign you?" I was like, "Are you crazy? Just watch." Then, after everything blew over, Erick came back.

Parrish Smith actually tried to sign Keith Murray after E went to Atlanta. I knew a guy named Alvin Toney who used to bodyguard for EPMD. One day Alvin Toney and Parrish came to my house. Parrish was like, "Are we gonna get these contracts signed?" And I said, "I'm not signing these contracts." Then Erick came back and I told him what happened. And then we recorded the song "Hostile" for Erick's album, and the rest is history.

"Hostile" was a great song. It still holds up seventeen years later.
"Hostile" is still the joint. Every night when I perform, I step out to that
song. [Starts rhyming] "Keith Murray, coming from the North, South,
East and left, rhymin' to death . . . "

**When you're working as part of a super group like Def Squad or the Un-
dergodz, does it make you write better? Is there a conscious effort not to
get outdone by the next man?**
It's a friendly competition. You know, these niggas are nice! They're your
boys, but at the same time you still battle with them. You're still trying to
outdo everything they do. At the end of the day, we make each other step
up their game. Writing with a group is way easier for me than writing by
myself. First of all, I don't have to write as much, and then, I don't have
to think as hard. They come up with something, then I come up with
something, and I play my part. It's very encouraging to be rhyming next to
Canibis or Redman or Erick Sermon. It makes me step it up 100 percent.
That doesn't mean I'm weaker when I do my solo thing, but it's a whole
different angle.

**You had an album titled *Rap-Murr-Phobia (The Fear of Real Hip-Hop)*.
Who do you feel fears real hip-hop, and why do they fear it?**
I think the fear of hip-hop comes from the people who misunderstand
the artists who come from the street. They fear the artists who speak from
their hearts. They'd rather see the artists who make some type of gimmicky
record to dull the culture of hip-hop for the sake of corporations making
money. If I make a record where I come on and I'm screaming, they fear
that. They say, "Why's he angry? Why's he so mad?" I'm not mad. That's
just the way I am sometimes. I'm high-strung. That's aggression and expression. They fear that. They say, "He's unpredictable. He's gonna do
something crazy."

Real hip-hop is the raw essence of the street. People don't want the
streets around them. They turn their back on the streets now.

Hip-hop is hurting right now. Who do you personally blame for that?
I don't blame anybody. I feel that hip-hop had to evolve. Every business
has its ups and downs. I don't feel that hip-hop is dead. I can't say that this
person killed it or that person killed it. Hip-hop is now worldwide, and
now everybody's gotten ahold of it, and they're going to interpret it the way

they want to interpret it and do it the way they want to do it. Hip-hop had to rise to a degree to get recognized. The corporations shape and mold and dictate what mainstream America wants to hear. It's different, but it's still hip-hop. It's a fact that cannot be disputed, just like saying that all people derived from black people. I know what Nas meant when he said hip-hop is dead; he meant hip-hop as we knew it to be pure and unadulterated is dead. Now everybody wants to get to the mainstream, and I'm not knocking them, because I want to go to the mainstream.

You're widely recognized as one of the finest lyricists in hip-hop. Today, hip-hop as a whole has kind of gotten away from lyricism. Why do you feel that is?
People have short attention spans. Nowadays, if people have to study something and take the time to understand it, they skip it. They'd rather hear something that feels good. Listeners today are like kids who don't want to do their homework.

DISCOGRAPHY

1. *The Most Beautifullest Thing in This World* (1994)
2. *Enigma* (1996)
3. *El Nino (1998)* [as Def Squad]
4. *It's a Beautiful Thing* (1999)
5. *The Most Beautifullest Hits* (1999)
6. *He's Keith Murray* (2003)
7. *Rap-Murr-Phobia (The Fear of Real Hip-Hop)* (2007)
8. *The Undergodz* (2009) [as the Undergodz]

CHAPTER SIXTEEN
PARADIME
Emcee/DJ

Paradime emerged on the Detroit hip-hop scene in 1991 with a street album. While the project only sold a few hundred copies, it established Paradime as a fierce and talented lyricist. In 1996, Paradime was discovered by Kid Rock, who took the young emcee under his wing. The partnership began with Paradime performing at local shows with Kid Rock, but soon grew into something much more. Paradime would ultimately co-write some of Kid Rock's biggest hits, such as "Cowboy," "Forever," and "Cocky." While still working on his own solo recording career, Paradime would eventually be enlisted by Kid Rock to tour with him as his DJ and hypeman.

In 1998, Paradime formed his own independent label, Beats at Will. He has since released four full-length albums. The first of these, *Paragraphs*, was hailed by local press as a "Detroit hip-hop classic." The album was named the top-selling album in Detroit (1999–2001) by the Detroit Music Retailers Collective. In 2001, Paradime released his second full-length album, *Vices*. Following the release of the album, Paradime won three Detroit Music Awards in 2002 for "Best Hip-Hop Artist," "Oustanding Live Performer," and "Album of the Year." (He has since won seven more Detroit Music Awards.) Additionally, Paradime was named *Real Detroit* magazine's "Hip-Hop Artist of the Year" three years in a row (2001–2004). He has also taken home awards for "Solo Artist of the Year," "Live Performer of the Year," and "Lyricist of the Year" from the annual Detroit Hip-Hop Awards.

In 2004, Paradime released *11 Steps Down* to great acclaim. He has since released the album *Spill at Will* in 2007, and was hard at work on his fifth album at the time of this writing.

What does hip-hop mean to you?

Hip-hop is my everything. It's like that Common song "I Used to Love H.E.R.," the way he describes her and went through so many relationship changes with the music. That's exactly how it is for me. It's just like a girl-friend—sometimes you hate its guts, and sometimes there's nothing better. [Laughs.] It's the first thing that goes into my ears when I wake up in the morning, and it's the last thing I listen to at night. I listen to all different types of music, but there is nothing else that moves me the way hip-hop does. I think it's the realness of the music that appeals to me; people say exactly what's on their minds, and there's nothing better than that.

What are some of your earliest hip-hop-related memories?

You know, people always ask who your favorite emcee is or whatever, and I always think about the first time I heard Rakim. The first time I heard "Paid in Full," his voice and his cadence made me pay attention. I was into breakdancing when I was a kid—I was an eighties baby—when hip-hop was still in its fledgling years. You know, *Beat Street* and *Krush Groove* . . . I was still really little during all of that. My older cousin was into everything, and I just did whatever he did. Once I watched *Beat Street* and started getting into it and feeling that music, there was nothing better. So you asked about my earliest memories? Really, honest to God, I remember being at my boy Mario's house—he's one of my close friends to this day—and listening to the *Paid in Full* cassette and thinking, Damn, that shit is fresh!

How did you hook up with Kid Rock?

In 1996, I had been making little four-track demos in the basement, and it got to the point where everyone in the neighborhood was really into it and bumping my music. One of the neighborhood dudes came up to us and was like, "I got some money, and I want you to actually record a real album." We'd press up little cassettes with our own little covers and pass them around and sell them; we practically lived off of them for a couple of years. And this dude was like, "I got real money to take you into the studio to actually record." So we went to this studio called the White Room in Detroit, and when we walked in, the very first person we saw was Kid Rock sweeping the floor. [Chuckles.] And we knew who he was at that point because he already had released the *Grits Sandwiches for Breakfast* album. But we were like, "Damn, dude, that's Kid Rock, sweeping the floors." So we met with the dudes who actually owned the studio and we told them what we wanted to do. They asked to hear some of the music, and Rock was right there, and he came in and said, "What's this?" We told him, and he said, "Tell you what," and he told the owners of the studio, "I want to work with these guys. If they end up recording here, I want to be an engineer; I want to be on this shit." He was really all about it.

We just built a relationship from there. We worked on this album that never came out, and around this same time his album *Early Morning Stoned Pimp* came out. Then I started to do some writing for him, and we've stayed boys for all these years. He signed me to Top Dog Records in 1999 to a production deal, and that was right when he blew up and [Kid Rock's former DJ] Uncle Kracker blew up. So when it came time to resign we said, "Dude, we can't. You're just too big. You'll never have time to do my music." So then, in 2001, Kracker went solo, and they called me up one day when I was broke as a joke, sitting at home with no money. They were like, "Hey, you want Kracker's job and make X amount of dollars?" I was like, "Hell yeah," and from then on the rest is history; I've been in the band for almost 10 years now.

How did you originally get into deejaying?

Well, that's the funny thing . . . I know people say they live hip-hop, but I literally lived it 24/7. In those mid-nineties, I would wake up in the morning, roll some weed, get in my car and drive to my cousin's house—he was a DJ and he had crates of *everything*—and we would seriously just sit around and fiddle with beats and rap. That's all we did all day! Then we'd go to a little telemarketing job at night and then we'd come home and do more. So just being around the turntables all the time—watching my cousin doing it and teaching myself little things here and there—was my introduction to deejaying. I never planned to be a serious DJ, but I was always fascinated with scratching and I thought that shit was so ill . . . When the Kid Rock gig came, my main focus with him is programming shit and lots and lots and lots of backup vocals. I have a couple of little scratch solos and shit like that, but as far as traditional deejaying, that's not my shit. I'm the best DJ that Kid Rock could possibly have in regards to the things that I do for him. I deejayed for Run when Run was out on tour with us. I can control when to drop beats. My timing, my backup vocals, and my knowledge of the songs are my bread and butter. If they ever want to stop and start something, I am on that shit. So as far as battle DJs? I couldn't hang, but then nobody else could hang doing what I do.

A lot of the younger kids don't remember this, but before Eminem blew up, it was nearly impossible to make it as a white emcee. What were your early experiences regarding race in hip-hop?
Well, Detroit always had this thing about it where it was accepted. I mean, when Kid Rock put out *Grits Sandwiches* on Jive, he was *huge* here. He might have had a little buzz in other places, but here he was the king shit. So there was already some acceptance of that here in Detroit. It wasn't really so bad. I mean, you always got that funny first look until you proved yourself. But this was Detroit, and in this city you had to prove yourself no matter who you were. A lot of times people would give you that look like, "Aw, shit, here's another white boy getting ready to spit . . ." But I was lucky because I always had respect in the streets and cats here knew me. To be honest, probably the hardest thing I had to deal with regarding race *was* Eminem. Because once Marshall came around, then cats started looking at you like, "Oh, you want to be Eminem."

Well, when I was rhyming back in the early nineties, I remember people saying, "Oh, you want to be Vanilla Ice," which was way worse.
Exactly! I didn't even think about him. See how little a part he plays in my memory? [Laughs.] But you're right. It was seen as cheesy, like white boys were just coming around to try and be poppy rappers. I mean, Marshall changed so much shit it isn't even funny.

I just think I was lucky to come up here, because Detroit had some of the biggest white emcees. It was kind of like you'd always get that first look, but then after that, I never had any problems.

How did you get the nickname "Microphone Bully"?
Around the time my first record came out—probably 1999—we were always doing shows in Detroit and Ann Arbor. I mean, this was right around the time that Marshall had just blown up. Kid Rock had just blown up. D12 was blowing up. That was the thing, we all ran in the same groups of people. Anyway, everyone knew I was a heavy drinker, and it just got to the point

where for this month and a half I wound up fighting someone in the club after the show every single night. It was kind of hilarious. It was just ridiculous. And that's actually how I met Trick-Trick and a lot of these other cats. They were like, "This crazy white boy is always coming around and fighting everybody!" I was just this short, chunky white kid who was tough as nails. I can't remember what the publication was, but there was this interview that I did, and something about that came up. They ended up putting that in the headline: "Paradime, the Microphone Bully." And then it just kind of stuck. It was a really wild time in my life and it was just fun as hell.

What are some things about the Detroit hip-hop scene that make it somewhat unique?
I'd say the camaraderie and the fraternity kind of feeling about it are different. There really isn't much beef here. I mean, there was stuff like I.C.P. and Proof, or I.C.P. and Eminem, but that was just sort of a given. But at any given time you can walk into a studio session with Trick-Trick and run into me and Black Milk or Guilty Simpson, or walk into a session with Street Justice and run into Monica Blair. The scene here is so big, but everybody wants to work with each other. Everybody's cool with each other. There will always be a couple of haters or a couple of people you roll your eyes at, but in the majority it's like a giant crew where everybody's just running with each other. The one thing that I always thought was unique about Detroit was the sarcasm, like the early Eminem shit; that really wild "I don't care"–type of shit. "Set fire to the carpet, and burn down your entire department . . ." All of that *wild* shit. Rappers here have always had a sense of humor, a kind of sarcasticness—a rowdiness. I've always found that to be sort of a backbone in so many artists from around here. We've all sort of got that "I don't give a fuck" attitude.

Both Kid Rock and Uncle Kracker have jumped from hip-hop to rock and then to country, and yet you've always stayed grounded in hip-hop.
Sometimes I get angry at myself and think that I'm being closed minded. I remember I heard "Follow Me," which is Uncle Kracker's biggest pop hit, early on. He played that song for me at his house one day and, I swear to God, I said, "You are out of your mind. That is the lamest shit I have ever heard in my life." I mean, a lot of people don't get this, but Kracker is a tough son of a bitch, and he came up doing some rowdy shit. He used to be this sick emcee—I mean *sick*—but he always had this ability to carry a

tune and write really good songs. I guess he was writing country songs at the same time he was writing rap shit in the late eighties and early nineties, so that's how far that goes back. So I was shocked—here's my buddy, who's covered in tattoos and has a gold tooth and was quick to go and sock somebody in their mouth—singing "Swim through your veins like a fish in the sea . . ." I was like what the hell is that? But then when it came out, it was so gigantic that I was like, "I'm an idiot." I think it's because of where they grew up at. The east side of Detroit and the west side of Detroit are as different as Los Angeles and New York. Sure, there are similarities, but then the people are just really different. Anybody will tell you that. And those guys are eastsiders, so where they grew up, they listened to rock, rap, and country. Where I grew up, it was just hip-hop, hip-hop, hip-hop. But in the same sense, as I'm working on my new album right now, I can see that this record is so much more musical than the stuff I've done in the past, and that's from being around those guys. My first single from the album, "Lovely Day," had a sax player in it. I want my music to be more like that—more timeless. I listen to hip-hop all the time, but on Sunday afternoons I've got this 72-hour playlist that I hit on my iPod called "Clorox," and it's all Steely Dan and Fleetwood Mac and Rolling Stones . . . That music is timeless.

I won't ever go the country route, but there's always a small element of rock in my songs. It's not rock/rap, by any means; I'm a hip-hop artist. I'm an emcee. But on this new album, you can see a lot more flavors of live music touching it.

A lot of emcees lose that hungry sound after achieving the kind of success that you've achieved, and yet you still sound as hungry as a new artist. How have you managed to keep those fires burning?
There's a real contradiction in what I do. What I mean by that is, you can listen to a Paradime album . . . I've had people who thought they were calling me out on this. "Hold on, man. This one song is called 'Rock Star Shit' and you're talking about flying on jets and trashing giant hotel rooms, and then on the next song you're bitching about not knowing when the next check is coming in to pay the bills." I'm like, "That shit's real." This Kid Rock lifestyle is *insane*. It's that real rock star shit like you see in the movies. I mean, for instance, one night we were in a hotel in Vegas and just for the hell of it Rock called downstairs and told them he wanted a baby carriage

and some bowling pins—just really random stuff to see if they'd bring it—and they brought all that shit up to the room! [Laughs.] That party lifestyle is real and the money is amazing. I've kept myself in my same surroundings, and what's funny is that Kracker did the same thing . . . When he got huge, he took the house he was living in and he knocked it down, and he bought the house next door and he knocked that down, and then he built this huge mansion in the middle of this tiny neighborhood! It's so crazy looking, and yet it's so fresh because he was like, "I want to stay in my neighborhood." I'm still where I want to be. I've got a little tiny house, but it's macked out to the gills. I've got money in the bank, which is nice, but if we don't tour for a year and I've been blowing my money and being Mr. Crazy Rock Star, then it catches up to you. And there's always the reality of coming home and finding out that one of my friends got shot or somebody overdosed or somebody broke someone else's jaw . . . The reality of where I'm from and where and what I represent never goes away.

I think that there are two of me. There's the me that goes out on tour and sings backup in a rock and roll band and has to play a tambourine every once in a while—*I hate that shit, by the way*—and then there's the me that still wants to go to St. Andrews and rock over a breakbeat and just spit. The guy who just wants to go and spit is frustrated, so I still am hungry. My pockets may have changed severely over the past decade, but my fire for hip-hop and my frustration over some things in hip-hop are still there.

You mentioned the baby carriage thing, which brings me to my next question. I get the feeling that you've probably seen some crazy stuff on tour. Tell me about that.
[Laughs.] It's funny. I always get that question and I can almost never answer it without getting anyone in trouble! [Chuckles.] It's basically like if you took the movies that you've seen about rock stars, and you take those stories that you've heard . . . I don't know. I've been in a hotel room where Chuck Lidell from the UFC is over in one corner talking to Suge Knight, and Xzibit is over here hammered on the couch, and some famous country singer is puking off the balcony. There are a couple of naked girls in the hot tub . . . sex and drugs and rock and roll . . . people doing coke off all kinds of other people. It's just crazy, and this is all true!

There are so many times when you just laugh to yourself like, This shit can't be real! But it is, and Kid Rock is my friend, and we've been in this business together for a long time, but I can say without fail that he is one of the last true rock stars. There aren't really rock stars like that anymore. You've got your pop stars and what have you, but Kid Rock really does this shit. He'll walk into any club and step up to the turntables and just murder it. I remember we did that show *Farm Club* and the Beat Junkies were there, and they were excited to meet Kid Rock because they knew the history. He got up and was cutting with those dudes, doing tricks, and standing up on the turntables and cutting between his legs and behind his back. And they were so geeked. People don't realize that Kid Rock is that guy, and he's also the guy who will walk into a country bar and pick up a guitar and rip a solo. The guy is ridiculously talented. But on top of that, he parties harder than anyone you know, or have seen, or have heard about. He is the real deal and there are times when I'm like, "Holy shit, you're nuts!"

DISCOGRAPHY

1. *Paragraphs* (1998)
2. *Vices* (2001)
3. *11 Steps Down* (2004)
4. *Spill at Will* (2007)

CHAPTER SEVENTEEN
R.A. THE RUGGED MAN
Emcee

Long Island emcee R.A. the Rugged Man was the product of a broken home. His father was a Vietnam veteran who suffered from the effects of Agent Orange. As a result of the chemical, R.A.'s brother Maxx was born handicapped and blind, ultimately dying at the age of 10, and his sister Dee Ann was unable to walk or speak. As a child, R.A. dreamed of becoming a filmmaker or a professional boxer. He then discovered hip-hop music, studying classic albums and honing his own flow. Soon R.A. established himself as one of the fiercest emcees on the New York battle scene. At the age of 17, R.A. found himself at the center of a nine label bidding war. After holding out for nearly a year, he ultimately signed with Jive Records and went to work recording his debut album, *Night of the Bloody Apes*. While recording a track for the album with the Notorious B.I.G., R.A. caught the attention of the legendary emcee, who was quoted as saying, "And I thought I was the illest." R.A. the Rugged Man was now seen as being the "next big thing," with magazines and other emcees testifying to his greatness. However, internal struggles with his label soon stopped the young emcee's rapid ascent to the top. Due to his refusal to allow the label to tamper with his music, R.A. was labeled as difficult to work with. As a result, the label decided to shelve his album (which would ultimately become a bootleg classic), and R.A. was subsequently banned from recording studios, record labels, and live appearances at just about every substantial venue in the United States.

Despite these setbacks, R.A. persisted, continuing to hone his skills and releasing his music independently. The emcee whom *Rolling Stone* magazine has compared to a blue-eyed Notorious B.I.G. has since become a go-to guy for collaborations and remix appearances. He has worked with the likes of Mobb Deep, Kool G. Rap, Wu-Tang Clan, Chuck D. of Public Enemy, and Sadat X, among others, as well as such noted producers as Erick Sermon, Trackmasters, DJ Quik, and Alchemist. In 2004, R.A. signed with the Brooklyn-based label Nature Sounds and finally had the opportunity to release an album through official channels. The album, *Die, Rugged Man, Die*, was met with heavy praise from both critics and fans worldwide. He has been featured on all three volumes of Rawkus Records' popular *Soundbombing* compilations, appearing alongside Eminem and Mos Def. He has also appeared on the platinum-selling *WWF Aggression* soundtrack. In 2009, Nature Sounds released the R.A. compilation *Legendary Classics Vol. One*, which featured "lost" tracks from *Night of the Bloody Apes*, as well as obscure collaborations.

In addition to his accomplishments as an emcee, R.A. has also written for magazines ranging from *Vibe* to *The Source*, co-written the screenplay for Frank Henenlotter's horror film *Bad Biology*, and directed his own feature film entitled *God Take, God Give*.

What does hip-hop mean to you?

That all depends on whom you ask, because there are different aspects to hip-hop: graffiti, deejaying, the beat-making. For me, as a lyricist, I don't live all of that other stuff. I see other emcees sign their autographs and make their signatures look like graffiti . . . I live my entire life for the lyricism in hip-hop. The culture is so much more broad than just what I do, but that's my entire life—lyricism and emceeing. That's what hip-hop means to me. It's personal expression in the truest, purest form possible.

How old were you when you first started rhyming?

I was 12 years old. There were a few kids in my neighborhood rapping, and one of them was this kid named Bub. He called himself Human Beat Box Bub. I saw this dude blowing up a shopping center window with an M-80. I pulled up on my bicycle and he said, "Check this out, kid! Check this out!" And all of a sudden the shopping center window blew up, and I thought, "This kid is cool." We then hung out all summer and we were doing stuff like breaking into houses. We were just on a rampage.

The kid also had a boom box, and he had all these cassette tapes; all the classic stuff. He started playing me some of this music, and I just fell in love with it. Within a year or two, I wound up being better than the dudes in my neighborhood, including Bub. That was surprising, because he was quite a few years older than me. Then I was kind of known around the neighborhood as the dope rapper. And that just came from hanging with these kids and becoming obsessed with rhyming.

Who are your biggest influences?
Kool G. Rap is the one I say all the time, and everyone knows I worship the guy. Kool G. Rap is the greatest lyricist who ever lived, and when I say that, I mean in the history of music, not just hip-hop. I mean, forget about John Lennon, forget about Jim Morrison, forget about all of those guys. Kool G. Rap is light-years ahead of them all. Most lyricists have no idea about wordplay and all of that. This man is a genius. Sure, all those rock guys are cool, but they can't compare to Kool G. Rap. He's the greatest cat to ever play with words in the history of music.

What prompted the song "Every Record Label Sucks Dick"?
I had just come off a nine record label bidding war the year before. I had all the labels after me. I had bidding wars with Def Jam, Priority, Warner Bros., Jive Records, Mercury Records, Tommy Boy . . . If you name a record label, they were throwing recording contracts at me. I saw how they all worked, and I saw how simple they were. They were all a bunch of followers. I went up to record labels the year before that, and nobody wanted to give me a deal. They kept saying, "You need more R&B in your music." Remember how in '91, '92, everything was like Father MC? They were throwing R&B into everything. A lot of these record labels like Def Jam and Warner Bros. were turning me down. Then I was in a recording studio with a bunch of famous rappers, and all of them loved me. So then, by the end of the day, I left the studio with offers for record deals from both Mercury and Giant. After I got those two offers, all of a sudden Def Jam wanted me. Then all of a sudden Jive wanted me. Then Priority wanted me. All of a sudden every label wanted me. They follow trends. The year before I couldn't get a big money deal, and all of a sudden I got two deals, three deals, four deals, and finally nine deals. So I played it off, and I wouldn't sign. It took eight months to negotiate. They started out like, "We'll give you $100,000." I was broke, so all of my family was like,

"$100,000? You better sign for $100,000!" And I said no, I wasn't signing for $100,000. They said, "What if you never get an opportunity like this again?" My lawyer was yelling at me. I said, "Shit, they're not all going to go away in one day." So I just sat on it, and I didn't sign. Eventually I was offered $340,000.

So the song came from me seeing how the industry worked. And then when I signed with Jive, I had a lot of issues with my label. I wrote that song while I was on Jive Records, and at the time it caused a lot of problems. There was a lot of controversy, and lot of people thought I was shooting myself in the foot. "You can't say that about labels! You'll never get a deal again!" And in the early Nineties, it wasn't like today where you can just go and release your album on an independent. There were some indie rap records back then, but you still needed tons of cash to do a record indie. It didn't exist the way it does now, where anyone can just go on their computer and put their record out worldwide. So if you weren't signed to a label, you had to have tons of cash to put out a record. Everyone thought I was hurting myself by recording that song, and in a way I did, but I'm glad I did. Look, here we are 15 years later, and you're asking me about that silly little record. [Laughs.]

Jive eventually shelved your album. What happened there?
There were a lot of internal problems. Record labels want to control their artists, and record labels want artists who are very grateful to be signed to them. You're supposed to think, "Yeah, my label always knows best." Here I was a young kid signed to this label, and I didn't know the politics of the game. You had to stroke these record executives' egos. That's what you do. You've got your manager in there saying, "Yes, that's right." You have to pretend that they're right and then do whatever you want to do anyway. That's the game, and I didn't play the game. In fact, I still don't play the game. So when a record executive would come into my session and tell me to lower a snare or to put something into a chorus, I'd say, "Get the fuck out of my session, you nobody! Get out or I'll smack you!" [Laughs again.] I really closed off a lot of the industry heads. They would say, "Why don't we put so and so on your song," and I'd tell them to get out and leave my music alone. "This shit is dope. If you know how to promote a record, this'll blow up. Go do your job."

I thought if your music was good, you blow up and you're successful. I thought the public was smart enough to know if you were dope. I didn't understand that it's a whole marketing machine, and the product is only 15 or 20 percent of it. The rest of it is marketing, getting it out there, and brainwashing the people who don't know the difference between good music and bad music. It's paying off DJs and paying off video channels. I didn't understand the game. I thought, "I don't need to listen to anybody, because my music is dope. When my album drops, it's gonna blow up." I was young and naïve. I didn't know that it didn't work like that. You can actually have wack music and have someone supporting you with the machine, and you're gonna blow up. I just had my way of making music, and they wanted to get their two cents in. I didn't let them get their two cents in, so I became the enemy. There was a lot of screaming and threats . . . a couple of physical things that went down. There was a sexual harassment lawsuit. Then I got banned from the building. They wouldn't even let me in the Jive Records office while I was signed to the label! I couldn't even step foot on the premises. Those were crazy times. And I was my own manager. Trying to manage your own career and being banned from your label at the same time is pretty tough.

That's crazy.
[Chuckles.] My life is crazy.

You recorded with the Notorious B.I.G. What was Biggie like?
He was the same as everyone else. He was a Brooklyn street emcee. You know, when you were in the studio it wasn't like, "Oh, my God, we're in the presence of the future of rap." He wasn't the icon that he is today. When you're working with someone, you don't really feel like that anyway. You're their equal. You're both in the studio working together. Before that, Biggie and myself and Akinyele worked on some stuff together, and at that time, Ak was the big man, not Big. I was like, "Ak is crazy. Ak is killing it." Meanwhile, we had this future icon in the studio with us. We weren't thinking that Big was the future . . . I was thinking that Ak killed it. [Laughs.] Ak had just done that album with Large Professor, so he was big at the time.

Big was coming up at the same time as me, so I saw him as an equal. You're competitive with cats. You're not thinking, "He's better than me." You're thinking, "I hope I do better than him, he hopes he does better than me, but I hope we all do good." There was no difference between working with Big as there was when I worked with Killah Priest. I just saw him as another tight lyricist.

You've done collaborations with just about everyone in the game. What are some collaborations that stick out in your mind as some of your favorite experiences?

The collaborations like Sadat X and Havoc meant a lot to me because they happened at a time when the music industry had turned on me. I was blackballed, and I wasn't really allowed to do anything with anybody. I was signed to a record label who wouldn't put out my material, and I couldn't get off that label even though I wanted to. I was stuck in a really horrible situation. My life wasn't happy at that time. I was very depressed. This was an extremely dark time in my life. The press had even turned on me. They said I was the best when I was coming up, but then after my label turned on me, they turned on me, too. They said I was uncontrollable and that I was a piece of shit.

I saw Sadat X at a club in the nineties, and he said he loved "Every Record Label Sucks Dick." We discussed collaborating, and he came to the studio. That meant a lot to me, because that was when I had nothing. He came on the strength of the music when I had nothing. It was the same thing with Havoc from Mobb Deep. I had known him since I was 16 years old, and we were coming up together. I went to the studio with a beat I had made, and it was too funky. You know, in Long Island we do that funk shit like Erick Sermon. I came with this beat that had some Roger Troutman funk stuff in it, and I said, "Yo Havoc, check this beat out. I want you to rap on it." I showed up at his session, which he was paying for, and tried to get a verse off of him. He said, "That beat is too West Coast. Let me make you a monster beat." And he just put on his MPC and laced up the hardest beat right there. This was right at the height of his career, when he was getting $20,000 a beat and selling millions of records. He hooked me up with a free beat and free verse. He was just like, "Do whatever you want to do with that." And those kinds of collaborations meant the most to me because they were when I was at the bottom.

You're one of the best lyricists in the game, yet it seems like you don't always get the respect you deserve. Why do you feel that is?

That's easy. It's because I don't have a machine behind me. Whether you believe it or not, even the streets are influenced by the machine. Everybody is. When you're constantly told that this person is the best, and that's the person that you hear, and the industry is forcing their music down your throat, people start to believe that. A lot of people don't know how the machine works. Like I said, I thought if you were dope, the world would love you, and they'd hear you. But that's not how it goes, and a lot of the world doesn't understand that that's not how it goes. So if you're everywhere on the TV, and everywhere on the radio, everyone believes that it's because you're the best. You know and I know that's not even the case. The wackest shit gets on the radio. It's just who's corporately run and who works with the machine better.

I do think in the underground a lot of kids think I'm one of the best modern day hip-hop artists. I get a lot of acclaim from the underground. If I was to work closely with the machine and have a few million dollars pumped behind me, then all of a sudden the fair-weather hip-hop fans would come to the table and say, "We love R.A. We always did. He's one of the best."

You have to brainwash the consumers, and that's what the record labels do.

What do you think of the people who say that white emcees are destroying hip-hop?
I think that if you're white, black, Spanish, Korean, or from Brazil or Colombia—wherever you're from—and you're spitting from the heart and practicing your art . . . If you're an incredible emcee, I don't think any of that other stuff matters. I mean, look at all the Latinos who were in hip-hop even back in the seventies. I don't think color, creed, or any of that shit matters at all. If you study the craft, you know your history, and you actually are good at what you do, then who cares about the other stuff? It's different when there's an Asher Roth or someone like that . . . He's not that good a rapper. I'm not going to diss him, but there were better emcees out there that didn't get the acclaim that he got. So you ask yourself, "Is that racism?" And it might be. I don't know. And then there's the fact that Eminem is considered by *Vibe* magazine to be the greatest of all time, which we all know is over the top. Are these guys ruining hip-hop? No, they're not ruining hip-hop. Hip-hop can't be ruined by a corporation if you know your music and you understand your music—you can look past the wack shit, the mediocre shit, and find what's great and what's phenomenal. You just have to understand hip-hop as an individual and not be swayed by what the machine is telling you. Imagine there were 500,000 wack white emcees . . .

[Chuckles.] Just ignore them and listen to the two or three dope brothers who are on the corner murdering tracks. No one has the power to destroy hip-hop unless we give them that power.

If someone is destroying hip-hop, I'm not sure you can say it's white rappers. I mean, they aren't the ones who have the money and the power. I think if you wanted to say that white *people* are destroying hip-hop, then that might be a better argument because the people with the money and the power . . . a lot of them are white. But on the flip side of that, when Jay-Z was the president of Def Jam, how did he help hip-hop? And he's a brother. Jay-Z had all the power to put hip-hop on the map and make it beautiful again and bring back the art form instead of putting out garbage. But did Jay-Z even put out a rap album by anybody? Did he even put any new artists on? So it's not just white people; black people aren't doing their part either.

You know what? It's not really white or black ruining hip-hop on the corporate level . . . It's green.

Recently online fans were trying to create a beef between Eminem and yourself where there really wasn't any animosity. It almost seems like hip-hop fans thrive on drama now. Why do you think hip-hop fans are so hungry for these conflicts between artists?
People love WWF wrestling. They love that shit. People love drama. They love soap operas. They love gossip. You know, so and so smacked so and so . . . then that'll be all over YouTube the very next day. They just love that conflict. The guys grew up on WWF wrestling, and the girls grew up on soap operas. Everyone loves that nonsense. In fact, it seems like fans like the drama more than they like the music. [Laughs.] You could put out the dopest album on the planet, and that'll get less hits online than footage of Rick Ross falling off the stage. "Oh, look, Rick Ross fell!" That nonsense will get 400,000 hits. Or Pitbull commenting on Kanye West and Taylor Swift. That shit got half a million hits in two days! Instead of people saying, "Yo, Pitbull's got a new album, check it out," they're saying, "Hey, Pitbull's speaking about Kanye!" People just love that drama.

In your songs you mention people like Tippi Hedren and Stanley Kubrick, and both of your album titles are references to fairly obscure films. Are you a big movie buff?
Oh, yeah, I'm a huge film buff.

As a hip-hop fan and a film buff, you've had some success in both arenas. Which was the bigger dream for you growing up—being an emcee or being a filmmaker?

I was a movie psychopath when I was a kid. I loved film more than anything. There were three things I wanted to be when I was a kid: I wanted to be involved with film, hip-hop music, and boxing. When I was seven or eight, I wanted to be Larry Holmes. I dreamed of being the heavyweight champion of the world, and it doesn't seem like that's going to be happening anytime soon . . . [Laughs.] And yeah, I wanted to be a filmmaker when I was a kid. My parents were broke when I was growing up, and my mother sort of raised me on her own. All I wanted in the world was a video camera, and one day for my Christmas and birthday presents combined—I think I was 11 at the time—she found a way to buy me a video camera. Today it's no big deal, but back then in that era, it was expensive. And this was the great big video camera with the VHS tape. This was a big gift. I was like, "Holy shit, I got a video camera!" So I started filming stuff, and we made our own movies; horror movies and ninja movies with Chinese throwing stars.

Then, when I was 12, I became obsessed with hip-hop music. As soon as I started rhyming, everything else got put behind me. None of it seemed important anymore. I remained a film fan, but hip-hop was my primary love.

DISCOGRAPHY

1. *Night of the Bloody Apes* (1994)
2. *Die, Rugged Man, Die* (2004)
3. *Legendary Classics Vol. One* (2009)

CHAPTER EIGHTEEN
ROB KELLY
Emcee

Born and raised in Wexford, Ireland, Rob Kelly was inspired by East Coast hip-hop artists like Big Daddy Kane, KRS-One, Redman, and Big L. The versatile emcee worked hard to sharpen his skills, first showcasing them with ferocious freestyles on Wes D'Arcy's 2FM radio show *The Big Smoke*. Kelly soon established himself as a formidable emcee and entered a spate of freestyle battles, winning several including the national championships sponsored by Universal Records in 2003. The young emcee began to garner attention from the United States, and he soon caught the attention of DJ Vlad, who named Rob to his website's prestigious Unsigned Heat, making him the first non-American to receive this honor. In 2004, Kelly released his first mixtape, *The Kellection*, which was mixed and hosted by DJ Pudgee P. His second mixtape, *Bragging Rights*, was given a full-scale release by English distributor Pickwick Records, and soon garnered him more attention from American and English audiences.

Kelly has since been selected to be a MySpace featured artist and has recorded tracks with celebrated American artists Memphis Bleek and Slaine of La Coka Nostra. His underground anthem "Dropkicked" became a major Internet sensation, and Kelly soon found himself featured in *XXL* magazine. With fans from around the world, Rob Kelly is one of the most celebrated free agents around. Even without a major label deal, *The Sunday Tribune* named Kelly one of the 30 "coolest people" in Ireland. In 2009, Kelly released *The St. Patrick's Day Massacre* and *The Best of Bobby Bars* on his own Acquisition label.

What does hip-hop mean to you?
Hip-hop is everything to me. I can't imagine my life without it. I'm in Spain as we speak, and on my iPod today I listened to a DJ set that Doo-Wop did at the Tunnel in the mid-nineties. I was playing that by the pool. Other people were relaxing and sunbathing, and I was listening to an hour of classics. Every defining moment of my adult life has been hip-hop related. Most Irish men my age, when they think back to making their Confirmation will think of looking forward to how much money they would get. I was looking forward to buying LL Cool J's album out of my Confirmation money and making sure my white boy flattop looked like Big Daddy Kane's.

What's the hip-hop scene in Ireland like?
The hip-hop scene in Ireland is nothing really; no scene. Ireland has traditionally always been like a rock band epicenter more than, say, hip-hop. For years I didn't even know there was a scene. It's gone backwards in the past few years, to be truthful. There are a handful of decent acts. I would say nothing more than decent, and then there are some up-and-coming acts, but their sense of what hip-hop is seems to be a little off. Even in a city as big as Dublin, the scene is tiny.

To be honest, I don't like the term "scene." It seems it's only ever applied to people outside of big cities. I always said that it's not scenes that blow up—it's good artists that put certain areas on the map. Bono couldn't tell you anything about the music scene in Ireland, but he knows he's doing well.

When did you know that you wanted to be an emcee?
I suppose I always knew. I knew when I first heard the Fat Boys and Salt-N-Pepa. I used to write even back then. I remember when I was 11 I did a rhyme for this girl I fancied. It was à la *The Fresh Prince of Bel-Air* about my bad day at school. I was always writing. In my teens I used to make tapes and pass them around school. I know someone has those. I used to loop a bassline with the pause button and do the same with the drumbeat; scratch over it and all that. Then it wasn't until I was in my twenties that I approached it seriously and did something about it. I knew I was talented, and I just wanted people to hear me.

Which emcees have most influenced you, and in what ways?
That changes all the time. I was talking about this the other day with someone . . . People's Top Five lists always change with what's current. How

many people do you know that have a Chuck D or an Ice Cube in your list now? Not too many, even though at the time those two would be automatic picks. I'm talking all-time lists. They are always so fickle. I am influenced by greatness, so I love Jay-Z. I like what he has done for the genre in that he has managed to stay relevant for the past 15 years; not only relevant, but he has managed to stay on top. Biggie. I was the biggest Biggie fan. I often think about how he was so nice, and he was only 24 years old when he passed? The imagery, the stories, the wordplay . . . He was just so nice. Big L, Redman, Nas. I like someone like Sean Price, too; just unadulterated rhyming and not giving a fuck, and conveying that on record.

You mentioned Jay-Z. I understand that, like Jay-Z, you don't write your rhymes on paper, but instead write and arrange them in your head.
That began because I started rhyming on the radio every Friday night. I didn't have any songs, so I would have to memorize the verses so I wouldn't fuck them up on live radio. It just came naturally after that. I do tend to write the odd line these days; I forget some stuff that comes to me, so I save some of the one liners on my Blackberry.

You've done quite a bit of emcee battling. Tell me about some of your favorite battle experiences.
Oh yeah, I did. At first I didn't really know how to do it. I ripped this guy from New Zealand, and he won anyway, because the crowd was comprised of people from his class in college. The next one, my friend G Leech beat me, because he was ready for me with a bunch of rhymes. But after that, I figured it out, and I never lost again. My favorite battle experience was against Rhymefest. He was coming to Dublin with Mark Ronson, and the people on the Internet were talking about how I had won all the battles in Dublin and that I should battle him. So I said I would do it. He must have thought I'd called him out or something, because he was acting crazy on the day, and when I met him he wouldn't shake my hand or anything. Mark Ronson was extra cool, though, and was enjoying all the tension. We had an interview for a radio station, and all of a sudden Rhymefest starts going in on me. The guy says, "If you had something to say to Rob, what would it be?" He was all, "I heard he's been on the Internet looking to find out shit to say. That won't work, though, because I'm spontaneous." So me being the smart arse that I am, I said, "I did Google him, but it came back 'who?'" Mark Ronson erupted with laughter. Then we went out and

had two rounds arranged, and I was killing him. Then he asked for a third round, and he kind of got me. But it was all good. We shook hands and remained in contact until he won a Grammy. [Laughs.] Actually, he said something about a group I know from the U.K. called S.A.S., and they wanted to really kill him. [Chuckles.]

Mark Ronson actually sent me a message on MySpace after he got super famous, which was nice.

It seems like the Internet provides a lot of new opportunities today for up-and-coming artists. You've certainly made the most of those opportunities.
The Internet is everything now. Kids don't listen to music like they used to. We used to see music on shows like *Yo! MTV Raps* or hear it on Westwood and then go order the single. These days kids listen to music first on the Internet. It's enormous, and it's so vital for me. Where would I be without it? I wouldn't have stood a chance. I couldn't be connecting with people all over the world without it.

However, I also think it's hurt the game in the short term. Sales are down, so artist development has become a thing of the past. Labels now look for people who have sold independently before signing them. What kind of bullshit is that? The A&R's work is already done. Today they are looking for something surefire, and as a result, some really great music is getting overlooked.

How does it feel to be getting attention and recognition in the United States, the birthplace of hip-hop?
I have always said that it is a blessing. To have recognition in the U.S. is what any European artist involved with hip-hop strives for, but I've always put it down to being talented. Any of the U.S. artists I have worked with have come looking for me to work with them. I haven't chased anybody or hassled them on MySpace. They wanted to do records with me. Playing shows in the U.S. and Canada opened my eyes as to what I can achieve with the right machine. People are coming up to you and telling you that you have made their favorite songs, and you can see in their eyes that when you perform they are so into it. To come from a little town like Wexford in Ireland, and then go to another country and have people fly in from other cities just to see you, or to have them know the words and relate to the music is a blessing. A lot of rappers can't do what I can do like that. People think they are big time, but I sell most of my merchandise, digital

records, et cetera in the United States, so I know with the right machine, I'll be golden.

You seem to be more popular in the United States than in Ireland. Why do you think that is?
I think because the community here is tiny, and also because there is not much support from the infrastructure here. The music industry here is comprised of a bunch of dinosaurs. The primary radio station is partially state owned. The program directors don't have a fucking clue about hip-hop, so why would they care about Rob Kelly? The States know me because of the affiliations I've made and because of the Internet. It's annoying to me sometimes because I go to the U.S. to play, and they know all the words to my songs, and I'm treated so well. But back home, they don't give a fuck. DJ Green Lantern knows me, DJ Vlad knows me, all the big DJs in the U.K. know me, and back home I'm still unknown. The Irish-Americans identify with what I'm trying to do though. They feel what I'm doing.

DISCOGRAPHY

1. *The Kellection* (2004)
2. *Bragging Rights* (2006)
3. *St. Patrick's Day Massacre* (2009)
4. *The Best of Bobby Bars* (2009)

CHAPTER NINETEEN
SADAT X
Emcee

ailing from New Rochelle, New York, socially conscious powerhouse Brand Nubian was formed in 1986. The group, comprised of Grand Puba, Sadat X, Lord Jamar, and DJ Alamo, released their self-titled debut single later that year. The group would ultimately be signed to Elektra Records in 1990 by noted A&R representative and producer Dante Ross. Brand Nubian's seminal debut offering, *One for All*, which was heavily influenced by the teachings of the Nations of Gods and Earths, is now considered one of the greatest hip-hop albums ever made. Three singles from the album—"Slow Down," "All for One," and "Wake Up"—were hits on *Billboard*'s Hot Rap Tracks chart in 1991. Despite these successes, Grand Puba and DJ Alamo left the group later that year. Sadat X and Lord Jamar, along with new member DJ Sincere, carried on the name Brand Nubian and released the hit single "Punks Jump Up to Get Beat Down" in 1992. The single proved to be controversial due to its use of the word "faggot," and many accused the group of being homophobic. Following on the heels of this notorious single, the group soon released their sophomore album *In God We Trust*. The album spawned four more singles and charted at number 12 on the *Billboard* pop chart and number four on the R&B/Hip-Hop chart. Two years later, the group released their third album, *Everything Is Everything*. This album produced two more Top 40 singles, "Word Is Bond" and "Hold On."

In 1995, Sadat X, Lord Jamar, and DJ Sincere disbanded to pursue solo careers. The following year Sadat X released his debut solo album

Wild Cowboys on Loud/RCA. The album, which featured the single "Hang 'Em High," would ultimately reach number 13 on the R&B/Hip-Hop chart. Sadat X released two more solo albums and two more Brand Nubian albums, worked as a sixth grade teacher's assistant, and taught children's basketball in the New York City Basketball League before being arrested on a weapons charge in 2005. He served a year at Rikers Island, and he walked away with a more positive outlook on life and a burning desire to make quality music.

Having recorded tracks with everyone from Wu-Tang Clan to Jay-Z to the Notorious B.I.G., Sadat X is one of hip-hop's living legends. With an impressive 13 albums beneath his belt—seven solo albums and six with Brand Nubian—Sadat X shows no signs of slowing down anytime soon.

What does hip-hop mean to you?
Hip-hop is a way of life. Hip-hop is Air Force Ones, gold chains, and sweat suits.

In the past you've stated "I do it out of love. It ain't about the money." What do you love about hip-hop?
I just love the feeling of being able to get on the mic. I love that feeling of hearing the beat, the drum—finding that rhyming pattern right behind it.

Along with groups like Public Enemy and X-Clan, Brand Nubian was part of a movement of socially and politically conscious groups. Today it feels like we're moving farther and farther away from that. In an age of songs like "Booty Dew," is there still a place for socially and politically conscious hip-hop?
There will always be a place for that. Right now, that's just not the money-maker for the industry. You know, there was a whole movement behind the movement. There were movies like *Do the Right Thing* and *Malcolm X*. "Fight the Power" was out at the time . . . It was a time when a lot of black people went back and regained their culture. That was around the time they were wearing the kente cloth clothing. There was an entire society that was tied up in that.

Do you feel that hip-hop has lived up to its potential in being an agent for social change, or do you feel that there's still room for growth?
There's always room for growth. You have to understand that hip-hop—as a musical form—is basically still in its infancy. It's still growing. You have

other types of music, like classical music, that has compositions that were written hundreds of years ago. Hip-hop is still growing and defining itself.

A lot of emcees that were big in the late eighties and early nineties have either fallen completely off the grid or the quality of their music has deteriorated. How have you managed to stay relevant?

I've stayed relevant by keeping with this. I've always been able to put out music continuously, whether people have heard it or not. By staying in there and continuing to put out new music, I've remained in tune with the community. Through no fault of their own, when a lot of emcees get to a certain point, they move away from the hood and they get complacent. When you're living well, it's easy to become a little bit lazy. And you can't really take a long break away from the music and then try to jump back on. This music is a constantly changing thing, and you have to be on the cutting edge of it.

Do you feel that artists should serve as ambassadors for the culture?

It's like movies; sometimes you get good movies, and sometimes you get bad movies. You get good hip-hop, and you get bad hip-hop. I don't feel that anyone has to go out there and carry the torch, per se. Sometimes people go out there and they step out of the boundaries. It's the same thing with actors; sometimes they go out there and they overstep those boundaries and do crazy shit too.

What are some of the differences between touring overseas and touring here in the States?

I would say that people are more into the cultural aspects of it overseas. In America, everyone with the hip-hop is real cool . . . There's not much dancing anymore, and it's not cool to be in there saying someone else's lyrics, because then it's looked at as you're trying to be that next man. In Europe, people are more likely to join in. They know the whole culture of hip-hop, and they know all the words to your songs, even when they don't have a full command of the English language.

Do you think that foreign audiences are more knowledgeable about hip-hop culture?

I do think they are more knowledgeable in regards to the history of the music and culture. Last year I went and performed shows in Europe where there were 16- and 17-year-olds that were singing songs off the *Wild Cowboys* album, and that album came out in 1996. Someone had to have told these kids that this was a good hip-hop album. They didn't just know that on their own. The traditions are passed down.

Why do you think more people don't know the history here?
A lot of times here—especially in the black community—the mother and father are working two jobs and aren't around to be a real parental figure. They're not there to teach their kids about things—not just music, but also about life.

You recorded a track called "Come On" with Notorious B.I.G. Tell me about working with Biggie.
Big was a cool dude, and he requested that I come and get on the song. We went to the studio, we sat there and listened to the beat. Then we went back to back and laid down our vocals. He was a very funny dude. It also helped that we had done shows together in the past and we had a rapport together.

How do you feel that the untimely deaths of Notorious B.I.G., Tupac Shakur, and Big L have affected hip-hop?
I think it's made it a little more introspective. If someone is abused, or people take something and twist it, the ramifications can sometimes be deadly.

The times have certainly changed. When emcees had beef in the past, they handled it on the microphone. There was no fear of a physical reprisal.
It is different. When you had beef back in the day, you kept it on wax. But sometimes, if you had beef—and there are a lot of beefs people don't know about—sometimes you fought. There were a lot of beefs where rappers threw their hands up and fought, and afterwards, you shook the dude's hand and respected him as a man. There were isolated incidents of the shootings we see today, but a lot of times, you know, if you had beef with somebody, you fought. It's not like today's beef. Today I see rappers who have beef with each other, and then they see each other, nothing happens. They see each other in the club, and one group is on one side of the club, and the other is on the other side. Then you see on the Internet the next day that words were supposedly said. Back in the day, if you had beef with a man, you went directly to that man. And if it came down to it, and you couldn't settle it any other way, then you put your hands up. And that was part of rap—fighting and getting knocked out. That was part of rap.

Today's rap is easier. I came up in a time of rap when you couldn't wear a chain to a party. Today there are a lot of dudes who have no business wearing jewelry in clubs that are doing it. I came up in a time when you didn't do that. If you were in the club and you had on a gold chain, that meant you were a serious person. Otherwise, it was getting taken. I'm talking about places like Latin Quarters, Rooftop, places like that . . . Hip-hop was scary then. It was new and it was undefined. When you went to a place like Latin Quarters, you knew you were going to a place that was semi-forbidden and that you had to be on your guard.

When you mention emcees fistfighting, it makes me think of when KRS-One jumped on the stage at the P.M. Dawn concert, threw them off the stage, and then performed his own material.
I was there when he jumped on the stage with P.M. Dawn. I was front and center. P.M. Dawn had started that song, and it was going along, and I guess KRS-One was feeling some type of way. He had to have already had somebody in place where he was like, "Listen, I'm getting ready to go on stage and get these dudes off. As soon as I get these dudes off the stage, I want my music to come on." I mean, it went down so well it was almost like it was scripted. But it wasn't. You knew it wasn't.

Your song "Punks Jump Up to Get Beat Down" was accused of being homophobic. Many other artists have made similar comments about homosexuals. What do you think it is about hip-hop music in particular that is conducive to homophobia? I mean, you don't see that sentiment expressed so openly in other types of music . . .
A lot of people said they had a problem with me saying "Freak the fly flow, fuck up a faggot/ Don't understand their ways, I ain't down with gays." I didn't really mean it like that. When I said "Freak the fly flow, fuck up a faggot," that was a term we used for somebody who was soft. Anyone who was soft was a faggot. And "Don't understand their ways, I ain't down with gays . . ." At that point and time when we were making that record—this was 1992, 1993—homosexuality wasn't as out in the open as it is now. Especially in the black community, where that was seen as being taboo. That's always been that way—in the black community that was taboo. It wasn't out in the open. We couldn't make that song today and get away with it, because the forces behind music and entertainment are mostly gay right now.

It really wasn't along the lines of us not liking gays. I just didn't understand gays, and anyone who was seen as being soft was a faggot. Was that ignorance on my part? Probably so. And as I've lived life and learned a bit,

I've probably changed my views a little bit on that. I probably wouldn't say that in that way now that I said it then.

Having spent time in Rikers Island alongside real criminals, what are your thoughts on the so-called gangsta rappers?
Having spent time beside real criminals and seeing exactly what it is, it makes me wonder sometimes what these dudes are talking about on some of these records. You know, they talk about going to buy cocaine . . . I lived in the cocaine blocks, and I didn't see too many of these guys out there. I did see a couple of rappers up there doing what they portray in the songs, but I didn't see the majority of them who are talking about that.

Having gone to Rikers Island, I don't think these dudes know what they're playing with. When you get in that jail and that door closes, it's a free-for-all in there. Especially in Rikers Island. I was in a dorm with 60 beds and two guards. We were in a giant enclosed area. So when that door closed, you were literally in that cage for the day. Whatever happened happened, and you had to be on your guard at all times. And this was a maximum security jail. That means you have people who are in transition who are going up north for crimes. You have people in there for petty crimes. It was just not conducive to a positive society of trying to get ahead. You know, they took all the programs out of Rikers Island, so the education value was gone. But on the other hand, Rikers Island was the greatest place in the world for someone who wanted to make connections in that world. If someone was trying to connect with someone selling cocaine on the outside, there were nine or 10 dudes in your dorm alone with whom you could compare prices. So when you came out of the system, you were more knowledgeable on things like where to find guns and how to pull credit card scams and things like that. This wasn't a positive society at all.

There was a time when New York completely dominated the hip-hop scene. Since then, hip-hop from other regions has taken center stage. Do you feel that we'll see a reemergence of New York hip-hop?
I do think we'll see a reemergence. Everything goes in a cycle. There was a time of resurgent music where you had groups like Brand Nubian, Poor Righteous Teachers, Public Enemy, and the Native Tongues. That was an era. And then you had a gangsta rap era of groups like NWA and Ice Cube. Then you had a Midwest era. Now you have a Southern era where rappers from the South are doing their thing.

I do think it'll come back around, but also you've got to understand New York. New York has always been a place of trendsetters. You also have to realize that a New York emcee is a different type of emcee. When I came up, I admired Big Daddy Kane. I admired Kool G. Rap. I admired Biz Markie. I admired them, but I didn't want to *be* them. New York emcees have always been kind of selfish in thinking that they were the best. A lot of times they're not willing to give another New York emcee his props. If you notice how Southern emcees got to where they are, they were always about helping each other. You hear Lil Wayne get on a record with Ludacris . . . Southern emcees got to the place where they're at by piggybacking off each other. They also did their thing at a good time in history. For instance, when New York was on top, you didn't have the Internet and stuff like that. And a lot of this Southern rap has come out at a time where communication and accessibility is at a high. You also have to understand that a New York emcee talks in a way that sounds different from most of the country. If you go to North Carolina, Georgia, Texas, or Watts, California, the dialect of those people sounds similar. The way they talk . . . "Eh, man." I can hear that "Eh, man" in Florida. Then I can go to my cousin's house in Oakland and hear that same "Eh, man." This made it that much easier for the rest of the country to connect with that type of style because there are more people who talk like that.

In rock, they encourage artists like Paul McCartney and Mick Jagger to continue performing past their sixties, whereas in hip-hop we start to dispose of emcees after the age of 30. What are your thoughts on that?
That's exactly right. Hip-hop is one of the only areas where they don't really honor their veterans. If you look at sports like baseball and football you'll see that they revere and hail their veterans. In rock, bands like the Who and the Rolling Stones go on tour without having had records out for 20 or 30 years. And they continue to get young and old fans. I don't know at what point this mentality came about that at a certain age you had to stop. People say, "When are you going to stop rhyming?" Is there supposed to be a specific day when all of a sudden the light goes off and I say, "I'm done with this"? It doesn't happen like that. It's just that we now have a different generation of people listening to it. Rap is still defining itself, and now we have people in the 30- to 40-year-old range who still love hip-hop. What are they supposed to do? Just not like it anymore?

You're 39 years old now. Do you feel that a 39-year-old emcee has different responsibilities than a 20-year-old emcee?
I feel that a 39-year-old emcee's perspective on life and rap is going to be different from a younger emcee just from the experience of living longer. There are going to be certain things that I'm going to talk about that might not seem relevant to a 20-year-old. The perspective changes once you get out into the workplace and you're not living with your mother anymore. You know, I've got to pay this bill here; I've got to pay for Sally's Catholic school or Johnny needs braces, but this kid needs that . . . In that situation, your perspective changes, and you start to talk about different things. Me, I'm going to talk about how I have to get up and get some money today, because the cable man is coming and this and that, as opposed to a Soulja Boy getting up and looking in the mirror and saying, "I'm in the mirror now/ I got my swag on . . ." You can do that at 18 because you aren't paying any bills. You're happy right then, and it's not their fault. That's why I don't fault the young emcees. You know, a lot of older dudes say, "These younger dudes aren't making any classics." Well, who's to say they're not making classics? My daughter is 17 years old, and some of these songs right now are the classics that she's going to remember from her youth.

DISCOGRAPHY

1. *One for All* (1990) [as Brand Nubian]
2. *In God We Trust* (1993) [as Brand Nubian]
3. *Everything Is Everything* (1994) [as Brand Nubian]
4. *Wild Cowboys* (1996)
5. *Foundation* (1998) [as Brand Nubian]
6. *The State of New York vs. Derek Murphy* (2000)
7. *Fire in the Hole* (2004) [as Brand Nubian]
8. *Experience & Education* (2005)
9. *Black October* (2006)
10. *Time's Runnin' Out* (2007) [as Brand Nubian]
11. *Generation X* (2008)
12. *Brand New Bein'* (2009)
13. *Wild Cowboys II* (2010)

SHOCK G
Emcee/Producer

Music has always come easily for Shock G. Even before becoming enamored with this new art form called hip-hop as teenager, Shock was an award-winning drummer. Despite these accomplishments, Shock soon traded in his drums for a set of turntables. In 1980, he dropped out of high school to pursue a career in hip-hop as a member of a group known as the Master Blasters. After returning to receive his diploma and attending college at Hillsborough Community College, he joined a number of hip-hop crews with such names as the Chill Factor and the Four Horsemen.

Shock G later relocated to Oakland and formed a group called Digital Underground, which also consisted of Chopmaster J and Kenny-K. (The group later expanded to include Money B, DJ Fuze, and Schmoovy-Schmoov.) In 1988, the group released the 12" single "Your Life's a Cartoon" on Macola Records. The following year, the group signed to Tommy Boy Records and released the single "Doowutchalike," which soon became an underground hit. Following on the heels of this single, Digital Underground released their full-length debut album *Sex Packets* in 1990. The album, which went platinum, spawned the number one hit "The Humpty Dance." (The single introduced the character Humpty Hump, the most famous of Shock G's many alter-egos.) The mega-selling single would later be ranked number 30 on VH1's 2008 list of the 100 greatest hip-hop songs of all time, and number 65 on VH1's 2007 list of the 100 greatest songs of the 1990s. In 1991, Digital Underground released the aptly titled gold-selling EP *This Is an EP Release*, which is notable because it featured the hit single "Same Song," which introduced the world to a young Tupac Shakur.

In 1991, Digital Underground released their third album, *Sons of the P.* The album, which went gold, featured the singles "No Nose Job" and "Kiss You Back." The group then released their fourth album, *The Body-Hat Syndrome*, in 1993. The album produced two singles "The Return of the Crazy One" and "Wussup wit the Luv," which once again featured Tupac Shakur. Digital Underground has since made five more highly qualitative albums—*Future Rhythm, Who Got the Gravy?, The Lost Files, Cuz a D.U. Party Don't Stop!!,* and *The Greenlight EP*—but none managed to find the larger audience that their earlier projects enjoyed.

Besides his work with Digital Underground, Shock has also worked extensively with other acts such as Tupac Shakur, Tha Luniz, Saafir, and Mystic. As well as producing, featuring, and performing with Tha Luniz, Shock also lent a guest verse to the remix of their multi-platinum smash single "I Got 5 on It." He is also responsible for producing two of Shakur's most successful singles, "So Many Tears" and "I Get Around," on which he also appeared as a featured guest. The latter, which featured Shock's drum programming and piano playing, was ranked number 14 on VH1's 2008 list of the 100 greatest hip-hop songs of all time. Shock also performed (as "Humpty Hump") with George Clinton and the P-Funk All-Stars as a guest vocalist at Woodstock 1999 before an audience of 250,000 people.

In 2004, Shock released his first solo album, *Fear of a Mixed Planet.* The album, which received critical acclaim, featured many Bay Area legends including Ray Luv and DJ Q-Bert.

What does hip-hop mean to you?
It always reminds me of music history. When I think of hip-hop, I think of jazz and then rock and roll. I see hip-hop as being this huge revolutionary force that revolutionized language and the way people relate to one another. I feel like hip-hop helped Obama get into office. It groomed the country to even be ready for something like that. I think it's amazing. I think it's an art form that revolutionized the world in the same way that jazz did,

and the same way that rock and roll then did. Those were both inner-city art forms that little by little crawled out of the inner city and then slowly became global crazes. Hip-hop did the same thing.

How was Digital Underground originally formed?

Me and Kenny-K were the last two members of the original four Master Blasters, which was a hip-hop group we had when we were in Florida. We all lived in Tampa; we were made up of people whose families had just moved to Tampa from New York. There was no hip-hop scene there when we arrived in the late seventies, so we put our own crew together. Then by the mid-eighties, life had gotten to all of us. Some of us had kids, some of us went back to school, some of us went into the military. I wound up roaming the country, and I eventually roamed out to California with my girlfriend. But we had all made a pact that if any of us made it into the music industry, we'd reach back and pull each other in. So it was just myself and Kenny-K working on the demo for Tommy Boy. So then later Chopmaster J got in it too, because he was the one who sent the demo to his old high school buddy who was now working in the music business. Because of that, we signed with Macola Records. This was one of two defunct deals before Tommy Boy. His offer had been, "Hey, my friend wants to sign you and put you guys in the studio, but if so you've got to put me in the group." So he was like the rich kid with the basketball. He wound up being a founding member of Digital Underground just based on his having the connection. So then for a while it was just the three of us.

While we were negotiating with Tommy Boy, they wanted to hear songs, so we sent them some songs. I think it was "Stick's Mix," "Hip-Hop Doll," a song called "Long Island Iced Tea," and "Doowutchya-like." Then those four songs got us an album deal with them, and they also asked to see a showcase; they wanted us to perform for them. So meanwhile, all of my crew from back in the day was now far from the art form—years out of it—and hadn't stayed with the changes in the music. So we needed current people. Chopmaster Jay was from the Bay area, and he said his girlfriend knew a DJ named DJ Fuze and we should check him out. We told Fuze we needed a DJ immediately for this showcase for Tommy Boy, which was gonna happen in two days. "We need a DJ. Can you help us out?" Then after that was successful, we asked him if he could go on tour with us. He said, "Yeah," but he didn't want to break up his own group MGM, which was him, Mac-Mone, and Money B. So that pulled them into the group. He was like, "Could you find something for them to do?" And we were like, "Yeah, no problem." So they became background vocalists and dancers for the tour, which just meant that little by little they got onto the record and became Digital Underground.

It was the same path with Tupac an album later. He was just kind of killing time with us. We had already recorded his album and his demo, and he was waiting to get a deal. But meanwhile he would tour with us. So if he was around when it was time to do a major record we'd be like, "Hey 'Pac, put a verse on this." So that just made the world consider anyone they saw on the videos with us a part of Digital Underground. Everyone always says that Tupac started out in Digital Underground, even though he was really just being a guest artist with us. I mean, he was only on like four or five Digital Underground songs *ever*. I think he's been on that many Snoop songs. But because the world saw him first with us, they consider him an official member. We never had that meeting with Tupac where we sat down and said, "You're part of Digital Underground now." We all just understood that his thing was more political and so-cially conscious stuff, so we wanted to keep a little distance between him and Humpty so that people would take him seriously.

But yeah, it just kind of evolved like that. In fact, some of the people in the picture on the front of the *Sex Packets* album weren't even group mem-bers. They were just our homies and our road manager. We always knew we were gonna let the posse evolve and grow, but we didn't have all the faces yet. So we took the picture with a lot of heads in the photograph. Then meanwhile I'm doing all these characters. Of the seven or eight people featured on the first album, I was about four of them. [Laughs.] We were keeping it a secret, but Piano Man was a different person. Rackadelic was a different person. Humpty and Shock G were brothers. MC Blowfish . . . I was just entertaining myself, to be honest.

I know people who still believe that Shock G and Humpty Hump are two different people. What are your thoughts on that? You pulled that off so well that there are people who are still confused.
Wow, that's funny. Well, it wasn't really done with the intention in mind to fool people into legitimately believing that I was another person. It was

just supposed to be, "Isn't this cool? This character is cool and funny." But then people started believing it and it was causing so much controversy, so we decided to roll with it and continue to create that confusion. So we would get doubles to appear in our shows. There have actually been four Humptys over the years. One was my actual brother, who's actually a grunge rock guitarist; my wife's ex-boyfriend Devin looked like me enough that we had him be Humpty; my friend Michael Webster was also Humpty. Yeah, we purposefully did things to make people come home from concerts *swearing* that there was no way that Humpty and Shock G were the same person because they saw them onstage standing next to each other.

How much did your life change after Digital Underground blew up?

My life didn't change much other than how busy I got. The busyness is what changed us. The doing shows and making music and goofing off in the studio had already been happening for 10 years, but the sizes of the audiences changed. But we still went about it the same way we had before. We rehearsed in the same place, and we still asked ourselves what we could do to make our shows special. We did those same things before we were Digital Underground. Before we were doing big tours we would ask ourselves what we could do to stand out from everyone else on the bill that night. "Yeah, I got an idea. Let's get some blow-up dolls and hump them onstage during 'Sex Packets'!" Shit like that was always part of our thing.

The framed gold and platinum record awards were nice, but they didn't change my sense of self-worth because I had Salesman of the Year plaques on the wall where I worked. So I was used to getting trophies. I was keyboard and drum machine salesperson at Music Unlimited in Oakland. Too Short, Sheila E, and Tone, Toni, Tony were all my customers. They all knew me as Greg Jacobs, keyboard sales. [Laughs.] So it freaked them out when Digital Underground happened. So that part wasn't new. What was new? The amount of ass we were getting all of a sudden! Hot chicks, too! Chicks that didn't usually mess with musicians. My clique, we weren't the baller types. We weren't drug dealers and we didn't have great jobs. We didn't have rich families. All of our money went into music equipment. We were all usually wearing the same pair of jeans the whole week and riding the bus, so chicks didn't look twice at us because we were just some broke-ass dudes. But all of a sudden when Digital Underground happened, we were bedding the *hot* chicks. That was the biggest difference to me. And you know, I came off as a ladies' man on the records. Humpty's lyrics on "Sex Packets"—it was all as if I was a ladies' man. But there was only one dude who understood it. He's a bass player and he teaches music in Oakland; his name is Jeff Hilliard. He said, "I knew you weren't a ladies' man all of your life because your whole album is about sex. Usually the people who are writing about sex are the people who aren't getting any." [Laughs.] I said, "You hit the nail on the head there." In high school and college it was the hardest thing in the world for me to do to get laid. People looked at us like we were cool and we should DJ the party and all that, but we were too wacky and weird to get the really hot girls. As you know, all the hot junior high school girls date high school guys. In high school all the hot chicks date college guys. In college all the hot chicks date athletes. It wasn't until I was 26 years old and on the radio that I started dating hot college chicks!

Your song "The Humpty Dance" has now been sampled in way over 50 songs. Has sampling clearance made you a wealthy man?
It doesn't make me wealthy, but it keeps some nice little surprises trickling in here and there. I own some of it but not all of it. I sold half of my publishing about 15 years ago for a big advance, but also to have a big company administer it. In regards to that song, I didn't even get that big of a piece of it because we had to share some of the publishing with Parliament; we gave them about 20 percent for that horn sample in there. It creates money, but it wouldn't be enough to retire on. My real bread and butter is doing live shows and touring. Touring has kept me wealthy.

Do you still tour a lot?
Touring is what pays my bills. I couldn't really survive off of just the publishing royalties. They get just a little bit smaller each year. But interestingly our price each year either holds or goes up because we become more classic with the passing of time. There was a point where our price was going down and down and down. When you very first fall off and the radio stations stop playing your songs is when a group is the coldest. But if you reach a 10 year mark where people are still playing your music and coming

to your shows, then a weird thing happens and it starts going in the other direction. With each year that passes you become a more classic, more revered act. And the price actually goes up. It's pretty cool, and it makes up for touring less or the less record sales. Now, back then, the publishing money was bigger; there were a lot of people who were sampling our songs or using them in films. As that pie gets smaller and smaller each year, the only thing that balances that out is the live shows.

It seems like "Kiss You Back" is really making a resurgence right now. I'm hearing that a lot more than "The Humpty Dance."
There are certain cities that are big for certain records. Like in New York City, "Kiss You Back" is bigger than it is in other places. There are a few cities where it's like that. Now up on the Northwest coast in cities like Sacramento and Seattle it's "Freaks of the Industry." In most cities, that's the record where if we play it too early in the show, the crowd thins out. Once in a while we still get those crowds where what they're waiting for is "The Humpty Dance," but 75 percent of the time it's "Freaks of the Industry." We have to play that one last or else we don't keep people in the audience.

Digital Underground participated in the "We're All in the Same Gang" project. What was that experience like?
Man, that happened so fast it was just like a whirlwind. They asked us if we would be interested in doing something like that and we said, "Sure." Then a day later we were in LA and they said, "Can you come by after soundcheck?" One day we were gonna do a show at the Palace and between soundcheck and when we did the actual show, they wanted us to come by. Dr. Dre was in the producer's chair at the keyboards, and some of the artists were there, but a lot of them had already laid their parts. Then there was someone else there, if I remember correctly, who hadn't laid their parts yet. The people who had already laid their vocals were the people who were on the song before our part, and the people who appear on the song after us were the people who hadn't come in yet. They were just letting it fly just like that. On the way there, Fuze was like, "Eazy-E is on the record, and Hammer is on there, and this person and that person, so we've gotta come up with something good." On the way there DJ Fuze said, "It would be cool if you could tie up the American flag in

it somehow." And that gave me the idea for the line about the red, the white, the blue . . .

When we got there, Michele was in the waiting room, where there was another piano. I sat down and we did some Anita Baker together and we did some Chaka Khan. We were just kind of goofing off. And they said, "Dre said come on in now." We went in, and he was finishing up with someone else. So I sat down at the piano and goofed off in the studio, and he wound up recording that and using that for the B-side of "We Want Eazy." It was some song that had the P-funk chords on it that I was fooling around on the piano with. So when we got into it, Dre was trying to make something about the music right there special. So I said, "This was all I did," and I started fooling with the keyboard and showed him how I set the bend to an octave, and enveloped the sound to make it sound more like it. And Dre was like, "Go ahead and lay that shit in there." He acted like he was just casually asking me how I did that bassline. By the time I finished showing him what I did, he had looked at the engineer and asked, "You got it?" And they had it already. And that's how we wound up having that little Humpty part come in under me.

You produced Tupac's first album. What was that experience like?
It wasn't really much different than working with Raw Fusion or Gold Money. When we were working on Tupac's album, he was still part of a threesome called Strictly Dope. I don't know who or how or why, but someone apparently convinced him at some point while he was working on that album to change the artist name to 2Pac and make it a solo album. I never questioned the decision; it just went like that.

I'm speaking for everybody here, and I don't know if everybody would admit this, but I know for sure that there's nobody out there that could say that Pac was as special as he is before he did what he did. He was just a *little* better than everybody else. He was a *little* better than the next guy. He seemed as good as Chuck D, or as good as LL Cool J or somebody. You didn't think, "He's about to be the crowned king or prince of hip-hop!" It wasn't like that. It was more like, "Yeah, 'Pac's hot," but his offstage and behind-the-scenes behavior was so wacky . . . He was just such a nut! He was so dysfunctional socially. He couldn't drive—he wrecked cars all the time! He didn't understand the job situation, the credit situation . . . We got him his first apartment. We got him his first bank account. Everything. He was just such a dysfunctional kind of social reject that it took away some of the believability that he was going to become this huge star if you knew him before he was a huge star. All you knew was that the chicks *loved* him! It was like, "'Pac gets as many girls as Money B and Humpty do, and he's not even in the video yet!" If you're onstage rapping and the girls see you, then definitely. If you're on the video and the girls see you, then definitely. But at the after parties after the shows, his swagger would pull as many chicks as we were pulling from actually being famous. You definitely knew he had it with the girls, but to envision him coherently pulling it together and putting out an album and keeping his career going just didn't seem possible. Even though he was a little better than everyone else rapping-wise, it was still like, "Oh, Lord, I'm working on this album with Tupac." Because there was always this thing in the back of your head like, "He might wind up getting shot or going to jail before this shit even comes out." You never felt guaranteed that you had your eggs in a good basket.

This nut . . . [Laughs.] He *always* got us arrested, and he was *always* in crazy fights. Sometimes it was worth it, sometimes it absolutely was not. Sometimes it was just a bunch of hot air and ego. But as he started climbing that ladder and then when the director of *Juice* noticed him to be something special and recast the lead part, then the writing was on the wall. "Yo, Tupac's next!" The chicks loved him, the directors loved him, he had a movie career coming up, he'd just ripped "Same Song" with us—when I said ripped it, I mean he didn't just put a verse on there; everyone loved it! He brought a lot more attention to that song than there would have been without him. He wasn't just on it, but he was *hot* on it.

So by the time we got to his second album, I made sure he got the best beat I had produced that year—

I think "So Many Tears" is not only his best song ever, but I think it's one of the best songs in the history of hip-hop.
I appreciate that, but I was actually speaking of "I Get Around." I wanted to give him something really hot. But yeah, "So Many Tears" was ghostly.

It's haunting. It has this dark-spirited soul of its own. It's mystical. I know what you mean . . . It's definitely a lot more now than it was as a track without Tupac on it. It sounded almost like a dance beat before he laid his vocals on it. It sounded like something Beyonce could have sung over. It didn't get dark until Tupac started chanting over it like he does. He poured those words over it in that tone he's got . . . And then Eric Baker added those guitar tracks to it that took it up a level too, and it just grew into this thing; it just became more than the sum of all of our individual parts. I was like, "Whoa!"

And speaking of "I Get Around," we performed it this year on the BET Hip-Hop Awards. The theme of the show this year is "when hip-hop was fun," and that's why they called us in. So we're going to celebrate the fun Tupac, as well.

What do you think happened to the fun in hip-hop?
I think the music grew up. Hip-hop became an adult. And you could say the same thing with all adults. Look at the timing: hip-hop began in the mid- to late-seventies, so when we were out in '89, hip-hop was a teenager. And like a teenager, it was fun. And then look at it in the nineties . . . When hip-hop was a late teen, it got gangster, and that's the age when teens get rough. That's when we start to get wild and crazy. We get that invincible feeling around 18, 19 . . . Then when hip-hop was turning 20—right at the age that responsibility hits a person—it became concerned with money all of a sudden, for the first time ever. Now hip-hop is approaching 40 years old, so hip-hop is a lot less loose and funny now, because it's an adult as an art form. And if you notice, jazz went through it, rock and roll went through it . . . It seems like all the art forms go through it, and hip-hop, being a big serious take-over-the-world art form, is going through all the struggles that other genres have gone through. Jazz and rock used to be the music with all the excesses with drug deaths and people like Elvis living beyond his means. Now hip-hop is the art form with all the excessive disgusts and deaths and material excess. And just like rock and roll, funk, jazz, you can still find whatever you listen to on the radio; it might only be once a week or it might be down in the eighties, but it all still exists. Each branch of the tree is still alive. It's just that all the new branches have taken on this really grown-up intense tone.

Another thing is the competition of it. When we were rhyming, it was this weird new art form out of New York City that most people hadn't even figured out yet. "Look at that! There's no band onstage! Just a DJ? I don't get it!" Now every dude in the audience wants to get onstage and battle the performer. Everyone in the audience has their demo in their pockets that they want you to check out that they made on their computer! It's like guitar players in the eighties—they were a dime a dozen; it was saturated. To be a special guitar player in the eighties was like the hardest thing in the world, and I think that's how it is right now with emcees. It's just saturated. All of the kids who listen to hip-hop have grown up now, and they can all rap. [Laughs.] *Everybody* can rap now. Old ladies know what good deejaying is! *The Golden Girls* used hip-hop slang on their TV show!

My mother used to tell me in the seventies and eighties—she used to point at the TV and say, "They said the word *cool*, or this or that . . ." And I would say, "What do you mean? Everybody says that." And she would say, "No, Gregory, there was a time when funk was a bad word," or stuff like that. And a lot of what we grew up thinking were normal words in our generation, my mother would say, "No, rock and roll and jazz brought those words in. That was considered nigger music. That was jig music. They thought it was poisoning the community and the planet! Things like ripped jeans—that's all part of the cool jazz period." Well, hip-hop has done that now. Our generation, our art form has fucking transformed the world, and it's a beautiful thing.

DISCOGRAPHY

1. *Sex Packets* (1990) [as Digital Underground]
2. *This Is an EP Release* (1991) [as Digital Underground]
3. *Sons of the P* (1991) [as Digital Underground]
4. *The Body-Hat Syndrome* (1993) [as Digital Underground]
5. *Future Rhythm* (1996) [as Digital Underground]
6. *Who Got the Gravy?* (1998) [as Digital Underground]
7. *The Lost Files* (1999) [as Digital Underground]
8. *No Nose Job: The Legend of Digital Underground* (2002) [as Digital Underground]

9. *Playwhutchyalike: The Best of Digital Underground* (2003) [as Digital Underground]
10. *Fear of a Mixed Planet* (2004)
11. *Rhino Hi-Five: Digital Underground* (2005) [as Digital Underground]
12. *Cuz a D.U. Party Don't Stop!* (2008) [as Digital Underground]
13. *The Greenlight EP* (2010) [as Digital Underground]

SPECIAL ED

Emcee/Producer

S ixteen-year-old Flatbush, New York, emcee Special Ed made a thunderous entrance into the world of hip-hop in 1989 when he released his critically acclaimed debut album *Youngest in Charge*. With producer Howie Tee behind the mixing boards and DJ Aksun on the turntables, he created the now classic single "I Got It Made." Special Ed's clever wordplay combined with West Indian–tinged intonations and unique rhyme flows immediately established him as one of the era's finest emcees. He then released a second classic single, "The Magnificent." (It should be noted that both of these singles have since been remade; Shaquille O'Neal covered "I Got It Made," and Rick Ross reworked "The Magnificent.") The following year, Special Ed released his follow-up album *Legal*, which spawned the successful singles "On a Mission" and "C'Mon Let's Move It." Special Ed has since released two more albums, *Revelations* and *Still Got It Made*, as well as *The Best of Special Ed*.

In 1994, Special Ed joined forces with Buckshot and Masta Ace to form the supergroup the Crooklyn Dodgers. The group recorded a single song, "Crooklyn," for the Spike Lee film of the same title. Special Ed has also displayed acting chops, having appeared on TV's *The Cosby Show*, as well as the films *Juice* and *Ganked*. In addition to these feats, he is also an accomplished producer who has made tracks for the likes of Tupac Shakur and the Notorious B.I.G.

Having influenced emcees as diverse as Snoop Dogg and Jay-Z, Special Ed has made an indelible mark on the rap game. At the time of this interview, Special Ed was preparing his fifth studio album for release on his own SEMI Records label.

What does hip-hop mean to you?
The unification of a culture.

You started battle rhyming as a teen. Tell me about those experiences and how they molded you into the emcee that you are today.
Basically, if I was walking through the neighborhood, or walking through school, and found that there was someone who was a self-proclaimed emcee, we would have to put it to the test. I used to battle walking home from school. I remember bugging out in the school yard. I just battled pretty much everywhere. One battle that really stood out happened when I first got to Erasmus Hall High School. There was a dude there who was supposedly the nicest emcee around. I was fresh and new in the school, and I had to get my weight up, so I stepped to him. I had heard him rhyme somewhere, and I thought it was wack. I was like, "Yeah, I'm gonna get him." So we got to the arch—under the arch was where we used to hang out—and the battle commenced. And we battled for names; so at the end of the battle, whoever lost would not be able to use their rap name anymore. And he lost. So that was that.

Those battles taught me to be confident. They taught me that I had the ability to achieve success. They taught me to fear no one.

Did you have many emcees trying to battle you after you became famous?
Nah. At that point the entire game changed for me. Nobody was on it like that at that point. The people in my hood, they already knew, so it wasn't really going in that direction. It more like "Congratulations. You've worked hard for it."

You landed your first record deal at the age of 15. How did that happen?
Well, I laid a few tracks with Howie Tee, and I came to the conclusion that I had to get someone to shop my demo around. And True Blue Management consisted of some cats from around the way. I was like, "If you can do something with this tape, then just do it." They then shopped the demo and came back with interest from Profile Records. From there it got pretty sticky because I was only 15. So it became a matter of how to sign me and make it legally binding. After they figured it out, going through the court system and all that, the deal became official.

I understand you struggled with some setbacks regarding your management and record label. What happened?

I think my management pretty much did as much as they were capable of. They were not experienced enough to take me to the point in my career where I needed to be. You know, they were almost as new to the music industry as I was. I won't say it was the blind leading the blind, but they were like, "What else can we do?" I don't know that they had the vision to go further than they went.

And the label . . . that situation pretty much spoke for itself. Profile Records was an independent label, and they weren't interested in the truth. They weren't interested in paying their artists. I was on the same label as Run-DMC, Dana Dane, and Rob Bass, and it's just a known fact that Profile Records didn't like to pay their artists. If you don't pay, you're going to have problems—especially with me. That was a problem. They didn't believe in that yet. Hip-hop wasn't large enough yet, and at that time, there was no SoundScan. Profile was doing their own manufacturing, their own distribution, and was their own label, so there was no way to contest their accounting. You couldn't prove or disprove anything, because they probably had five sets of books. So that was the problem with Profile Records.

How did you get out of that situation?

My third album, *Revelations*, was my last one with Profile. By this time, they had frozen my contract and set my career back quite a bit. By the time we got to court, the situation was that they had to pay me X amount of money to keep me, and they didn't want to do that. So I found a way to get out through the court system.

You've always stated that it's your primary goal to be different from everyone else. How so?

I'm the type of person where if I'm writing something and it sounds similar or anything like anything anyone else has done, I cross it out and start over fresh. I don't like any of my stuff sounding like anyone else. I want to be the first one to say something like that, or the first one to rhyme that particular word. I mean, there are only so many words in the English language, but I try not to use the obvious ones or to do what everyone else is doing.

You frequently experimented with an internal rhyme scheme. Did that come natural for you, or was that something you focused on consciously?

It kind of came naturally, but then once I realized it was happening, I ran with it because it worked. It's different when you're saying something and when you're writing something. So when I was saying it, and it was coming out hot, I was like, "Yeah, I've got to get some more of this going." It worked and it fit my style. Plus, it made the rhyme that much more interesting.

You were part of the legendary Crooklyn Dodgers, and you recorded the song "Crooklyn" for Spike Lee's film of the same title. Tell me about that experience.

I believe Q-Tip reached out to me, and he was like, "Spike Lee is making this movie *Crooklyn*, and he wants this song." I was honored, because up until that point I had never been asked to do anything with anyone in that capacity. It was just an honor and a privilege. It also gave me the opportunity to get down on a film soundtrack, which was another experience I had never had before. I was already working with Buckshot on some other projects; when the Boot Camp Click first got together, they used my studio a lot. So we already had a relationship. And then Masta Ace is just so super cool already, so there was no problem. We all got together in the lab and formulated the song, and then we took it to the city where we recorded it.

You made a cameo in the film *Juice*. What was that experience like, and what was Tupac Shakur like?

The *Juice* experience really came about because of Tupac. I had originally read for a different role, but I had not gotten the part. So when 'Pac was making the film, he hit me up like, "Yeah, we're in the city and we're making a movie." So we went up to just chill with him, and I casually mentioned that I had tried out for the movie and had not gotten the role. And he was kind of shocked like, "They didn't give Special Ed the part?" So he went to the producers of the movie and said, "Special Ed is here. Why didn't you guys give him a part?" So due to his influence, I got that cameo. I got to use my own vehicle. Initially they wanted to use an old hardtop Wrangler without the hardtop, and it looked really silly. So I ended up using my own car for the scene, and it was a good look.

In what ways is hip-hop different for a 36-year-old man than it is for a younger man?

I think the whole attitude toward hip-hop is, for someone of my age, more refined and experienced. Because of this, I have a different outlook. Someone starting out today is going to have a completely different outlook—they'll probably be where I was 20 years ago. You know, wanting to rhyme all the time; wanting to cypher; wanting to battle and freestyle. I'm past all of that now. I want to make money and I want to put out quality music. I want to kind of teach the youth how to act. I want to try and set an example at this point, whereas before, when I first started out 20 years ago, I was in a different mind-set. I just wanted a name—I wanted to be recognized as a talented emcee. Now that I am, my goals are different. A younger artist's concerns are going to be different from those of an older one. A young kid listening to hip-hop is probably just interested in the money and the flashiness of it all; "I want money, I want chains, I want cars, I want to be famous," etc. My goals are completely different from all that. I think that's just a difference that comes with age and wisdom.

Today, you're a father. Has that affected the way you look at your own music and at the music of other artists?
Definitely, because I'm concerned with what my kids listen to and what they repeat. For me it's like, if I'm even writing a rhyme and I start to write something that's a little bit too reckless, I think about my kids listening to it. I think, would this be okay for them to hear? What could I do to make this more suitable, or less reckless? The images that we put into the minds of the youth leave a lasting impression, so these days I'm much more conscious about what I'm saying.

It's kind of hard to control what your children are hearing on the radio now because there is less censorship. When we were coming up, you couldn't say certain things. I mean, even just on the album version. The label would censor what you were saying, and you couldn't just be reckless. And nowadays you can pretty much say or do anything you want with no recourse.

How do you feel when someone like Shaquille O'Neal covers one of your songs or someone like Jay-Z references you in one of his songs? A lot of emcees acknowledge you as a legend. Do you feel like a legend?
I'll tell you the honest truth: I don't feel like it personally because I'm me, and I'm a humble person. I could act the way some artists choose to act and let it go to my head, but I don't feel that that's the right thing to do. That's not righteous. In my mind, you have to remain realistic about life and the world. Entertainment and show business are completely separate

from the rest of the world; you have to separate the two things. But I'm honored by those things that you mentioned. I do understand it. Twenty years is quite a bit of time, and there are kids who actually grew up listening to me. The same way I grew up listening to and idolizing certain artists, there are kids who grew up idolizing and listening to me. It's an honor for me to even be a part of the history of hip-hop, much less to be considered a legend. You know, I accept it humbly, and I'm honored by it. I just appreciate the fact that I'm appreciated. When people reference me and do covers of my songs, it's just a testament to the fact that I did do something that was honorable or great to the extent that someone would mimic me or even acknowledge me. Sometimes I just wish that artists were more truthful and honest and had the persona where they didn't have too much pride to give another man props. I find that, as a grown man, that's one of the most difficult things to do—to acknowledge or give respect to another grown man for something that he's done. And when people do give me those props, I'm honored by it. I'm glad to have been able to have done what I've done in this short amount of time, and the fact is that I'm not finished. There's more to come.

You've been vocal about the deterioration of hip-hop as we know it. Who or what do you feel is responsible for watering down this once mighty art form?
The media and the large corporations. They came in and saw the income potential for hip-hop, and then they moved in. Now what sells is pretty much whatever they push onto you. People are programmable in that sense—whatever is repetitive is what sticks now. They kind of beat you over the head with whatever music they want to force-feed you. Real hip-hop and the cultural aspect of hip-hop is no longer being respected as it was by the masses. This is because the media has injected us with bullshit for so long. So it's kind of difficult to stay true to what you're doing when the music that's selling is something that's completely different. That comes along with genocide and the attempt to corrupt a race or a culture; they infest us with bullshit in the hopes that we'll either kill each other off or do what the records say and become drug addicts and victims. That's pretty much where it's at right now. There's still a chance to take hip-hop back, but we have to work at it.

DISCOGRAPHY

1. *Youngest in Charge* (1989)
2. *Legal* (1990)
3. *Revelations* (1995)
4. *The Best of Special Ed* (2000)
5. *Still Got It Made* (2004)

CHAPTER TWENTY-TWO

SPINDERELLA
DJ

Cheryl "Salt" James and Sandra "Pepa" Denton formed the group Salt-N-Pepa (originally dubbed "Supernature") in 1985. The following year, they released their debut album, *Hot, Cool & Vicious*. That same year, the group replaced their DJ, Latoya Hanson, with a 16-year-old turntablist named Deidra Roper (a.k.a. Spinderella). The group scored moderate hits with the singles "My Mic Sounds Nice," "Tramp," and "Chick on the Side," but would become enormously successful with the smash hit "Push It." Both the single and the album would sell more than a million copies, making Salt-N-Pepa the first female hip-hop act to go gold or platinum. The group would also receive a Grammy nomination for the single. Two years later, Salt-N-Pepa released their second album, *A Salt with a Deadly Pepa*, which featured the hit collaboration with Washington, D.C., go-go group EU, "Shake Your Thang." The album would ultimately go platinum, making Salt-N-Pepa the first female hip-hop act to go gold or platinum more than once. They also received their second Grammy nomination for "Shake Your Thang."

The group's third album, 1990's *Blacks' Magic*, would feature a slightly different sound. The album, which went platinum, was the first to feature Spinderella on vocals, as well as the first of their albums not produced entirely by Hurby "Luv Bug" Azor. The album featured three hit singles in "Expression," "Do You Want Me," and the Grammy-nominated "Let's Talk about Sex." In 1993, the group released their fourth album, *Very Necessary*. The album featured three smash hits with "Shoop," "Whatta Man," and "None of Your Business," and sold more than five million copies. Salt-N-Pepa would ultimately receive two Grammy nominations for "Whatta Man" and "None of Your Business," winning for the latter. In 1997, Salt-N-Pepa released their fifth album, *Brand New*, which again went gold. In 2002, the group disbanded but has reunited to perform their hits on the 2005 Hip-Hop Honors and the 2008 BET Hip-Hop Awards.

Today, Spinderella is a respected radio personality on KKBT 100.3 in Los Angeles, where she cohosts the nationally syndicated old school radio show *The BackSpin*. She has also appeared in the films *Stay Tuned* and *Kazaam*.

What does hip-hop mean to you?
It's a culture. It's a feeling. It's the voice of the street. It's the voice of a generation that basically didn't have a voice.

When did you first become aware of hip-hop?
The first time I heard something that was different was when I was about 10 years old, and it was a Fatback Band song. I was pretty young, but I realized at the time that what I was hearing was something different. I had grown up on my dad's music, which was the soulful classics; you know, the old funk and disco. To hear this type of sound, it was really something different. But I didn't really know what it was, and I didn't really fall in love with it, until I heard Boogie Down Productions. That was when I really fell in love with hip-hop.

When did you know that you wanted to be DJ?
I never really realized I wanted to be a DJ. I just kind of picked it up along the way. In high school, my boyfriend was a local DJ. He basically showed me different types of scratches and stuff. I used to help him carry his records at parties. One day I got up there on his set and just started messing around, and he was like, "Let me hear you do this . . . Now let me hear you do that . . ." And then that would become the routine. I would practice with him, and he would show me different cuts. We would listen to music and cut up breakbeats.

You stepped in and replaced Latoya Hanson just after Salt-N-Pepa released *Hot, Cool & Vicious*. How did you hook up with them?
I auditioned for them. They were needing a DJ for their first tour, which was the Fat Boys' Wipe Out Tour. Someone that I knew from school

asked me if I would be interested in deejaying for a group. She didn't say what it was or who it was. So I was like, "All right, cool. That sounds cool." And by this time, I had really started deejaying. I was in the process of learning, and that night I got a call from Hurby Azor, who was Salt-N-Pepa's manager at the time. He told me that it was Salt-N-Pepa, and I was like, "Wow, this is crazy." I auditioned for them immediately after that, and I got the job.

Salt, Pepa, and yourself became very successful in a very male-dominated genre. What were some of the obstacles you had to overcome as women in hip-hop?

Basically they were the same obstacles that any woman has to overcome in any career choice. You know, proving your worth, your talent . . . We just basically tried to avoid looking at what those obstacles were. Instead we looked beyond them and continued to grow past them. Some of the obstacles were these guys who would say, "Well, they're one-hit wonders," or "They're cute," or something like that. We proved otherwise. We proved that we had actual talent.

Do you feel that you had to work twice as hard to achieve the same things as male artists?

Yeah, but you know, it was good. When you work twice as hard, you become better than those who are against you. It made us sharper.

Salt-N-Pepa kind of paved the way for the female artists of today. Do you have many contemporary artists thank you for your contributions?

Yeah, I get a lot of respect. A lot of artists seem to respect the path that we laid. There were female artists who came before us that we owe a debt of gratitude to, as well. We were not the first, although we did open some doors to the mainstream. We weren't the first. You have to respect the bricklayers; the pioneers. But yes, we do get a lot of respect from the female artists of today and of the past. But it wasn't just us. There were a handful of females who were making noise. Some of them could break into the mainstream, and some couldn't, but that doesn't take away from their talent or their contributions to hip-hop.

You toured the world with Salt-N-Pepa. What are some of your fondest memories with the group?

Just being on the road. We had a lot of fun on the road, although sometimes it was brutal. We basically grew up together on the road. I think of the pranks, the shows themselves, and practicing for the shows. Back in the day, you couldn't be a hip-hop act and sell out an arena without having an R&B-type artist on the bill with you. So for us to be able to do that—to sell out arenas—was amazing. I'm very proud to be able to say that we did that, because at that time, they weren't allowing hip-hop to play in arenas like that. So for Salt-N-Pepa to be able to perform at that level, and to sell out those arenas, was beautiful. We had a great run. Our performances would probably be the most memorable moments for me.

You did some rhyming with Salt-N-Pepa. Have you ever considered making the transition to full-fledged emcee?
No. [Laughs.] Simply no. I don't mind doing it, but it was just one of the talents I was exhibiting. I had a lot of fun with it, but no. I'm a DJ. That's what I am. That's my love.

Hip-hop lyrics by male emcees can often be quite misogynistic. As a female working in hip-hop, are you ever offended by the depictions of women in these songs?
Oh yes, of course. I wouldn't say that I'm personally offended, but I do feel that artists have a responsibility to the generation listening to the music. Artists don't get into the industry to be censored. They just want to do them; they want to be themselves. Most of them—not all, but most—tell their own stories and speak from their own truths and experiences. But the fact is that these songs are an influence on a large part of a generation. So when you speak that way to women, continuously calling them out, then you're going to have young women believing those things about themselves. They'll start reciting it, and believing it. So I'm not really taking offense to it, because I know they're not talking about me, but I would hope that artists would take into consideration just how influential their music is. Songs like that could potentially destroy a woman's self-esteem. Artists may not want to be a role model, but once you are thrust into that light, you become a role model because young people look up to you. So what you say is important.

You host a radio show which plays music from the "golden era" of hip-hop. What are some things that you miss from that era?

It was young, it was fun, there was a variety, it was wide open. It wasn't so taxed or so controlled. It was at its best when it was uncontrolled. And everything wasn't rosy back then either. Let's not forget that. But there was more variety, and you could choose what you liked. If you liked the Fat Boys, you liked the Fat Boys, if you liked EPMD . . . if you liked Salt-N-Pepa . . . You could listen to what you wanted to. But then when the music started becoming more controlled, it removed the integrity from it. Back then it was a lot more fun. You would run home to listen to it, because back then, they didn't play your favorite song 20 times an hour. The old school radio DJs made you appreciate the music. And it wasn't just about money back then, it was about an actual love for the music.

In the past, there was a time when the DJ got overshadowed by the emcee. But today, there's been a little bit of a shift, and the DJ is getting a lot more attention. What are your thoughts on this?
I'm a DJ, so I love it. [Laughs.] But both the DJ and the emcee should be respected, because both are integral parts that make up the whole. It's important that the DJ respects the emcee, and the other way around. And back in the day, the emcees did have respect for the DJ. Artists used to dedicate entire songs to the DJs and big up the DJ. Salt-N-Pepa put me out front. Run-DMC put Jam Master Jay out in the front. You had DJ Jazzy Jeff and the Fresh Prince. They made sure the DJ was a part of the group. If we could get that back again, it would probably change the entire setup, and one wouldn't be above the other. But DJs are getting it right now, and it's a beautiful thing, but I have mad respect and love for the emcee.

DISCOGRAPHY

1. *A Salt with a Deadly Pepa* (1988) [as Salt-N-Pepa]
2. *Blacks' Magic* (1990) [as Salt-N-Pepa]
3. *A Blitz of Salt-N-Pepa Hits* (1990) [as Salt-N-Pepa]
4. *Very Necessary* (1993) [as Salt-N-Pepa]
5. *Brand New* (1997) [as Salt-N-Pepa]
6. *Salt-N-Pepa: The Best of* (2000) [as Salt-N-Pepa]
7. *The Best of Salt-N-Pepa* (2008) [as Salt-N-Pepa]

CHAPTER TWENTY-THREE
STICKY FINGAZ
Emcee

Brooklyn emcee Sticky Fingaz joined the group Onyx after they had already released the 1990 single "Ah, and We Do It Like This" on Profile Records. In 1992, the group, which also included Fredro Starr, Sonsee, and Big DS, released the underground anthem "Throw Ya Gunz." This was followed by the highly anticipated debut album *Bacdafucup*, which was executive produced by Run-DMC's Jam Master Jay. The album, which spawned the platinum-selling number one single "Slam," would eventually be listed to *The Source* magazine's 1998 list of the 100 greatest hip-hop albums ever made. The album established the group, and its loudest member, Sticky Fingaz, as ferocious emcees willing to battle anyone. Their trademark style of dress, which consisted of bald heads, black fatigues, and Timberland boots, had a tremendous impact on hip-hop and soon became a popular style of dress for legions of hip-hop fans, as well as other groups such as Run-DMC and Da Youngstas. The group's raspy growling vocal delivery would also be imitated by many, many hip-hop acts in the years to come. The group then dabbled in hip-hop/rock fusion by collaborating with the heavy metal group Biohazard on both the "Slam" remix and the title song from the *Judgment Night* film soundtrack.

The group's second album, *All We Got Iz Us*, was released in 1995. While the album wouldn't find the same commercial success their debut album had, it would ultimately reach number two on the Top R&B/Hip-Hop Albums chart and receive glowing critical reviews. The album, which went gold and produced the singles "Last Dayz," "All We Got Iz Us,"

"Live Niguz," and "Walk in New York," was later named the best-produced album of 1995 by *Vibe* magazine and selected as one of the magazine's "Twenty Albums All Hip-Hop Fans Must Own (But May Have Missed)."

The group's third album, *Shut 'Em Down*, was released in 1998. The album once again received stellar critical reviews and featured the singles "React" (featuring 50 Cent), "Shut 'Em Down" (featuring DMX), and "The Worst" (featuring Wu-Tang Clan). The album marked the group's highest debut on the *Billboard* 200, peaking at number 10.

In 2000, Sticky Fingaz made a memorable appearance on the Eminem classic "Remember Me," providing a legendary verse and managing to outshine Eminem on his own album. The following year Sticky Fingaz released his first solo album, *Blacktrash: The Autobiography of Kirk Jones*, on Universal Records. The album, which showcased a more mature Sticky Fingaz, featured the single "Get It Up" and was critically well received. Two years later, he released his follow-up album, *Decade: " . . . but wait it gets worse.*" The album, released by D3 Entertainment, featured production by Scott Storch and appearances by Missy Elliott, Omar Epps, and Fredro Starr.

Sticky Fingaz has also found a prospering career as an actor. He made his acting debut in the 1995 Spike Lee film *Clockers*. He has since appeared in many films including *Dead Presidents*, *Next Friday*, and *Leprechaun: Back 2 tha Hood*. He has also made a big splash in television, playing a recurring character on *The Shield*, appearing as a regular on the series *Over There*, and playing the lead role in the short-lived series *Blade*. In 2009, he wrote, directed, and starred in the film *A Day in the Life*. The film, notable for being the first film ever made in which all of its dialogue is rapped, also starred Mekhi Phifer, Omar Epps, Michael Rapaport, and Bokeem Woodbine.

What does hip-hop mean to you?
I think the standard answer that everyone would give is that it's a culture, and da-da-da-da, but I don't really look at it like that. I just look at it like it's my life. That's what I've been doing for as long as I can remember.

What are your earliest hip-hop-related memories?
I was probably 10 or 12, and the big thing to me was deejaying. I always wanted to be a DJ back then. I wanted to be a DJ so bad that I asked my mother to get me some turntables for Christmas, and as poor as we were, she got me turntables and a mixer. These weren't the Technic 1200s with

the swivel arms; these were some straight-arm turntables. But I still made it work. I grew up to Run-DMC. You know, one of the dudes I liked back in the day was Fresh Prince. And it wasn't like "Parents Just Don't Understand." I mean, that was cool, but he had some harder, witty freestyles that he was doing. And I used to memorize everybody's rhymes. My big thing, for a long period of my life, from like 15 to my early 20s, was that there wasn't anything that I didn't know in hip-hop. I knew every artist and I knew every song. I knew all of their lyrics, and I could recite them frontwards and backwards. I could probably say it better than the actual artist was saying it. Slick Rick was one of my all-time favorite rappers on the planet. You know, he had the stories and everything. He was just so ill. He used to play other characters and shit . . . In fact, I think Slick Rick made me want to rap. Then you had Big Daddy Kane, who was hardcore, but was still doing the dance moves with Scoop and Scrap Lover. Those were my earliest memories . . . back in the Sparky D days. Roxanne Shante, UTFO, Biz Markie . . .

When did you start rhyming?
I started out biting everybody's rhymes. Like I said, I knew everybody's rhymes, and I would say them. I wouldn't use their rhymes in a battle. Well, one time I did. I stole Fresh Prince's rhyme from an underground freestyle he had done back when he was making pause tapes. That rhyme was so ill that when I was freestyling against somebody one day, I used that rhyme. And nobody ever knew about it, because unless you were on the underground circuit making pause tapes like I was, you would never have heard that rhyme. He never put that rhyme out on a record or anything. So when I first started rhyming, I was stealing people's rhymes! [Laughs.] Then in time, slowly but surely, I started making my own rhymes. And then I found out that I was a lot better than a lot of the people whose rhymes I had been biting at first.

How did you get involved with Onyx?
Onyx had signed a single deal with Profile Records. The single was called "Ah, and We Do It Like This." It was a dope song. It wasn't the Onyx sound that we know today, but actually I think they were ahead of their time. They were kind of singing, and that's where hip-hop is at right this second. So they were like 20 years ahead of their time. But they weren't getting along with Profile, and Profile probably wasn't getting along with

them. So it was a mutual thing, and they got off the label. Then they started to shop for a new deal.

Now I wasn't even in the group at that time. I was just Fredro Starr's little cousin from Brooklyn. And they were from Queens. So they shopped their record to Jam Master Jay from Run-DMC, and he took a liking to it. But just like any label exec, he said he liked it but he wanted to hear some more stuff. At that time they had a manager who was like a fast talker; a one tooth missing, working for the garbage company, 40-year-old still living with his parents type dude. But he had a lot of big ideas, and I'll give him that. So Sonsee and Big DS were stranded in Connecticut or someplace like that. So Jam Master Jay wanted to hear some more stuff, and I just happened to be there. So their manager at the time was like, "We don't want to lose this deal and those guys are stranded. So Fredro, why don't you take your cousin into the studio and just record something so we won't lose this deal." I always used to rap back then, but I wasn't a part of their group. I was like a solo artist, and I was younger than everybody else. So I wasn't really looking for a record deal. I was working in the barbershop at the time, so I was comfortable making a thousand dollars a week cutting high school.

When we went to the studio we made two records. One was called "Stick and Move" and the other was called "Exercise." And they both were crazy! When Jay heard the songs he was like, "Yo, I love the group." And we found out years later that it was between Onyx and Common Sense! Then when it came time to sign the group, it was just the other three guys there. I had just been doing them a favor, and I didn't expect to be a part of the group or anything like that. And Jay was like, "Wait a minute. Where's the nigga with the deep voice? I'm not signing y'all without him." And Big DS didn't even want me in the group. Sonsee didn't care either way, and Fredro was petitioning for me. He said, "Well, if my cousin isn't in the group, then I'm not in it either!" And that's how I got inducted into Onyx.

What was Jam Master Jay like to work with, and how important was he in the creation of that first Onyx album?
He was incredible to work with. He was a great dude, and he brought incredible energy and ideas. He was like a Dr. Dre to me. When I went into the studio with Dre, I saw that he just has a way of pulling the best out of you without even trying. And Jam Master Jay was like that. He was so important that he was like the unofficial fifth member of Onyx. He helped

with the production and he let us know what was hot and what was not. He was the executive producer, and he was the one who brought us to Def Jam. He was very, very important.

You came into the industry during a very special time in hip-hop. What was that time like for you?
It was like a whirlwind. It was like a 10 to 15 year whirlwind. It was like I jumped into that whirlwind and then 15 years later I was like, "Holy shit! What just happened?" It was crazy.

And when Onyx first started, I was going through a crazy time in my life. I had just run away from home, and one of Onyx's main producers had just gotten murdered. And we should have seen the signs. He sold his SP-1200 and then went to Maryland to try and hustle some money. He got murdered; they shot him in the head, shot him in both of his hands. Fredro got kicked out of his house. Then we met Jay. I was out there wylin' out, doing acid at the time, and I was 16 or 17 years old. I was going out to clubs until six in the morning . . . When I was 15 I gave my mother an ultimatum. I was like, "Either you let me go and you'll see me again, or I'll run away and you never see me again." So she had no choice. All of that was happening, and that's why you see that transition from Onyx's first single on Profile. It was still street and ghetto, because that was where we were living at the time, but it was also on a happier, lighter side. Then when we came out with the full-fledged Onyx album, *Bacdafucup*, it was just aggressive and going at the world. We were experiencing all these different things in our lives at that point.

I was a very depressed person around that time, and I never smiled. There were seriously three years of my life in which I never smiled. I mean *never*. And that has an effect on your body and your mental state. All I wanted to do at that time was destroy other emcees. That was my only purpose in life. Once we signed that deal, everything changed, and I just wanted to destroy *everybody*! We would go to clubs and we would be on the line battling niggas, just going for their throats. And the line was crowded, so we had a whole crowd to battle, and we were just tearing people's heads off! I was the illest nigga *ever* at that point in time. Not only was I the illest nigga ever in my own mind, but I think other people recognized me as that, as well. Writing rhymes was about saying the illest shit that you could think of, but not like someone like Bizarre from D12, who tries to say the illest shit but is more like on some comedy shit. I was more on some "I hate your fucking ass and I hope you fucking die" type of shit! It was just aggressive, ill shit.

What was it like when you saw other groups imitating you by rocking the bald heads or growling on the mic? Did that make you angry, or did you see that as a sign of respect?

I was probably angry. I wasn't old enough to recognize that imitation is the most sincere form of flattery. I just thought niggas was bitin', you know what I'm saying? And I was like fuck everybody. That was my mentality. I just wanted to destroy everybody. At first, we even used to try and fight our fans! [Laughs.] I remember the first show we did, Jam Master Jay took us to this community center, and we performed in front of a couple hundred people. And we were like, "Fuck you," to the crowd. And when we got off the stage, Jay was like, "Whoa! What are you doing? You don't wanna diss the crowd! You want them with you and on your side. You show them love and they'll show you love, but don't diss the crowd." And I was like, "Oh, okay, cool." [Chuckles.] But that was my mentality at that time: fuck the world.

On songs like "Judgment Night," the "Slam" remix, and "The Black Rock," you guys have experimented with rap-rock fusion. Unlike a lot of artists who attempt to bridge these sounds, you guys have always managed to maintain the vibe and integrity of both forms of music. What do you feel that you do differently than these other groups who try to merge rock and hip-hop?

Well, first of all, before we combined rock and hip-hop, we were already a rock group. We're screaming at the top of our lungs; we're slam dancing; we're stage diving; we're throwing water; we're aggressive and we fight with each other onstage. I remember myself and Big DS had a real fight on-stage in front of the crowd, while we were performing! [Laughs.] We kept performing, and we kept fighting. And everybody just thought it was part of the show, like hey, that's Onyx. So what we do differently is that we're already rock. When we mash it up with rock groups, it's not like we're stepping out of our lane and doing something that's not the norm for us. But we were also so street that we almost didn't do the Biohazard collaboration. That was Lyor Cohen's idea, and probably Jam Master Jay's, too. He was like, "Lyor sent us this offer. He wants you to do a song with this group called Biohazard, and they're hardcore too." We were so street and so hood that we were like, "Hell no, we don't want to do no fucking rock and roll shit!" And Jay was like, "Trust me, this'll be a good move." Jay cosigned it, because they had done that joint with Aerosmith back in the day. "Slam" was already platinum before we even did the Biohazard remix, so we did it, and it came out dope. We bonded with the Biohazard dudes. Even though they were white, they were niggas just like us. It was crazy; it was wild; it was hardcore. It worked out, so we did some more songs with them. Then I went on to do songs with guys like Slipknot. It just fit because that was our natural energy. Plus, when we were making the *Bacdafucup* album, we were listening to groups like Das-Efx and Nirvana. We were influenced by both kinds of music, so it was incorporated into our music.

Your verse on Eminem's "Remember Me" is legendary. How did that collaboration take place, and what was your mind-set when you wrote that?
That was originally supposed to be for Dr. Dre's album, and actually, Fredro named Dre's album *Chronic 2001*. I was in the studio with Dre, and that was when he found out that Suge Knight was putting out that *Chronic 2000* project, trying to beat him to the punch. He was like, "This is some bullshit." So I was on the phone with Fredro when Dre heard about that, and I told Fredro. He said, "Yo, just tell Dre to call that shit *Chronic 2001*." So I told Dre and he was just like, "Word?" He heard it, but he kind of acted like it didn't even register. Lo and behold, when the album came out it was called *Chronic 2001*! He didn't even acknowledge that it was a good idea, but when the album came out it was titled that. So he listened to Fredro; Fredro named that shit.

But that Eminem joint was originally for Dre's album. I had just filed bankruptcy to get out of my Def Jam agreement. I had been like, "Yo, I wanna make a solo album," and Fredro and Sonsee were like yeah, go do that. There was no beef. They *wanted* me to do a solo album. So I went to Lyor and told him I wanted to do a solo album, and he told me that under our contract he only had to give me $250,000. I was like, "$250,000? I'm on fire right now. I could probably get a million dollars from anybody right now. Are you crazy?" So I suggested that I go to another label and get a million dollars to make an album and then he could just take an override. And he said, "I'm not in the business of overrides." I was like, "Word?" Then my lawyer told me I could get out of my contract by declaring bankruptcy. He told me it would mess up my credit for seven years, but that all my contracts would be dissolved. I was like, "Fuck credit. I'd rather dissolve my contracts and go get that million dollars and have cash. Who needs credit when you've got cash?" So I filed bankruptcy and I went out to LA to do movies. When I got there the first person I called was Dr. Dre. I said, "Remember you told me if I ever got out of my deal to come and see you and you'd give me a solo deal, right?" He said, "Yeah," and I said, "Well, I'm free and I'm in LA right now." He asked me where I was, and I told him I was at some girl's crib and I didn't have a car or a place to stay. That nigga got me a rental car and threw me up in a nice hotel. The next day I'm in the studio with him, and he was working on a Snoop Dogg record. He said, "I want you to do this song. It's gonna be you, RBX, and Eminem for my album."

I murdered that shit. I wrote that rhyme in two hours. Then the illest part of the whole thing is that Eminem recorded his verse later, and he told me, "Yo, it took me two months to write that rhyme to come after you." I thought he was just talking shit and trying to make me feel good, but later Dre told me the same thing. "It took Eminem two months to write that verse to come after you." And I was like, "Damn, that's ill." I wrote that shit in two hours. But like I said, Dre just pulled the best out of me. Plus it's so easy to write to Dr. Dre beats because they're so ill. If you can't write a rhyme to a Dr. Dre beat, you need to find a new career.

I wanted to body everybody with my own solo shit. I told Fredro, "You watch: my album is gonna sell 10 million copies. I'm gonna go diamond." And it didn't do that. But the nigga who did that was 50 Cent, whom we gave his start to on our song "React." He went diamond. He did what I wanted to do, and he did it with Dr. Dre. I was supposed to sign with Dre, but I didn't. I went back to New York to shop my dude X1, and I went to Universal. They were like, "We like him, but we want to hear some of your shit." But I didn't want to play my shit; I wanted to sign with Dr. Dre. I wanted to get my man X1 signed. And they said, "That's cool, but can we just hear some shit?" So I let them hear it, and they were like, "X1 is dope, but we want to sign you." They said, "We don't want to get into a bidding war with Jimmy Iovine, because we will lose, but we'll give you a proposal." And they gave me a proposal for $800,000. Dre had gone to Jimmy Iovine and told him that I wanted a million dollars, but Jimmy Iovine said he would only give me $500,000. So I weighed that $500,000 at Aftermath against the $800,000 they were offering me at Universal. I should probably have taken the $500,000 just to work with Dre. You know they had that comic book called *What If?* Well, I always wonder what would have happened if I had signed with Dre instead of Universal. But that $300,000 difference was the money that I used to buy my mother the first house that she ever owned in her entire life, so I would never change that.

And that was when Dre was going through all that beef and craziness with Suge Knight and Tupac Shakur. I'm a hotheaded nigga. I used to carry guns and wild out. So if I had been with Dre during all that beef shit, I would probably either be dead or in jail for murder. So who knows? Maybe I did choose the right road. I mean, I'm still here and I'm still alive and kicking. I've still got great potential, and now I'm directing and making my own movies.

I really respect your film *A Day in the Life*, which is a musical in which all of the dialogue is rapped. How did you conceive the film, and what were some of the obstacles you had to overcome to make it?
It all started with *Blacktrash*. I always wanted to do an album that was a movie, and since I make both movies and albums it made sense. It started with this one song called "Can You Hear Me?" I wrote this song for me and Fredro. Remember the time when the cell phones would break up all the time and they had the commercials and all that? I wrote the song like we were just talking on the phone, as opposed to the normal rap. I've got a friend who said he knew someone who had cameras and would shoot it for free. I was like, "Word?" I was so excited about shooting that I hadn't even finished the script. I had the entire script in my head already, and I would just write it scene by scene. I would say, "Today we're gonna shoot this scene. You say this and this." Then the next week I would write another scene. "Okay, now we're gonna shoot this scene." I didn't want to do it properly, which was to sit down and write the entire script and then go out and film it. I wanted to get it done. So I had maybe 15 minutes shot and one of my homeboys told me, "Whatever money you raise, I'll match it." That made it easier on me. Then my homeboy Omar, who was basically the Dame Dash of the situation, told me that Lionsgate wanted to see the movie. But the messed up part is that the place where we were editing didn't have a DVD burner, so I couldn't put it on DVD to bring it to Lionsgate. So I said, "Yo, if I was Jay-Z and you were Dame Dash, Dame Dash

would make Lionsgate come to the editing studio to see the film." And he said, "All right, I'll call you back." So we played the footage for Lionsgate in the editing studio and they were like, "Don't show this to anyone else. We'll have a proposal for you by the end of the week." And by the end of the week they gave me the proposal, and it got put out by Lionsgate.

First I would start shooting with good unknown actors, and then I would call my good known actor friends and show them the footage. They were all like, "This is dope. I've never seen any shit like this. I'm on board." So I would use one actor to get another actor to get another actor. One of the first actors to sign on was Faizon Love. Then Ray J. got down. Then Mekhi Phifer got down. Then Omar Epps got down. Then Michael Rapaport got down. I would show Mekhi Faizon's scenes. Then I would show Omar Epps Mekhi's scenes. Then I would show Michael Rapaport all of their scenes! It was just like dominoes.

You know, I never really liked the song-and-dance type movies. And I didn't like that they had regular dialogue scenes. I felt like if it was going to be a musical, it should be a complete musical from beginning to end.

It seems to me like more emcees looked at hip-hop as an art form when you guys first came out. Today it seems like there are a lot of people who just look at it as a means to get paid. What are your thoughts on this?
Not only are some of the younger guys throwing out some bullshit, but they're not taking the time to perfect their craft. And the Internet is making it accessible for them, too. Before you had to have a record deal to be heard by the public. Now Joe Blow can get heard and even get his video out there for people to see. Remember how I said Eminem took two months to write his rhyme for "Remember Me"? That's the craft of the whole thing right there. People don't spend that kind of time on their shit anymore. Sometimes it would take me two months to write a rhyme. That's the craft. That's perfecting it and trying to make it perfect. It's like cooking food to perfection as opposed to just throwing something in the microwave. Nowadays people are just throwing something in the microwave instead of really cooking something meaningful and good. I come from that age and I still work hard on my music.

You once said that radio stations are "saturated with bullshit." Radio stations today play a lot less real hip-hop than they used to. Why do you think that is?

It's totally not the radio station's fault. A radio station is a business just like any other, and they have to keep their lights on. If you've got one emcee that you really love and you want to play his music, you might play it on a mix show level, but you want to add it so it's on the daytime playlist as well. But then you have a label come by and they say, "Here's $50,000 and we want you to play *this* song instead." And they've got to do what they have to do to keep their lights on. The payola is the problem. It's the record labels who are paying radio stations to play their records. That's how you blow a record up today. Everybody knows that. It's not a secret. So if I'm a DJ at a radio station, I have to listen to my program director. And the program director has to listen to whoever's paying him to play that shit. And there are some mix show DJs like Funkmaster Flex or Kay Slay or DJ Clue who try to spin some real records on that level, but as far as real hip-hop getting added to the regular rotation, that doesn't happen because the record companies are paying to have this other stuff played. And most record execs are old and white, and the ones that are black are old and scared of losing their jobs. And sometimes that probably means signing some pop artists that they don't really feel in their bones as opposed to signing a really ill artist that they do feel. They've got to do what they've got to do. That's why some artists, no matter how hood or street they may be, have to have some kind of commercial record to get the record companies to get behind financially.

Right now there's a big discussion about the importance of street credibility. Back in the day, having street cred was extremely important for an artist. Do you feel that having street credibility is still important for emcees today, or is that a thing of the past?
What do you mean?

If the kind of information that recently came out about Rick Ross had come out about an artist 15 years ago, their career probably would have ended. You recorded with Boss, and you'll remember that it basically ended her career when it was revealed that she wasn't really the kind of person she portrayed herself to be in her songs. Today it's becoming more and more common to learn that artists are really completely different people than the personas that they convey in their music. But they still sell. So do you think having street credibility is still important?
Obviously that no longer matters. Rick Ross is a great example. It completely baffles me. When that shit came out [that he was a former prison

guard and not a drug dealer] and he completely denied it, and then they had pictures to prove that he was lying, I really believed his career was over. And so did 50 Cent. That's why he was going at him so hard. And I think that Rick Ross is really the only person who's beaten 50 Cent in a battle. And the reason I say he beat him is because he's still current. He's still making songs with guys like Jay-Z and Puffy and all of the top artists of today, whereas when 50 had a beef with Ja Rule, niggas were afraid to do a song with Ja Rule! They didn't want 50 mad at them. Even me . . . When 50 and myself were throwing jabs at one another, I felt like I bodied him. He said the shit about me on "How to Rob," right? Then I did that shit "Jackin' for Beats," and I felt like I bodied him. So I didn't feel a need to keep dissing him. Then I heard that he had two more little jabs that he threw at me in songs, but I took that as being like when you beat a nigga's ass and he still wants to talk shit because everybody knows you beat his ass. I just figured I'd leave it at that, and I really wasn't that disrespected by him talking about me in "How to Rob." I actually would have been more offended if he hadn't talked about me in that song, because he was talking about all the top artists. So if he hadn't mentioned me I would have been like, "So I'm not a top artist?" So it was cool. I wasn't really mad at him. Fredro was more angry with him than I was, and that's why Fredro and him got into a fight at some awards show. I just felt like it was all in the fun of it.

A lot of times we as older guys talk about what we see as being wrong with hip-hop. Do you think there's more merit to the new music today than we often give it credit for?
Yeah, I think there is actual merit to *some* of it. I think when you're used to eating soul food all the time and then somebody takes you to a sushi restaurant for the first time, you're gonna be thrown off a little bit. And you know how they say that everything goes in full circle? It's true and I can prove it. When Onyx first came out, Run-DMC wasn't wearing skinny jeans, but they were wearing fitted jeans. And then we came out with our cultural revolution with the baggy jeans and everything, and all the older dudes who were the same age you and I are now, were like, "Boy, what are you wearing those baggy-ass jeans for? Pull your pants up!" So now it's the complete opposite. The youth are now wearing skinny jeans. And back then it was all colorful just the way it is now. Think about it: back then you had Salt-N-Pepa, Kid 'n Play doing dances. Even Big Daddy Kane

was doing dances! They were all doing dances! And it did a complete 360 and came back around. Now we're the older dudes and we're saying, "Boy, what are you wearing those skinny-ass jeans for?" And we complain about all these funny-ass dances they're doing now, but we were doing the same thing back then: the Wop, the Pee-Wee Herman, the Running Man, all that shit. So it's a complete 360, and yeah, some of the music today does have merit.

DISCOGRAPHY

1. *Bacdafucup* (1993) [as Onyx]
2. *All We Got Iz Us* (1995) [as Onyx]
3. *Shut 'Em Down* (1998) [as Onyx]
4. *Blacktrash: The Autobiography of Kirk Jones* (2001)
5. *Bacdafucup Part II* (2002) [as Onyx]
6. *Decade: "... but wait it gets worse"* (2003)
7. *Triggernometry* (2003) [as Onyx]
8. *Cold Case Files: Murda Investigation* (2008) [as Onyx]
9. *A Day in the Life: Soundtrack* (2009)
10. *Black Rock* (2011) [as Onyx]

YOUNG MC
Emcee/Producer

Hollis, Queens rapper Young MC first discovered hip-hop at the age of 10. Influenced by such varied artists as Chic, Bob Marley, the Eagles, and Parliament, he soon started writing and reciting his own rap lyrics. By the time he attended the University of Southern California in the late 1980s, he had honed his skills and was recognized as a talented emcee. In 1987, he landed a recording contract with Delicious Vinyl Records after displaying his rapid flow on a telephone call with the label's owners. Young MC soon went to work co-writing the songs "Wild Thing" and "Funky Cold Medina" for another up-and-coming rapper named Tone Loc. Young MC was still recording his own album when "Wild Thing" became one of 1988's biggest hit singles, selling more than four million copies. During this same period Young MC released the 12" singles "I Let 'Em Know," "The Fastest Rhyme," and "My Name Is Young," all of which became regional hits and landed in rotation at KDAY in Los Angeles. He then released "Know How," which became his first release to have major distribution. In 1989, Young MC released his debut album *Stone Cold Rhymin'* and saw his single "Bust a Move" become a smash hit. The song, which featured vocals by Crystal Blake and a bassline by Red Hot Chili Peppers bassist Flea, would remain on the *Billboard* Top 40 list for an impressive 40 weeks. That same year Tone Loc's "Funky Cold Medina," which Young MC had co-written, also became a huge hit, reaching number three on the *Billboard* singles chart. *Stone Cold Rhymin'* would ultimately achieve multi-platinum status, and Young MC would receive accolades from the American Music Awards (Best Rap Artist), the *Billboard* Music Awards (Best Pop Artist), and the Grammy Awards (Best Rap Performance).

Young MC soon left Delicious Vinyl and signed with Capitol Records, where he released his gold-selling sophomore album *Brainstorm* in 1991. Two years later Young MC returned with his third offering, *What's the Flavor?*, which featured production by Tribe Called Quest producer Ali Shaheed Muhammad. In 1997, Young MC released his first independent album, *Return of the One-Hit Wonder*, on Overall Records. Although the album would fail to make a dent on the charts, it did spawn two charting singles ("Madame Buttafly" and "On & Poppin'"). In 2000, the artist established his own recording company, Young Man Moving Records, and released his fifth album, *Ain't Goin' Out Like That*. The album would mark a return to the *Billboard* charts for Young MC, and the title single would also appear on the charts. That same year Young MC co-wrote Anastacia's hit single "Not That Kind," which appeared on the hugely successful album of the same title.

In 2002, Young MC appeared on (and won) *The Weakest Link—Rap Stars Edition*, which also featured Run, DJ Quik, Jermaine Dupri, Da Brat, B-Real, Xzibit, and Nate Dogg. That same year he released his sixth album, *Engage the Enzyme*, on Stimulus Records. The album featured the hit single "Heatseeker," which reached number three on the *Billboard* Hot R&B/Hip-Hop sales chart and later number two on the *Billboard* Hot 100 Singles Chart.

Young MC has since released the albums *Adrenaline Flow* and *Relentless*, appeared on the VH1 reality show *Celebrity Fit Club*, and made appearances in the films *The Zero Sum* and *Up in the Air*. In addition, his music continues to appear on television series like *Glee* and *Scrubs*, in films like *Four Brothers* and *The Blind Side*, and in commercials for everything from hamburgers to soft drinks.

What does hip-hop mean to you?

I think of a form of expression. I think of a familiar place, at least for me, as a black kid in the eighties who grew up in New York. It was something that was out in the streets, but it was constructive. There were a lot of kids who'd been out there getting into trouble—especially if you weren't an athlete looking to get a scholarship or something like that. It was a good release for me, and a good counterbalance to my schooling because everything was focused on my being in school and going to college. This was something I could do and feel like it was mine.

In terms of it being a culture and the like, I was part of it in its infancy, so I didn't really see it as this big culture. It was just something that I did with my friends that grew into a culture outside. Then I realized the impact of what I had done when it was just me and my friends in a basement.

What are some of your earliest hip-hop-related memories?
Block parties, basement parties, house parties. People switching on the microphone. A beat would come on and then one guy would rap and then switch off, doing a little bit of battling but not really. It was more just watching what the other guys did. And then there were kids from other neighborhoods . . . We'd hear about a guy just a few blocks away that was pretty nice on the microphone. Where I was in Hollis, it was really localized. I heard about what was happening in Manhattan and the Bronx, but I was too young to get into the clubs. So it really didn't make much sense for me to get on the train and travel into another borough if I was going to get to a place where I couldn't get inside.

When did you realize that you wanted to be an emcee?
I think I realized when I would see the looks on the faces of other guys in the neighborhood whenever I got on the mic. I had studied other rappers and felt that I would be able to do it. Then when I was able to develop my own style and create my own rhymes, to learn what biting was and then make my style something that was different from everyone else's, and really personalize it. Then most people who heard me were shocked that I could do it and was good at it because I was known as more of a nerd or a bookworm. Then I would go to house parties where people who had never heard me before would be impressed by what they heard, and then I found that I liked that attention. So I just kind of went with it.

Your musical influences are quite diverse. As an artist, do you believe that it's important to listen to diverse types of music?
Yeah. I mean, for the most part, I don't listen to a lot of hip-hop. When something's huge, I'll listen to it just to kind of find out what's going on.

But I'm not tracking down every single release to try and get ideas from it. A lot of times I'll listen to stuff in other genres, whether it be rock or dance or even some more melodic types of music, and then let myself be fed artistically from those. I find that if you're only listening to your competition, then it's really difficult to think outside of the box that your competition is in. With me, for instance, with all of the records—"Wild Thing," "Bust a Move," "Funky Cold Medina," and even "Principal's Office" to a certain extent—my contributions would not have been the same lyrically had I been concerned with what everybody else was making.

How did you get your first record deal?
I grew up in New York City, and I graduated high school in 1985 and went to USC in California. In the summer of 1987, I hooked up with a guy at a record store called Rock and Soul in New York; I think it was 35th Street and Seventh Avenue. We went to the studio and made a couple of demos and tried to get some attention from a record label in New York, but that didn't work out. He knew the guys from Delicious Vinyl, so when I came back out to school for my junior year, I got on the phone with them. I rapped for them and then within a week of my rapping over the phone they sent me a contract. I didn't have a lawyer; I didn't have anything. So I went and signed the contract and started recording with them.

Did you write the Tone Loc songs first or were you recording your songs simultaneously during this period?
No, I actually recorded a few singles beforehand. "My Name Is Young," "I Let 'Em Know," and "Fastest Rhyme" were all over KDAY. Then at that point I co-wrote "Wild Thing." I wrote four verses and I think they kept three of them. And then after that I released another song called "Know How," and then around the same time I co-wrote "Funky Cold Medina" because they wanted a follow-up single for Tone. And that came out at the end of 1988, and then "Bust a Move" came out towards the next summer.

"Wild Thing" was a smash before "Bust a Move" came out. How much did your life change after that song was released?
Especially in hip-hop, it was kind of an inside thing. I wasn't going around saying that I wrote the song. Nobody really knew who I was nationally, so Tone was just doing it. There was no reason for my name to even come up. My co-writing of "Wild Thing" and "Funky Cold Medina" only came up

and became news once I came out with "Bust a Move." I was well known in LA, and I had a lot of support there, but in terms of a nationwide buzz, even as a songwriter, that didn't really happen until "Bust a Move" started happening.

I read that you didn't have a car of your own and had to be driven to the studio sessions. Is that right?
Absolutely. That was when I was at USC, and I was coming from New York City, and as a teenager you don't drive in New York—at least back then. It was all trains and buses. So then I went to the campus and everything was pretty much self-sufficient there, so I really had no need for a car and I didn't really start driving until my junior and senior years of college.

What can you tell me about the recording of "Bust a Move"?
I wrote it in an hour and a half, and that was pretty much the first draft. I had first come up with the title "Make That Move," and we then decided to change that to "Bust a Move." Once we made that change I just went in and spit it. It wasn't something where there were a lot of retakes or rewrites or anything like that. That song is pretty much a flow of consciousness. I mean, it's pretty much just story upon story, and I was just so eager to write something that a professor hadn't told me to write . . . [Laughs.] And also the track was a lot different at that point. By this time Tone had already sold two to three million with "Wild Thing," and "Funky Cold Medina" was already platinum, and I was sitting here with "Bust a Move" that was slower and didn't have a rock edge to it. So I had no idea how people were going to respond to it. And the song cadence was a lot different than it was in those songs. When I was writing for Tone, I was writing for Tone. So writing for myself, and with the beat being slower, I felt I could be a bit more active with it, but I didn't know if people would get into it as much as they had with Tone's stuff. So there was a bit of nervousness until the record really took hold and people responded to it.

As far as the recording process, I don't really remember much. I know that things were done separately. I was not there for the recording of the background singer or for Flea playing bass. I just kind of came in, the stuff was there, and I went in and did the track. The funny thing is that it's four 16-bar verses with a 16-bar break, and no one edited the record. So the record was like 4:20 to 4:30 and everybody played it at the full length, which to me is still shocking. I've never heard the record edited, because everybody knows the arrangement as it is.

I understand that your parents were initially skeptical of your decision to be a rapper. Tell me about that.

Initially, yeah. I mean, look, you send your kid to go to college and then he comes back from college and says, "Yeah, I got my degree, but . . ." They basically gave me the summer after graduation to make this work, because "Bust a Move" came out finals week of my senior year. So I had that summer to determine whether that was going to be my career or if I was going to get a regular job and go to grad school, and then I just started doing shows and the record started taking off. The video hit, and I just kept pushing, and that was it.

What were things like for you after "Bust a Move" blew up?

It was not like it is now. I tell people this all the time and they don't understand it. This was pre-Internet and pre–cell phone. I felt bad a few years ago because I had to throw out a box full of fan letters, because you're getting all of this stuff and you don't have time to respond to it in due time. It was not instantaneous like it is now, so I was sheltered a lot from what was going on. Not everybody had cable, not everybody had MTV. You could see the *Billboard* numbers and the like, but if you're not terribly savvy in terms of what that means industry-wise, you're somewhat in a bubble; you're going through it and you don't know what's happening every place at the same time. Right now it would be a lot easier to see that, and it would be a lot easier for an artist to blow up nationwide, whereas then it was very regional.

What are your thoughts on this onslaught of technology, from an artist's perspective?

It helps in that it gets a record out to everybody very quickly, so there aren't a lot of secrets anymore. You no longer see a regional record kind of bubbling up in one place and then people slowly finding it. "Bust a Move" was on the charts for 40 weeks, and it outlasted my second and third singles. And basically a lot of the reason for that is that a lot of people had to grow into that record. It didn't hit at all places at one time. The video push, and then retail did okay, and then radio started kicking in, and those things all kind of fed each other. And this was pre-Soundscan, as well, so there wasn't that concentrated promotion of trying to get the most sales after six weeks or on a certain weekend or something like that. So those are the positives.

I think the negative is that there's no longer a personal story that people have about the first time they heard a record. You know, "the first time I heard this record I was in this place, and then I heard it on the radio, and then I saw the video, and then I heard it was in other cities . . ." That process used to take months, and then by the time the album came out you were like, "I'm gonna go get this album" because you feel like you have a personal relationship with how the artist and the record took off. That really doesn't exist anymore. All of that stuff is being manipulated to try and get the Soundscan numbers, and the only reason the label will work regions isn't because there is or isn't a demand, but because it's more convenient for them to work certain regions like that. People don't have the personal relationship with the artist and watching an artist grow. It no longer feels like it's part of someone's personal story the way it was back when my record came out. The artist development aspect isn't really there, and that's the biggest thing that's missing in terms of artists being able to have careers with longevity or being able to have songs that really stick where fans know every word of the song when they go to the concert. That doesn't really happen for anyone who's over the age of 20 now. Teenagers might do it because it's fun, but in terms of a record being five or 10 years old and you knowing every word, that really doesn't happen that much anymore.

Hearing a song on the computer doesn't really provide much of a memorable first experience, either.
Right, or "someone told me about this" or "someone sent me a link." I have nothing against that, but it's just not that organic thing. "I was digging around on YouTube and I found this." It's just not the same kind of thing, and then so much stuff gets put out like that or leaked—especially with people looking toward the Soundscan numbers—that even if you hear something, it may get to the point where it doesn't come out or it's only available digitally. And radio stations . . . When was the last time you were able to call a radio station and request a song that they don't play and actually have them end up playing it? That doesn't happen. Now the only requests that radio stations take are the stuff that they're already playing.

Which feels like about five songs played over and over again.

Right. I think the actual number is 13, as opposed to Top 40. So if you listen to most stations, you're going to hear the same songs twice.

You come from a proud tradition of fun hip-hop, which is something we don't see much of anymore. Today hip-hop takes itself very seriously. Why do you think that is?

I think what happened is that the major labels got involved, and they started focusing on whatever the newest, hottest thing was, and then when it went gangsta, they just decided that all of it should go that way. And then trying to turn it back around and have some fun stuff . . . There are a few artists who have some fun records, but it isn't the way it was when I first came out, where you had guys like me, and Tone Loc, and Hammer, and Vanilla Ice, at the same time as having Poor Righteous Teachers and Public Enemy and Digital Underground and De La Soul and NWA and Geto Boys all going platinum at the same time and it wasn't an issue. And there was no one sitting around saying that we all had to sound like this or like that. Now I will say that I did hear from artists who, after "Bust a Move" came out, had an A&R tell them that they had to make an uptempo record with a girl singing on it because that was the sound right now. I didn't make records to establish a sound; I made records to establish *me*. Then A&R guys started saying, "If you don't sound like the hottest thing on the radio right now, then that's it." So when NWA, and Snoop, and Dre came out, then everyone had to sound like them. Then when Puffy or whoever else you had came out, then everybody had to sound just like them because that was the sound of the moment. Also, you no longer have albums made with a central producer. Now everybody's got to get a Kanye track, or a Dre track, or a Just Blaze or 9th Wonder track. It wasn't like that. Today people say, "If Dre was able to make a hot track for Eminem or whoever, then we'll just get a Dre track and we should do just fine." And that's what made a lot of the stuff today sound the same. And you can't blame the producer, because they're going and getting the work wherever they can. But the labels say, "Eminem just sold X amount of records, so we've got to get that sound or some piece of that to tie it in." But the fans are looking for diverse sounds, so as soon as people started worrying about that and running away from that diversity, then hip-hop started going downhill.

And then with Soundscan you could no longer let a record grow organically. What Soundscan did was it caused people to begin selling records the way films are sold. The way a film comes out is you see the commercials for a while, then maybe a preview either on a DVD or a movie you go to, and then you go see the film on the first week. People don't consume music like that; especially not albums. You hear a single, you like it, you get into it. You may not buy anything, but you know it's there. Then you hear a second single, you may like it, get into it or hear it on the radio or whatever, and then at some point between that single and a third single you begin hearing both of those first singles playing in different places. Then you say, "Okay, that's enough to prompt me to go out and buy an album." No matter what a record company does, you can't coordinate a fan's response in that way to go out and buy an album. This is because you listen to an album over and over and over again, whereas you watch a movie for two hours and you're done with it. And that's what Soundscan did—it forced the promotion of music to be handled like film.

You mentioned that groups rarely record with a central producer today. It seems like having one central producer—or maybe two producers—lent itself to crafting a cohesive album. It seems like the art of constructing a solid album is dying out today.

Just listen to the interviews. Whenever someone would interview me about my record, they would interview me about the concepts on the record, what I was feeling, what I was thinking, what I was trying to do. When they interview *any* hip-hop artist today, they ask who did the tracks and who are the guest stars. Those are the first two things they ask, not what were you feeling, what are you trying to say with the record. That has nothing to do with it. "Who did you get on here with you?" That's what they ask, and that's why albums aren't cohesive.

Nas famously stated that hip-hop was dead. Do you agree with that assessment?

Hip-hop is not dead, but the hip-hop I knew is no longer the prom queen. And different people have different views of what they think hip-hop is. A lot of us older guys can point to 1986 through 1993 as the "golden era." Maybe you can squeeze that down a little bit, but in there, if you're starting with Run and going all the way through to Dre and Snoop, is what would essentially be considered the golden era. But if you're asking younger people, they'll say it's after that. "Oh, no, it's Biggie and Tupac." "It's Kanye or Eminem." A lot of it in terms of what the greatest era of hip-hop is depends on when people consumed it in their formative years. To me, it seems like there's not as much foundation of hip-hop to the music that comes out today. A lot of people who really get into hip-hop end up going back five, 10, 15 years, maybe more. And a lot of the artists who can do shows are artists my age, as opposed to guys who came out with records around 2000 or 2001 with a lot of gangsta stuff. That's one thing that labels didn't see: The 14- or 15-year-old kids who wanted to hear that gangsta stuff are now 30 and they have kids at home and they're not going to get a babysitter to go out and listen to some gangsta stuff, and there are a lot of venues that won't book those groups. So me, 20 years after my hit, I can get shows where guys who came out a decade after me and sold more records than me can't.

DISCOGRAPHY

1. *Stone Cold Rhymin'* (1989)
2. *Brainstorm* (1991)
3. *What's the Flavor?* (1993)
4. *Return of the One-Hit Wonder* (1997)
5. *Ain't Goin' Out Like That* (2000)
6. *Engage the Enyzme* (2002)
7. *Adrenaline Flow* (2007)
8. *B-Sides, Demos and Remixes* (2007)
9. *Relentless* (2009)

INDEX

INDEX

ABOUT THE AUTHOR

Andrew J. Rausch is a freelance journalist whose essays, critical reviews, and celebrity interviews have appeared in numerous publications. He has worked on a handful of motion pictures in a variety of capacities, including producer, screenwriter, actor, cinematographer, and composer. Rausch is also the author of numerous books on the subject of popular culture, including *Turning Points in Film History, Fifty Filmmakers: Conversations with Directors from Roger Avary to Steven Zaillian, Reflections on Blaxploitation* (with David Walker and Chris Watson), *Making Movies with Orson Welles* (with Gary Graver), and *The Films of Martin Scorsese and Robert De Niro. I Am Hip-Hop* is his tenth book.